Rick Steves ®
SNAPSHOT

Dubrovnik

W9-BRX-617

CONTENTS

Dubrovnik

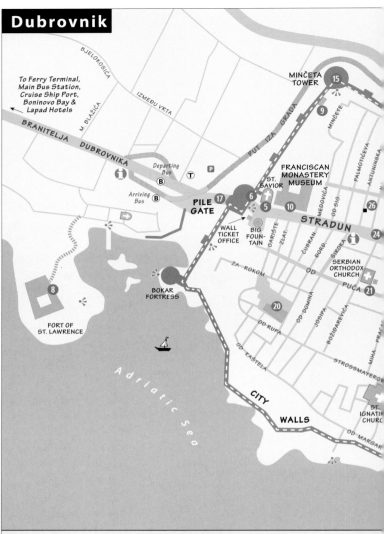

SIGHTS

1. Bell Tower
2. Buža Gate
3. Cable Car
4. Cathedral
5. Church of St. Savior
6. City Wall Entrances (3)
7. Dominican Monastery Museum & Church
8. Fort of St. Lawrence
9. Foundry Museum
10. Franciscan Monastery Museum & Church
11. Jesuit St. Ignatius' Church
12. Lazareti (Old Quarantine Building)
13. Luža Square & Orlando's Column
14. Maritime Museum & Aquarium
15. Minčeta Tower
16. Old Port
17. Pile Gate
18. Ploče Gate
19. Rector's Palace
20. Rupe Granary & Ethnographic Museum
21. Serbian Orthodox Church & Icon Museum
22. Sponza Palace & Memorial Room of Dubrovnik Defenders
23. St. Blaise's Church
24. Stradun (a.k.a. Placa)
25. Synagogue Museum
26. War Photo Limited

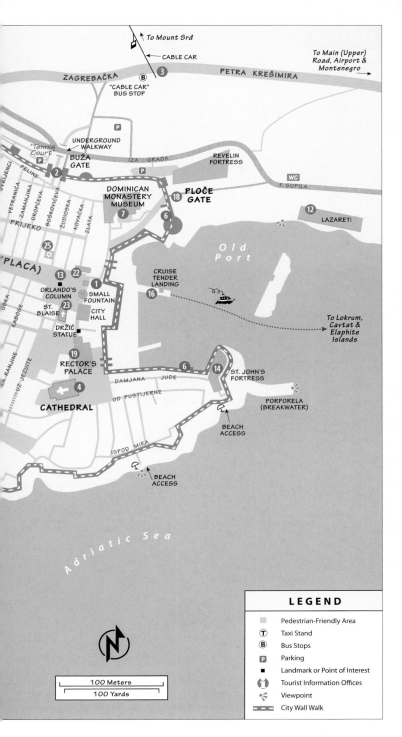

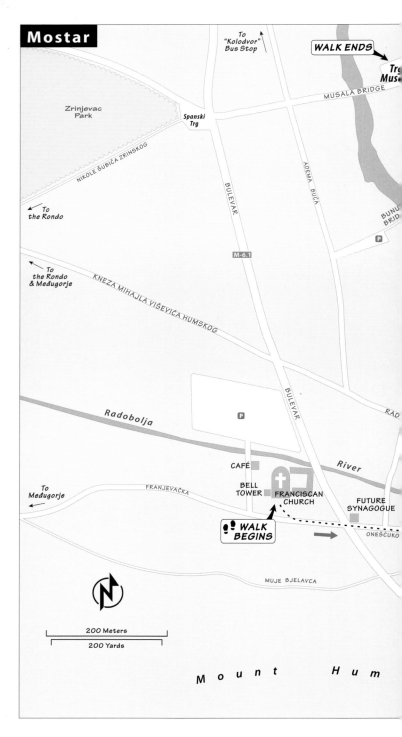

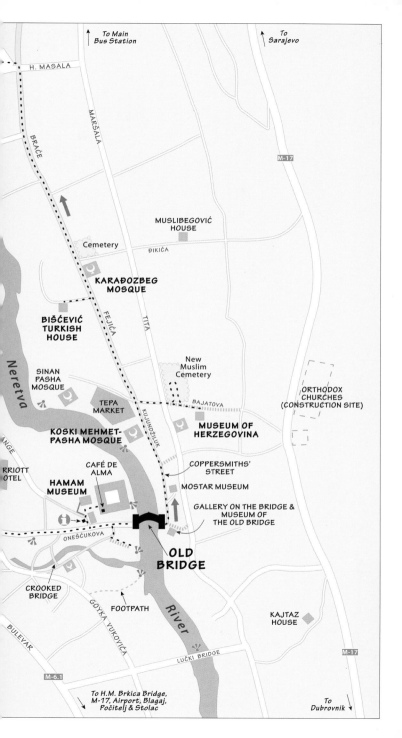

Dalmatian Coast

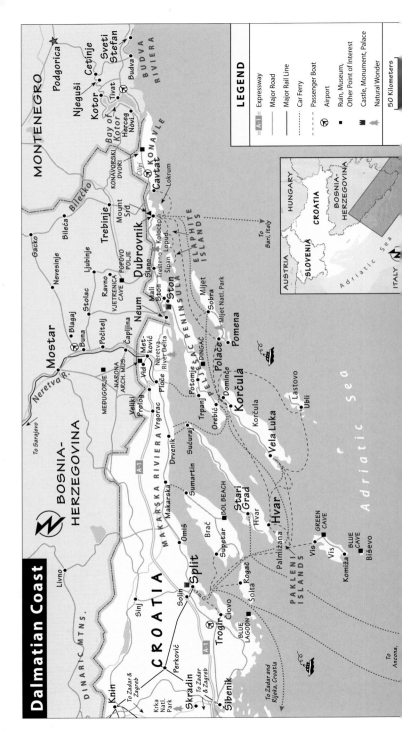

LEGEND

- = = Expressway
- —— Major Road
- —— Major Rail Line
- ········ Car Ferry
- – – – Passenger Boat
- ✈ Airport
- ■ Ruin, Museum,
  Other Point of Interest
- ■ Castle, Monument, Palace
- ◄ Natural Wonder

50 Kilometers

AUSTRIA
SLOVENIA
HUNGARY
CROATIA
BOSNIA-
HERZEGOVINA
ITALY
Adriatic Sea

MONTENEGRO

BOSNIA-HERZEGOVINA

CROATIA

DINARIC MTNS.

Adriatic Sea

INTRODUCTION

This Snapshot guide, excerpted from my guidebook *Rick Steves Croatia & Slovenia*, introduces you to Croatia's single best destination, the "Pearl of the Adriatic"—Dubrovnik. This magnificent medieval city, encircled by a stout wall and poking proudly into the sea, comes with an epic history and plenty of ways to idle away your vacation days. Climb steep steps to the top of the city's imposing stone walls, and stroll high above Dubrovnik's patchwork of red roof tiles. Promenade down the inviting main drag, dropping into an eclectic smattering of fine museums—history, art, folk life, war photography, and the Jewish and Orthodox faiths. Hit the beach and go for a swim in the crystal-clear waters of the Adriatic.

While there are many island and resort-town side-trips from Dubrovnik, this book emphasizes a diverse pair of neighboring countries that offer a more culturally stimulating look at the region: Bosnia-Herzegovina and Montenegro. Mostar, one of Bosnia-Herzegovina's leading cities, is a fascinating combination of Ottoman (Turkish) history, Muslim faith, welcoming locals, lingering war damage, and inspiring postwar reconciliation. Rugged, scenic Montenegro, just south of Dubrovnik, is an emerging Mediterranean hotspot—especially the historic old town of Kotor—but deep in its mountains, you'll find echoes of a bygone mountain kingdom.

To help you have the best trip possible, I've included the following topics in this book:

• **Planning Your Time,** with advice on how to make the most of your limited time

• **Orientation,** including tourist information (abbreviated as TI), tips on public transportation, local tour options, and helpful hints

- **Sights** with ratings:

  ▲▲▲—Don't miss

  ▲▲—Try hard to see

  ▲—Worthwhile if you can make it

  No rating—Worth knowing about
- **Sleeping** and **Eating,** with good-value recommendations in every price range
- **Connections,** with tips on driving, buses, and boats

The **Understanding Yugoslavia** chapter offers a simplified explanation of the history of this complex part of Europe.

Practicalities, near the end of this book, has information on money, staying connected, accommodations, transportation, and other helpful hints, plus Croatian survival phrases.

To travel smartly, read this little book in its entirety before you go. It's my hope that this guide will make your trip more meaningful and rewarding. Traveling like a temporary local, you'll get the absolute most out of every mile, minute, and dollar.

Sretan put! Happy travels!

Rick Steves

DUBROVNIK

DUBROVNIK

Dubrovnik is a living fairy tale that shouldn't be missed. It feels like a small town today, but 500 years ago, Dubrovnik was a major maritime power, with the third-biggest navy in the Mediterranean. Still jutting confidently into the sea and ringed by thick medieval walls, Dubrovnik deserves its nickname: Pearl of the Adriatic. Within the ramparts, the traffic-free Old Town is a fun jumble of steep alleys, low-impact museums, al fresco cafés, and kid-friendly squares. After all these centuries, the buildings still hint at old-time wealth, and the central promenade (Stradun) remains the place to see and be seen.

The city's charm is the result of its no-nonsense past. Busy merchants, the salt trade, and shipbuilding made Dubrovnik rich. But Dubrovnik's most valued commodity was always its freedom— even today, you'll see the proud motto *Libertas* displayed all over town (see *"Libertas"* sidebar).

Dubrovnik flourished in the 15th and 16th centuries, but an earthquake (and ensuing fire) destroyed nearly everything in 1667. Most of today's buildings in the Old Town are post-quake Baroque, although a few palaces, monasteries, and convents displaying a rich Gothic-Renaissance mix survive from Dubrovnik's earlier Golden Age. Dubrovnik remained a big tourist draw through the Tito years, bringing in much-needed hard currency from Western visitors. Consequently, the city never acquired the hard socialist patina of many other Yugoslav cities.

As Croatia violently separated from Yugoslavia in 1991, Dubrovnik became the only coastal city to be pulled into the fighting (see "The Siege of Dubrovnik" sidebar, later). Imagine having your youthful memories of good times spent romping in the surround-

Libertas

Libertas—liberty—has always been close to the heart of every Dubrovnik citizen. Dubrovnik was a proudly independent republic for centuries, even as most of Croatia became Venetian and then Hungarian.

In the Middle Ages, the city-state of Dubrovnik (then called Ragusa) bought its independence from whichever power was strongest—Byzantium, Venice, Hungary, the Ottomans, the Vatican—sometimes paying off more than one at a time. Dubrovnik's ships flew whichever flags were necessary to stay free, earning the derisive nickname "Town of Seven Flags." It was sort of a Hong Kong or Singapore of the Middle Ages—a spunky, trading-oriented statelet that maintained its sovereignty while being completely surrounded by an often-hostile mega-state (in Dubrovnik's case, the Ottoman Empire). Dubrovnik persevered partly because of the inherently corrupt nature of the Ottomans; always susceptible to bribery (or "tribute"), the sultans were more than happy to let Dubrovnik thrive...provided they got their cut.

As time went on, Dubrovnik's status grew. Europe's big-league nations were glad to have a second major seafaring power in the Adriatic to balance Venice; Dubrovnik emerged as an attractive alternative at times when Venetian ports were blockaded by the Ottomans. A free Dubrovnik was more valuable than a pillaged, plundered Dubrovnik.

In 1808, Napoleon conquered the Adriatic and abolished the Republic of Dubrovnik. After Napoleon was defeated, the fate of the continent was decided at the Congress of Vienna. But Dubrovnik's delegate was denied a seat at the table. The more powerful nations, no longer concerned about Venice and fed up after years of being sweet-talked by Dubrovnik, were afraid that the delegate would play old alliances off each other to reestablish an independent Republic of Dubrovnik. Instead, the city became a part of the Habsburg Empire and entered a long period of decline.

Libertas still hasn't died in Dubrovnik. In the surreal days of the early 1990s, when Yugoslavia was reshuffling itself, a movement for the creation of a new Republic of Dubrovnik gained some momentum (led by a judge who, in earlier times, had convicted others for the same ideas). Another movement pushed for Dalmatia to secede as its own nation. But now that the dust has settled, today's locals are content and proud to be part of an independent Republic of Croatia.

DUBROVNIK

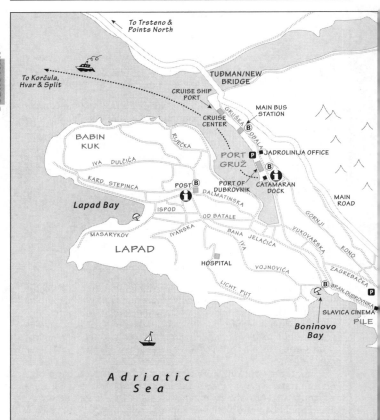

ing hills replaced by visions of tanks and warships shelling your hometown. The city was devastated, but Dubrovnik was repaired with amazing speed. The only physical reminders of the war are lots of new, bright-orange roof tiles. Locals are often willing to talk openly about the experience with visitors—offering a rare opportunity to grasp the realities of war from an eyewitness perspective.

Though the war killed tourism in the 1990s, today the crowds are most decidedly back—far exceeding prewar levels. In fact, Dubrovnik's biggest downside is its popularity. When several cruise ships are in town, it can be mobbed. And, with more and more locals priced out of the Old Town and moving to the suburbs, the center can feel, at times, like a very pretty but soulless theme park. But those who dig deeper find that the city still has a strong sense of identity and a lovable personality. And, like Venice, Dubrovnik rewards those who get off the beaten path and savor the town early and late, when cruisers and day-trippers have cleared out. If you

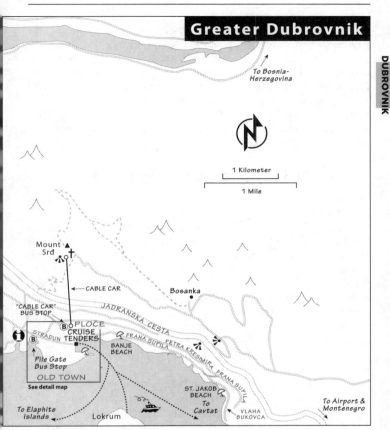

haven't discovered your own secluded, laundry-draped back lane... then you haven't looked hard enough.

For many, Dubrovnik makes an ideal home base. Build some slack into your Dubrovnik stay for a wide array of worthwhile side-trips (outlined in the Near Dubrovnik, Montenegro, and Mostar chapters).

PLANNING YOUR TIME

While Dubrovnik's museums are nothing special, the real attraction here is the Old Town and its relaxing, breezy ambience. While Dubrovnik could easily be "seen" in a day, a second or third day to unwind (or even more time, for side-trips) makes the long trip here more worthwhile. I enjoy staying at least three or four nights, for maximum side-tripping flexibility.

To hit all the key sights in a single day, start at the Pile Gate, at the entrance to the Old Town. Walk around the city's walls to get your bearings (before it gets too hot and crowded), then work your way down the main drag (following my "Stradun Stroll"). As you explore, drop in at any museums or churches that appeal to you. Ride the cable car to the top of Mount Srđ for the sunset, then descend to the Old Town for dinner. With a second day, spread out these activities, hit the beach, or take a boat excursion from the Old Port (Lokrum Island, just offshore, requires the least brainpower). With even more time, fit in side-trips to a pair of particularly striking international destinations: Bosnia-Herzegovina's Mostar and Montenegro's Bay of Kotor.

Orientation to Dubrovnik

Nearly all of the sights worth seeing are in Dubrovnik's traffic-free, walled **Old Town** (Stari Grad, STAH-ree grahd) peninsula. The main pedestrian promenade through the middle of town is called the **Stradun** (STRAH-doon); from this artery, the Old Town climbs steeply uphill in both directions to the walls. The Old Town connects to the mainland through three gates: the **Pile Gate,** to the west; the **Ploče Gate,** to the east; and the smaller **Buža Gate,** at the top of the stepped lane called Boškovićeva. The **Old Port** (Gradska Luka), with leisure boats to nearby destinations, is at the east end of town. While greater Dubrovnik has about 50,000 people, the population within the Old Town is around 1,500; most property owners here have converted their homes into tourist apartment rentals.

The **Pile** (PEE-leh) neighborhood, a pincushion of tourist services, is just outside the western end of the Old Town (through the Pile Gate). In front of the gate, you'll find the main TI, ATMs, a post office, taxis, buses (fanning out to all the outlying neighborhoods), a bus ticket kiosk, a cheap Konzum grocery store, and a DM pharmacy. This is also the starting point for my "Stradun Stroll."

A mile or two away from the Old Town are beaches peppered with expensive resort hotels. The closest area is **Boninovo Bay** (a 20-minute walk or 5-minute bus trip from the Old Town), but most cluster on the lush **Lapad Peninsula** to the west (a 15-minute bus trip from the Old Town). Across the bay from the Lapad Peninsula is **Port Gruž,** with the main bus station, ferry terminal, and main cruise port. (Additional cruise ships tender to the Old Port.) While accommodations prices in these areas can be lower, you'll be competing with lots of other day-trippers (and cruise passengers) on your daily "commute" into your Old Town sightseeing. I'd much prefer to stay within walking distance of the walls.

TOURIST INFORMATION

Dubrovnik's main TI is just outside the Old Town's **Pile Gate,** at the far end of the big terrace with the modern video-screens sculpture (June-Sept daily 8:00-21:00, May and Oct until 20:00, off-season until 19:00 and shorter hours on Sun; Brsalje 5, tel. 020/312-011, www.tzdubrovnik.hr). There are also locations at **Port Gruž,** across the street from the Jadrolinija ferry dock (same hours except closes earlier in off-season, Obala Ivana Pavla II, tel. 020/417-983); in the **Lapad** resort area, at the head of the main drag (Masarykov put 2, in Dvori Lapad building, tel. 020/437-460); on two of the Elaphite Islands, **Lopud** (Obala Iva Kuljevana 12, tel. 020/759-086) and **Šipan** (Luka b.b., tel. 020/758-084); and at the arrivals area of the **airport.** While not an official TI, the handy **Cultural Information Desk** (at the base of the Bell Tower, on Luža Square) is more central and can answer many questions (open long hours daily).

All TIs sell the Dubrovnik Card and hand out copies of two similar booklets: the annual *Dubrovnik Riviera Info* (lots of glossy photos and telephone directory) and the monthly *The Best in Dubrovnik* (with tons of ads, a current schedule of events and performances, and bus and ferry schedules).

Sightseeing Passes: If you'll be doing any sightseeing at all, choose between Dubrovnik's two passes. The 120-kn **"nine museum ticket"** is good for a week and covers several major museums, including the Rector's Palace, Rupe Museum, and Maritime Museum. Since you can't buy individual tickets at these sights, you'll have to get this ticket to see any of them. But assuming you're climbing the City Walls—Dubrovnik's top attraction—you might as well buy the **Dubrovnik Card** instead, which includes the same museums, the walls, and public transit. To squeeze all of your sightseeing into one day, get the 24-hour pass (190 kn, includes unlimited transit); with more time, consider one of the longer tickets, which cover the same sights and add a few more bonuses and discounts—including for side-tripping to Cavtat (250 kn/3 days includes 6 transit rides, 350 kn/7 days includes 10 transit rides; cards sold at TIs and many sights and hotels; slightly cheaper if you prebook online).

ARRIVAL IN DUBROVNIK

Most of Dubrovnik's arrival points—ferry dock, cruise terminal, bus station—are at **Port Gruž,** about 2.5 miles northwest of the Old Town. To get into town, hop on a bus (#1a, #1b, #3, or #8) or take a taxi (around 70-80 kn) to the Pile Gate, at the entrance to the Old Town.

By Boat

Passenger **catamarans** and car **ferries** all arrive at Port Gruž, two miles northwest of the Old Town. On the road in front of the ferry terminal, you'll find a bus stop (wait on the embankment side of the street) and a taxi stand. Across the street is the Jadrolinija office (with an ATM out front) and a TI.

Some **cruise ships** anchor just offshore from the Old Port, then send their passengers into the Old Town on tenders. Others put in just beyond the bus station at Port Gruž, where you can catch a bus or taxi to the Old Town.

By Bus

Dubrovnik's main bus station (Autobusni Kolodvor) is just beyond the ferry terminal along the Port Gruž embankment. On arrival, walk straight ahead through the bus stalls then bear right at the main road to the city bus stop, or hop in a taxi.

Alternate Bus Stop for Outbound Buses: For buses that are leaving Dubrovnik toward regional destinations to the south (such as the airport or Cavtat), there's another bus stop that's much closer to the Old Town, saving you the long journey out to the main bus station. The **"cable car" bus stop** (a.k.a. "fire station" bus stop) is just uphill from the Buža Gate, overlooking the old wall, right next to the bottom station of the cable car up to Mount Srđ.

By Plane

Dubrovnik's small airport (Zračna Luka) is near a village called Čilipi, 13 miles south of the city. A bus meets arriving flights for most major airlines at the airport, and brings you to the Pile Gate just outside the Old Town, then continues to the main bus station (40 kn, 40 minutes). Legitimate cabbies charge around 250-270 kn for the ride between the airport and the center (though some cabbies charge more than 300 kn; consider arranging your transfer in advance with one of the drivers listed under "Tours in Dubrovnik—Private Drivers" or through your *soba* host; airport code: DBV, tel. 020/773-333, www.airport-dubrovnik.hr).

To get *to* the airport, you can take the same bus, which typically leaves from Dubrovnik's main bus station 1.5 hours before each Croatia Airlines or Austrian Airlines flight, or two hours before other airlines' international flights (the schedule is posted the day before—you must ask at the TI). The airport-bound bus stops at the main bus station and at the "cable car" bus stop just above the Old Town's Buža Gate (see "By Bus," earlier)—but *not* at Pile Gate.

By Car

Coming from the north, you'll drive over the modern Tuđman Bridge (which most locals, mindful of their former president's tarnished legacy, call simply "the New Bridge"). Immediately after crossing the bridge, you have two options: To get to the main bus station, ferry terminal (with some car-rental drop-off offices nearby), and Lapad Peninsula, take the left turn just after the bridge, wind down to the waterfront, then turn left and follow this road along the Port Gruž embankment.

Alternatively, to head to the **Old Town,** continue straight after the bridge. You'll pass above the Port Gruž area, then take the right turnoff marked *Dubrovnik* (with the little bull's-eye). You'll go through a tunnel, then turn left for *Grad/Old City.* This road passes the big Old Town parking garage (described below), then twists around over the top of the Old Town, until you can see the lower station for the cable car. Here you have two choices, which will determine which one-way loop you'll get stuck in: If you want to reach the Pile Gate (at the eastern end of the Old Town), make a sharp right turn just before the cable car (watch for *Grad/Old City* signs), then turn right again (passing the entrance to the small "tennis court" parking lot) to curl around the back of the city wall and pop out at the Pile Gate (with another small parking lot), then back up out of town toward Boninovo Bay and Lapad. Or, if you want to head east of the Old Town, continue straight past the cable-car station for a long, scenic drive above the Viktorija area, then (after a sharp right turn) past luxury hotels and to the Ploče Gate.

Parking: Near the Old Town, parking costs are exorbitant (rates constantly in flux and may exceed what's listed here). Ideally, make Dubrovnik either the first or last stop of your car rental, so you won't have to pay to park here. But if you must, ask your *soba* host for their best advice (many have a line on relatively reasonable options, though they may be distant).

There are a few small parking lots **near the City Walls**—so expensive and crowded that they're useful only for dropping off luggage before retreating to a more affordable alternative. The most expensive is just behind the DM pharmacy near the Pile Gate (75 kn/hour, no daily rate); somewhat cheaper—but still pricey and usually often full—is the "tennis court" lot, huddled behind the wall at the Buža Gate, at the very top of the Old Town (40 kn/hour or 600 kn/24 hours—you have to buy the daily ticket at a Tisak kiosk or the machine, www.sanitat.hr).

For longer-term parking, choose between close and expensive or far and cheap: The **Old Town parking garage** costs 40 kn/hour or 480 kn/day in July-Aug, 35 kn/hour or 420 kn/day in June and September, and less off-season. Important: If you'll be staying overnight, request a daily ticket *(dnevna karta)* at the ticket office within 15 minutes of when you park—this is essential to avoid exorbitant hourly rates. From this garage, it's about a 10-minute downhill walk to the Old Town—and a much steeper, 20-minute hike back up. Or you can park at the big lot at **Port Gruž,** just north of the Jadrolinija ferry terminal (10 kn/hour, 130 kn/day); from here, you can take a bus or taxi to the Old Town's Pile Gate.

HELPFUL HINTS

Festivals: Dubrovnik is most crowded during its **Summer Festival,** a month and a half of theater and musical performances held annually (July 10-Aug 25, www.dubrovnik-festival.hr). This is quickly followed by the **Late Summer Festival,** designed to continue the festivities into September.

Crowd-Beating Tips: Dubrovnik has been discovered—especially by cruise ships (hundreds of which visit each year, bringing more than one million passengers—on very busy days, there may be four ships in at once, sending 9,000-plus passengers ashore). Cruise-ship crowds descend on the Old Town roughly between 8:30 and 14:00 (the streets are most crowded 9:00-13:00). Bad-weather days are a perfect storm, when people staying locally—who'd otherwise hit the beach—come into the Old Town for sightseeing, along with all the cruise passengers. On busy days, try to avoid the big sights—especially walking around the City Walls—during these peak times, and hit the beach or take a siesta midday, when the town is hottest and most crowded. It can also make sense to schedule out-of-town side-trips for busy cruise days; you can check the day-by-day cruise schedule at www.portdubrovnik.hr. There's a lot of talk about how Dubrovnik could strategically limit the number of cruise passengers allowed in town—but until that happens, your best strategy is to be aware and to avoid the busiest places.

No Euros: Dubrovnik's merchants (even some of the city's top sights, such as the City Walls and cable car) can be stubborn about accepting only kunas—no euros.

Wine Shop: For the best wine-tasting selection in a cool bar atmosphere, don't miss **D'Vino Wine Bar** (described later, under "Entertainment in Dubrovnik"). If you want to shop rather than taste, **Vinoteka Miličić** offers a nice variety of local wines in a shoebox space. Jolly Dolores can explain your options, most of which are their own Miličić wines, and she can bubble-wrap bottles—handy to travel with (daily June-Aug 9:00-22:00, shorter hours off-season, near the Pile Gate end of the Stradun, tel. 020/321-777).

Laundry: Lavaman is most central and offers full service. Drop your clothes and let them do the dirty work (daily 7:00-18:00, same-day service usually possible if you drop it off in the morning, Dropčeva ulica 2, tel. 020/321-233). The retro, self-service **Sanja and Rosie's Launderette** is just outside the Ploče Gate (cross the bridge and look left, clear English instructions, machines take bills, daily 8:00-22:00—or later in peak season, put od Bosanke 2, mobile 091-896-7509). If you're sleeping near the top of town, it may be easier to hike up to the self-service **Laundry Spin,** in the tunnel just outside of the Buža Gate (daily 8:00-20:00, Wi-Fi, Iza Grada b.b., tel. 020/456-855).

Car Rental: The big international chains have offices at the airport; a few also have branches near the Port Gruž embankment where the big ships come in, or in Lapad hotels. In addition, the many travel agencies closer to the Old Town also have a line on rental cars. Be sure the agency knows if you're crossing a border (such as Bosnia-Herzegovina or Montenegro) to ensure you have the proper paperwork.

Best Views: Walking the **City Walls** late in the day, when the city is bathed in rich light, is a treat. The cable car up to **Mount Srđ** provides bird's-eye panoramas over the entire region, from the highest vantage point without wings. The **Fort of St. Lawrence,** perched above the Pile neighborhood cove, has great views over the Old Town. The **panoramic cruises** that loop around the Old Town are another fine choice. A stroll up the road east of the walls offers nice views back on the Old Town (best light early in the day). Better yet, if you have a car, head south of the city in the morning for gorgeously lit Old Town views over your right shoulder; various turnoffs along this road are ideal photo stops. The best one, known locally simply as **"panorama point,"** is where the road leading up and out of Dubrovnik meets the main road that passes above the town (look for the pullout on the right, usually crowded with tour buses). Even if you're heading north, in good weather it's worth a quick detour south for this view.

GETTING AROUND DUBROVNIK

If you're staying in or near the Old Town, everything is easily walkable. But those sleeping in outlying areas will want to get comfortable using the buses. Once you understand the system, commuting to the Old Town is straightforward (though the buses can be quite crowded).

By Bus: Libertas runs Dubrovnik's public buses. Tickets, which are good for an hour, are cheaper if you buy them in advance from a newsstand or your hotel (12 kn, ask for *autobusna karta,* ow-toh-BOOS-nah KAR-tah) than if you buy them from the bus driver (15 kn). A 24-hour ticket costs 30 kn (only sold at special bus-ticket kiosks, such as the one near the Pile Gate bus stop).

When you enter the bus, validate your ticket in the machine next to the driver (insert it with the orange arrow facing out and pointing down). Because most tourists can't figure out how to vali-

Game of Thrones in Dubrovnik

Fans of the HBO television series *Game of Thrones* may feel the tingle of déjà vu during their visit to Dubrovnik. For years, much of the series was filmed here. Many locals have been extras, and they grew accustomed to seeing Peter Dinklage strolling down the Stradun in full costume.

On the show, Dubrovnik and the surrounding coastline and islands provided a setting for two main storylines: the royal family intrigue at King's Landing; and Daenerys Targaryen's conquest of the continent of Essos, from idyllic Qarth to Slaver's Bay. Of course, in most cases, the real-life Croatian settings were dressed up with special effects—the sea, rocks, and bottoms of the buildings were real, while the fanciful towers and spires (and the dragons) were pure fantasy.

For die-hard *GoT* geeks, here are some specifics (spoilers ahead!): The real-life Fort of St. Lawrence looks over a pleasant cove that becomes Blackwater Bay. Trsteno Arboretum (described in the next chapter) is where Sansa Stark had many heart-to-hearts with Olenna and Margaery Tyrell. The eventful royal wedding of Joffrey and Margaery was filmed in Gradac Park. The epic duel between Oberyn Martell and The Mountain was filmed at the amphitheater below Hotel Belvedere, facing Dubrovnik's Old Port. The island of Lokrum played host to the Qarth garden party, and the tower where Daenerys' dragons were held captive was Minčeta Tower (in the City Walls). And Cersei was humiliated by being forced to walk naked through town, beginning at the top of the grand staircase below the Jesuit Church (which I now think of as the "Steps of Shame! Shame! Shame!").

Filming has also taken place in Split, where Diocletian's cellars became the dungeon where Daenerys safely locked up her dragons. And the fortified town of Klis, just north of Split, was the location for the slaving town of Mereen.

To please *GoT* pilgrims, various companies offer walking tours of filming locations (see "Tours in Dubrovnik," later). A shop on Boškovićeva street (just above Prijeko street) has a replica of the Iron Throne (a great photo op, but only if you buy an overpriced souvenir). And the monastery on Lokrum Island hosts a small museum of *Game of Thrones* memorabilia.

Game of Thrones kicked off a new trend of Hollywood filming in Dubrovnik. The town stood in for the casino city of Canto Bight in *Star Wars: The Last Jedi,* and 2018's *Robin Hood* was shot here. (Locals were pleased with the construction of wood-frame castle extensions to the City Walls at the Old Port—and then were disappointed when they got burned down for the film's finale.) And recently, the new James Bond film (featuring Daniel Craig's final appearance as 007) used Dubrovnik as one of its primary settings, while *Mamma Mia 2* was shot on the nearby island of Vis. For the latest on what's been filmed here, ask around town.

date their tickets, it can take a long time to load the bus (which means drivers are understandably grumpy, and locals aren't shy about cutting in line).

All buses stop near the Old Town, just in front of the Pile Gate (buy tickets at the newsstand). From here, they fan out to various parts of town; the routes you're most likely to use are buses #1a, #1b, #3, and #8 to Port Gruž (cruise port, ferry terminal), or buses #4 or #6 to the resort cove at Lapad. For more information, visit www.libertasdubrovnik.hr.

By Taxi: Taxis start at 25 kn, then charge 8 kn per kilometer. The handiest taxi stand for the Old Town is just outside the Pile Gate. The biggest operation is Radio Taxi (tel. 0800-0970 or 020/435-650). Uber, which is often cheaper, also works well in Dubrovnik.

Tours in Dubrovnik

Walking Tours

Two companies—**Dubrovnik Walks** (www.dubrovnikwalks.com) and **Dubrovnik Walking Tours** (www.dubrovnik-walking-tours.com)—offer similar one-hour walking tours of the Old Town several times daily (90-100 kn). I'd skip these tours—they're pricey and brief, touching lightly on the same information explained in this chapter. Both companies (and others) also offer themed tours covering *Game of Thrones* locations, wartime Dubrovnik, and the historic Jewish quarter. For the latest offerings, pick up their fliers (sales kiosks by Pile Gate bus stop, in front of TI) or check their websites.

Local Guides

For an in-depth look at the city, consider hiring your own local guide. **Roberto de Lorenzo** and his mother **Marija Tiberi** are both warm people enthusiastic about telling evocative stories from medieval Dubrovnik, including some off-the-beaten-path stops tailored to your interests (500 kn/2 hours, mobile 091-541-6637, dubrovnikgardens@gmail.com); ask about guided transfers to Bosnia-Herzegovina, Split, or beyond. **Štefica Curić Lenert** is a sharp professional guide who offers a great by-the-book tour and an insider's look at the city (550 kn/1.5 hours, other tour options explained on her website, reserve at least one day ahead, mobile 091-345-0133, www.dubrovnikprivateguide.com, stefe@dubrovnikprivateguide.com). If these guides are busy, they can refer you to another good guide for a similar price.

FROM DUBROVNIK

For information on tour boats and guided big-bus excursions from Dubrovnik to nearby destinations, see the next chapter.

Private Drivers

If you're more comfortable having someone else do the driving to sights near Dubrovnik, hire your own driver. While the drivers listed here are not licensed tour guides, they speak great English and offer commentary as you roll, and can help you craft a good day-long itinerary to Mostar, Montenegro, or anywhere else near Dubrovnik (typically departing around 8:00 and returning in the early evening).

Friendly **Pepo Klaić** is enjoyable to get to know and has a knack for making the experience both informative and meaningful. Ask about his tennis-phenom son (€180 for Bay of Kotor, €200 for Mostar, airport transfer for about €30—cheaper than a taxi, these prices for up to four people—more expensive for bigger group, mobile 098-427-301, www.dubrovnikshoretrip.com, pklaic@gmail.com). **Petar Vlašić** does similar tours for similar prices, and specializes in wine tours to the Pelješac Peninsula, with stops at various wineries along the way (€30 airport transfers, €190-200 for 2-person trip to Pelješac wineries, €230 to Mostar or €250 to Montenegro including local guide, these prices for 1-3 people—more for larger groups, mobile 091-580-8721, www. dubrovnikrivieratours.com, info@dubrovnikrivieratours.com).

If your destination is Mostar, likeable Bosnian driver **Ermin Elezović** will happily come pick you up for less than the Dubrovnik-based drivers (€120 for one-way transfer from Dubrovnik to Mostar with a few brief sightseeing stops en route, €240 for round-trip to Mostar with same-day return to Dubrovnik; for contact information and details, see page 159).

Stradun Stroll

Running through the heart of Dubrovnik's Old Town is the 300-yard-long Stradun promenade—packed with people and lined with sights. This self-guided walk (rated ▲▲▲) offers an ideal introduction to Dubrovnik's charms. It takes about a half-hour, not counting sightseeing stops.

• *Begin at the busy square in front of the west entrance to the Old Town, the Pile Gate.*

Pile Neighborhood

This bustling area is the nerve center of Dubrovnik's tourist industry—it's where the real world meets the fantasy of Dubrovnik (for details on services offered here, see "Orientation to Dubrovnik," earlier). Behind the odd, modern, mirrors-and-LED-screens monument (which honors the "Dubrovnik Defenders" who protected the city during the 1991-1992 siege) is a long and leafy café terrace. Wander over to the balustrade at the terrace's end and take in the imposing walls of the Pearl of the Adriatic. (*Game of Thrones* fans might feel a twinge of déjà vu for Blackwater Bay.) The huge, fortified peninsula just outside

the City Walls is the **Fort of St. Lawrence** (Tvrđava Lovrijenac), Dubrovnik's oldest fortress. Imagine how this fort and the stout walls worked together to fortify the little harbor—and the gate just behind you. You can climb 208 steps up to this fortress for great views over the Old Town (50 kn, covered by same ticket as City Walls on the same day)...or just hike up to the little terrace in front of the door, which has views nearly as good. The view from up top offers a perfect illustration of how Dubrovnik's walled Old Town is shaped like a V—with two formerly separate hill towns joined by a covered-over canal.

• *Back along the busy main drag, cross over the moat (now a shady park) to the round entrance tower in the City Walls. This is the...*

Pile Gate (Gradska Vrata Pile)

Just before you enter the gate, notice the image above the entrance of **St. Blaise** (Sveti Vlaho in Croatian) cradling Dubrovnik in his

arm. You'll see a lot more of Blaise, the protector of Dubrovnik, during your time here—he is to Dubrovnik what the winged lion of St. Mark is to Venice.

Inside the first part of the gate, dead ahead you'll see another image of Blaise.

Turn left and go down the ramp, to the little hole in the wall. Step through it to enter a tranquil **playground park,** where locals play with their toddlers in serenity (surrounded on all sides by tourists). Back inside the gate, look for the **white map** (next to the tourist map) that shows where each bomb dropped on the Old Town during the siege. Once inside town, you'll see virtually no signs of the war—a testament to the townspeople's impressive resilience in rebuilding so well and so quickly.

• *Continue down the ramp and pass the rest of the way through the gate.*

On the other side, you'll find a lively little square surrounded by land-marks.

St. Savior Square

The giant, round structure in the middle of the square is **Onofrio's Big Fountain** (Velika Onofrijea Fontana). In the Middle Ages, Dubrovnik had a complicated aq-

ueduct system that brought water from the mountains seven miles away. The water ended up here, at the town's biggest fountain, before continuing through the city. Three things helped make little, inde-pendent Dubrovnik very siege-resistant: this plentiful supply of water, large reserves of salt (a key source of Dubrovnik's wealth, from the town of Ston—see page 83), and a massive granary (now the Rupe Granary and Ethno-graphic Museum, described later).

Stand with your back to the fountain and face the small **Church of St. Savior** (Crkva Svetog Spasa). Townspeople built this votive church to thank God after Dubrovnik made it through a 1520 earthquake. When the massive 1667 quake destroyed the city, this church was one of the only buildings left intact—its Renais-sance interior stands at odds against the predominantly Baroque styles in other town churches. And during the Yugoslav Wars, the church survived another close call when a shell exploded on the ground right in front of it (you can still see faint pockmarks from the shrapnel).

To the left of the church, a steep stairway leads up to the im-posing **Minčeta Tower.** It's possible to enter here to begin Du-brovnik's best activity, walking around the top of the City Walls (tickets are sold across the square)—but this walk ends near a bet-ter, less crowded entry point.

The big building to the right of the Church of St. Savior is the **Franciscan Monastery Museum.** This tourable building has a delightful cloister and one of Europe's oldest continually oper-ating pharmacies (described later; enter through the gap between the small church and the door of the big church). Historically, the monastery's **Franciscan Church** was the house of worship for Du-brovnik's poor people, while the Dominican Church (down at the far end of the Stradun, where our walk ends) was for the wealthy. Services were staggered by 15 minutes to allow servants to drop off their masters there, then rush up the Stradun for their own service here. If you peek inside the church, you'll find a Baroque interior—

typical of virtually all of the town's churches, which were rebuilt after the 1667 quake.

Back outside, still with your back to the round fountain, look up and notice the **bell tower** of the Franciscan Church—with its rounded top—which is integrated into the structure of the building. If your travels have taken you beyond Dubrovnik, you'll notice the difference from other Croatian towns, where church steeples follow Venetian convention: Set apart from the church, and with a pointy top. This is just the first of many contrasts we'll see between Dubrovnik and Venice—two powerful, rival maritime republics.

Finally, notice the stubby little, shin-high, mustachioed **gargoyle** embedded in the wall, just left of the Franciscan Church's door. You may see a commotion of tourists trying to balance on the small, slippery surface of the gargoyle's head. Tour guides enjoy spinning a variety of tall tales about this creature—for instance, if you can balance on one leg for three seconds, your fondest wish comes true—but these are a recent innovation.

• *When you're finished taking in the sights on this square, continue along...*

The Stradun

Dubrovnik's main promenade—officially called the Placa, but better known as the Stradun—is alive with locals and tourists alike.

This is the heartbeat of the city: an Old World shopping mall by day and sprawling cocktail party after dark, when everybody seems to be doing the traditional evening stroll—flirting, ice-cream-licking, flaunting, and gawking. A coffee and some of Europe's best people-watching in a prime Stradun café is one of travel's great $5 bargains.

When Dubrovnik was just getting its start in the seventh century, this street was a canal. Romans fleeing from the invading Slavs lived on the island of Ragusa (on your right), and the Slavs settled on the shore. In the 11th century, the canal separating Ragusa from the mainland was filled in, the towns merged, and a unique Slavic-Roman culture and language blossomed. While originally much more higgledy-piggledy, this street was rebuilt in the current, more straightforward style after the 1667 earthquake. The ensuing fire raged for three weeks and consumed much of the city.

The distinctively shaped doors—with P-shaped shop windows built right in, to provide maximum views of goods, but minimum

DUBROVNIK

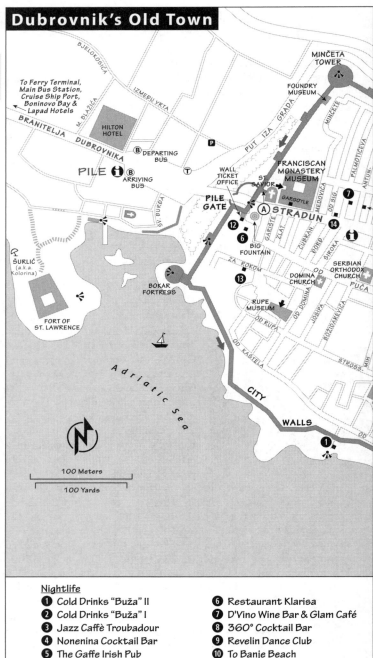

Dubrovnik's Old Town

MINČETA TOWER

FOUNDRY MUSEUM

To Ferry Terminal,
Main Bus Station,
Cruise Ship Port,
Boninovo Bay &
Lapad Hotels

BJELOKOSIĆA

IZMEĐU VRTA

M. BLAŽIĆA

SV. ĐURĐA

BRANITELJA DUBROVNIKA

HILTON HOTEL

P

B DEPARTING BUS

T

PILE **ⓘ** **B**

ARRIVING BUS

PUT IZA GRADA

WALL TICKET OFFICE

ST. SAVIOR

PILE GATE

FRANCISCAN MONASTERY MUSEUM

MINČETE

PALMOTIĆEVA

ANTUN-

Ⓐ STRADUN

GARGOYLE

OD SIG

7

12

6

14

ⓘ

GARIŠTE

ZLAT

CUBRAN

POBJ

SIROKA

BIG FOUNTAIN

ŠURLIĆ
(a.k.a.
Kolorina)

BOKAR FORTRESS

ZA ROKOM

13

DOMINA CHURCH

SERBIAN ORTHODOX CHURCH

PUČA

OD DOMINA

LOJISTRA

BOŽIDAREVIĆA

RUPE MUSEUM

FORT OF ST. LAWRENCE

OD RUPE

OD KAŠTELA

STROSS. MIH.

Adriatic Sea

CITY

WALLS

OD

1

N

100 Meters

100 Yards

DUBROVNIK

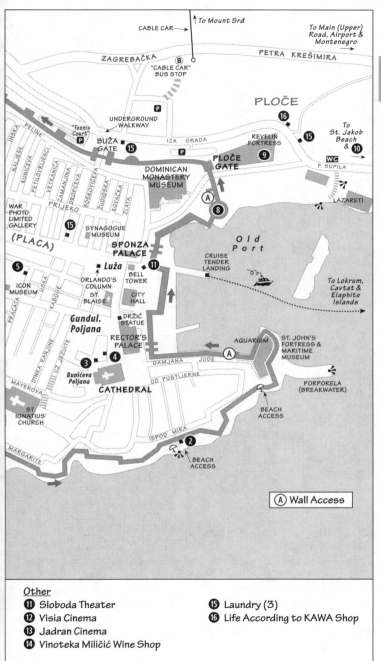

access—indicate that this was the terrain of the merchants...and it still is.

The austerity of Dubrovnik's main drag disappoints some visitors. Rather than lavishing funds on ostentatious palaces, as in Venice, Dubrovnik seems eager to downplay its wealth. For much of its history, Dubrovnik paid a hefty tribute to the sultan of the Ottoman Empire to maintain its independent status. Flaunting wealth would have raised Ottoman eyebrows...and, likely, Ottoman taxes. Think about the stark contrast between restrained Dubrovnik and its rival Venice, which was desperate to impress. Venice was surrounded by Italians, Austrians, Germans—some allies, some rivals, but all Christian. Dubrovnik sat five miles from the frontier of the Ottoman Empire; leaving the city felt like leaving the known world and the safety of what we'd today call "Western Civilization."

Let me guess—the Stradun is crowded, right? When multiple cruise ships drop anchor, the many excursions into town feel more like incursions. But try some attitude adjustment: The maritime republic of Dubrovnik has always been a crossroads of merchants, sailors, and other travelers from around the world. While today they may be following their tour guides' numbered paddles rather than trading exotic spices, the legions of visitors are still part of the city's tapestry of history.

If you're here on a summer evening (June-Sept), you might hear the rat-a-tat-tat of a drum echoing through the streets from the Stradun. This means it's time to head for this main drag to get a glimpse of the colorfully costumed **"town guards"** parading through (and the cavalcade of tourists running alongside them, trying to snap a clear picture). You may also see some of these characters standing guard outside the town gates. Begun only recently, this "tradition" is part of the local tourist board's efforts to make their town even more atmospheric.

• *Branching off from this promenade are several museums and other attractions. At the end of the Stradun is the lively Luža Square. Its centerpiece is the 20-foot-tall...*

Orlando's Column (Orlandov Stup)

Dubrovnik erected this column—a northern European symbol—in 1417, soon after it had shifted allegiances from the oppressive Venetians to the Hungarians. Whenever a decision was made by the Republic, the town crier came to Orlando's Column and announced the news. The step he stood on indicated the importance of his message—the higher up, the more important the news. It was also used as the pillory, where people were publicly punished. The thin line on the top step in front of Orlando is exactly as long

as the statue's forearm. This mark was Dubrovnik's standard mea-
surement—not for a foot, but for an "elbow."

• *Now stand in front of Orlando's Column and orient yourself with a...*

Luža Square Spin-Tour

Orlando is looking toward the **Sponza
Palace** (Sponza-Povijesni Arhiv). This
building, from 1522, is the finest surviving example of Dubrovnik's Golden
Age in the 15th and 16th centuries. It's
a combination of Renaissance (ground-
floor arcade) and Venetian Gothic (upstairs windows). Houses up and down
the main promenade used to look like
this, before the 1667 earthquake and fire.
This used to be the customs office *(doga-
na),* but now it's an exhaustive archive of
the city's history, with temporary art exhibits and a war memorial.
The poignant **Memorial Room of Dubrovnik Defenders** (inside
and on the left) has photos of dozens of people from Dubrovnik
who were killed fighting Yugoslav forces in 1991. A TV screen and
images near the ceiling show the devastation of the city. Though
the English descriptions are pointedly—if unavoidably—slanted
to the Croat perspective, it's compelling to look in the eyes of the
brave young men who didn't start this war...but were willing to fin-
ish it (free, long hours daily in peak season). Beyond the memorial
room, the impressive **courtyard,** which hosts temporary exhibits,
is worth a peek (25 kn, generally free after-hours).

To the right of Sponza Palace is the town's **Bell Tower** (Grad-
ski Zvonik). The original dated from 1444, but it was rebuilt when
it started to lean in the 1920s. The big clock may be an octopus, but
only one of its hands tells time. Below that, the golden circle shows
the phase of the moon. At the bottom, the old-fashioned digital
readout tells the hour (in Roman numerals) and the minutes (in
five-minute increments). At the top of each hour (and again three
minutes later), the time is clanged out on the bell up top by two
bronze bell-ringers, Maro and Baro. (If this all seems like a copy
of the very similar clock on St. Mark's Square in Venice, locals
are quick to point out that this clock predates that one by several
decades.)

The clock still has to be wound every two days. Notice the
little window between the moon phase and the "digital" readout:
The clock-winder opens this window to get some light. The Kra-
sovac family was in charge of winding the clock for generations.
During the 1991-1992 siege, their house was destroyed—with the
winding keys inside. For days, the clock bell didn't run. But then,

DUBROVNIK

The Siege of Dubrovnik

In June 1991, Croatia declared independence from Yugoslavia. Within weeks, the nations were at war (for more on the war, see the Understanding Yugoslavia chapter). Though warfare raged in the Croatian interior, nobody expected that it would reach Dubrovnik.

As refugees from Vukovar (in northeastern Croatia) arrived in Dubrovnik that fall, telling horrific stories of the warfare there, local residents began fearing the worst. Warplanes from the Serb-dominated Yugoslav People's Army buzzed threateningly low over the town, as if to signal an impending attack.

Then, at 6:00 in the morning on October 1, 1991, Dubrovnik residents awoke to explosions on nearby hillsides. The first attacks were focused on Mount Srđ, high above the Old Town. First the giant cross was destroyed, then a communications tower (both have been rebuilt and are visible today). This first wave of attacks cleared the way for Yugoslav land troops—mostly Serbs and Montenegrins—who surround-ed the city. The ragtag, newly formed Croatian army quickly dug in at the old Napoleonic-era fortress at the top of Mount Srđ, where just 25 or 30 soldiers fended off a Yugoslav takeover of this highly strategic position.

At first, shelling targeted military positions on the outskirts of town. But soon, Yugoslav forces began bombing residential neighborhoods, then the Pearl of the Adriatic itself: Dubrovnik's Old Town. Defenseless townspeople took shelter in their cellars, and sometimes even huddled together in the city wall's 15th-century forts. It was the first time in Dubrovnik's long history that the walls were actually used to defend against an attack.

The people of Dubrovnik refused to flee their town. Though severely outgunned and outnumbered, Dubrovnik's defenders managed to hold the fort atop Mount Srđ, while Yugoslav forces controlled the nearby mountaintops. All supplies had to be carried up to the fort by foot or by donkey. Dubrovnik wasn't prepared for war, so its citizens had to improvise their defense. Many brave young locals lost their lives when they slung old hunting rifles over their shoulders and, under cover of darkness, climbed the hills above Dubrovnik to meet Yugoslav soldiers face-to-face.

After eight months of bombing, Dubrovnik was liberated by the Croatian army, which attacked Yugoslav positions from the north. By the end of the siege, 100 civilians were dead, as well as more than 200 Dubrovnik citizens who lost their lives actively fighting for their hometown (much revered today as "Dubrovnik Defenders"); in the greater Dubrovnik area, 420 "Defenders" were killed, and another 900 wounded. More than two-thirds of Dubrovnik's buildings had been damaged, and more than 30,000 people had to flee their homes—but the failed siege was finally over.

Why was Dubrovnik—so far from the rest of the fighting—dragged into the conflict? Yugoslavia wanted to catch the city off-guard, gaining a toehold on the southern Dalmatian Coast so they could push north to Split. They also hoped to ignite pro-Serb passions in the nearby Serb-dominated areas of Bosnia-Herzegovina and Montenegro. But perhaps most of all, Yugoslavia wanted to hit Croatia where it hurt—its proudest, most historic, and most beautiful city, the tourist capital of a nation dependent on tourism. It seems their plan backfired. Locals now say, "When Yugoslavia attacked Dubrovnik, they lost the war"—because images of the historic city under siege swayed international public opinion *against* Yugoslavia.

The war initially devastated the tourist industry. Now, to the casual observer, Dubrovnik seems virtually back to normal. Aside from a few pockmarks and bright, new roof tiles, there are scant reminders of what happened here more than two decades ago. But even though the city itself has been repaired, the people of Dubrovnik are forever changed. Imagine living in an idyllic paradise, a place that attracted and awed visitors from around the world...and then watching it gradually blown to bits. It's understandable if Dubrovnik's citizens are a little less in love with life than they once were.

It's clear that in the case of this siege, the Croats of Dubrovnik were the largely innocent victims of a brutal surprise attack. But keep in mind the larger context of the war: The cousins of these Croats, who were defending the glorious monument that is Dubrovnik, bombarded another glorious monument—the Old Bridge of Mostar. It's just another reminder that the "good guys" and "bad guys" in these wars are far from clear-cut.

Dubrovnik has several low-key attractions related to its recent war, including the museum in the ruined fortress atop Mount Srđ and the Memorial Room of Dubrovnik Defenders in the Sponza Palace on Luža Square. Another sight, War Photo Limited, expands the scope to war photography from around the world.

miraculously, the keys were discovered lying in the street. The excited Dubrovnik citizens came together in this square and cheered
as the clock was wound and the bell chimed, signaling to the soldiers surrounding the city that they hadn't won yet.

To the right of the Bell Tower, you'll see the entrance to the
Sloboda theater (marked *Luža*), which hosts cultural events (such
as folk-dancing shows) in the summer, and movies year-round.
There's also the helpful Cultural Information Desk inside. Next
to that, **Onofrio's Little Fountain** (Mala Onofrijea Fontana) is
the little brother of the one at the other end of the Stradun. The
big building beyond the fountain is the **City Hall** (Vijećnica). The
terrace at the near end of City Hall is occupied by the **Gradska
Kavana**, or "Town Café." This hangout—historically Dubrovnik's
favorite spot for gossiping and people-watching—has seating all
the way through the wall to the Old Port.

Behind Orlando is **St. Blaise's Church** (Crkva Sv. Vlaha),
dedicated to the patron saint of Dubrovnik. You'll see statues and
paintings of St. Blaise all over town,
always holding a model of the city in
his left hand. According to legend, a
millennium ago St. Blaise came to a
local priest in a dream and warned
him that the up-and-coming Venetians would soon attack the city. The
priest alerted the authorities, who
prepared for war. Of course, the pre-
diction came true. St. Blaise has been a Dubrovnik symbol—and
locals have resented Venice—ever since.

The church, like most churches in this city, was built following the 1667 earthquake and fire. And, while we've heard plenty on
this walk about Dubrovnik's rivalry with Venice, there's no deny-
ing that the Venetians were some of Europe's top cultural trend-
setters at that time. So Dubrovnik invited a Venetian architect to
design the church dedicated to their favorite saint. That's why St.
Blaise's looks like it would be right at home reflected in a Venetian
canal...right down to its bulbous dome, which seems to have been
transplanted here from the top of St. Mark's.

Just down the street from the "Town Café" is the Rector's Palace, and then the cathedral (both described later, under "Sights in
Dubrovnik"). Just before the palace, on the left, notice the statue
of Dubrovnik poet **Marin Držić** (1508-1567). This beloved bard's
most famous work concerns "Uncle Maro," an aristocrat who's
as stingy as he is wealthy. His son cleans out his savings account
and goes on a bender in Rome...until his father gets wind of it and
comes calling. The shiny lap and bright nose of this statue, erected
in 2008, might lead you to believe it's good luck to rub his schnoz—

and, sure enough, you'll see a steady stream of tourists doing just that. But the truth is that when the statue went up, local kids were drawn to his prominent proboscis, and couldn't resist climbing up on his lap and grabbing it. Tourists saw the shine and assumed they were supposed to do it, too. A legend was born.

• *Your walk is finished. From here, you've got plenty of sightseeing options (all described next). As you face the Bell Tower, you can go up the street to the right to reach the Rector's Palace and cathedral; you can walk straight ahead through the gate to reach the Old Port; or you can head through the gate and jog left to find the Dominican Monastery Museum. Even more sights—including an old synagogue, an Orthodox church, a modern exhibit of war photography, the medieval granary, and the ruins of an old foundry—are in the steep streets between the Stradun and the walls.*

Sights in Dubrovnik

Keep in mind that many of Dubrovnik's museums require you to have either a "nine museum ticket" or a Dubrovnik Card (which also covers the City Walls and public transit); for details on both options, see "Tourist Information," earlier.

▲▲▲CITY WALLS (GRADSKE ZIDINE)

Dubrovnik's single best attraction is strolling the scenic mile-and-a-quarter around the City Walls. As you meander along this lofty perch—with a sea of orange roofs on one side and the azure sea on the other—you'll get your bearings, peer into secluded gardens, and snap pictures like mad of the ever-changing views. Bring your map, which you can use to pick out landmarks and get the lay of the land. Speed demons can walk the walls in about an hour; strollers and shutterbugs should plan on longer.

Cost: 150 kn to enter walls, also includes the Fort of St. Lawrence outside the Pile Gate (kunas or credit cards only—no euros).

Hours: From April through October, the walls open daily at 8:00; the closing time depends on the season (June-mid-Aug until 19:30, late Aug until 19:00, May and Sept until 18:30, Oct and April until 18:00). Off-season (Nov-March), the walls are open daily 9:00-15:00. The "closing time" indicates when the walls shut down, *not* the last entry. Attendants begin circling the

walls 30 minutes after the posted closing time to lock the gates, so if you want to make it all the way around, ascend at least 30 min-

Dubrovnik at a Glance

▲▲▲**Stradun Stroll** Charming walk through Dubrovnik's vibrant Old Town, ideal for coffee, ice cream, and people-watching. See page 16.

▲▲▲**City Walls** Scenic mile-long walk along top of 15th-century fortifications encircling the city. **Hours:** June-mid-Aug daily 8:00-19:30, progressively shorter hours off-season. See page 27.

▲▲▲**Mount Srđ** Napoleonic fortress above Dubrovnik with spectacular views and a modest museum about the recent war. **Hours:** Mountaintop—always open; cable car—daily June-Aug 9:00-24:00, progressively shorter hours off-season; museum—same hours as cable car. See page 45.

▲**Franciscan Monastery Museum** Tranquil cloister, medieval pharmacy-turned-museum, and a century-old pharmacy still serving residents today. **Hours:** Daily 9:00-18:00, Nov-March until 14:00. See page 34.

▲**Rector's Palace** Sparse antique collection in the former home of rectors who ruled Dubrovnik in the Middle Ages. **Hours:** Daily 9:00-18:00, Nov-April until 16:00. See page 36.

▲**Cathedral** Eighteenth-century Roman Baroque cathedral and treasury filled with unusual relics, such as a swatch of Jesus' swaddling clothes. **Hours:** Church-daily 8:00-17:00, treasury-generally open same hours as church, both have shorter hours off-season. See page 38.

utes before the posted closing if you're speedy, and an hour or more before if you want to linger.

Entrances and Strategies: There are three entry points for the wall (see "Old Town Hotels & Restaurants" map, later), and wall walkers are required to follow the one-way route counterclockwise. One good strategy is to begin at the far side of the Old Town, using the entrance **near the Ploče Gate** and Dominican Monastery (this is where my self-guided tour of the walls begins). This entrance is the least crowded, and you'll tackle the steepest part (and enjoy some of the best views) first. The most popular—and most crowded—entrance is **just inside the Pile Gate,** next to the Church of St. Savior (for this location, you must buy your tickets at the desk across the square from the stairway entry). If you manage to arrive before the hordes descend, it can make sense to enter here and get this (most congested) section out of the way first. Finally, there's a

DUBROVNIK

▲**Dominican Monastery Museum** Another relaxing cloister with precious paintings, altarpieces, and manuscripts. **Hours:** Daily 9:00-18:00, Nov-March until 17:00. See page 39.

▲**Synagogue Museum** Europe's second-oldest synagogue and Croatia's only Jewish museum, with 13th-century Torahs and Holocaust-era artifacts. **Hours:** Daily 9:00-21:00; mid-Nov-April Mon-Fri 10:00-13:00, closed Sat-Sun. See page 41.

▲**War Photo Limited** Thought-provoking photographic look at contemporary warfare. **Hours:** May-Sept daily 10:00-22:00; April and Oct Wed-Mon until 16:00, closed Tue; closed Nov-March. See page 42.

▲**Foundry Museum** Excavated foundry with explanation of medieval metalworking. **Hours:** Daily 10:00-17:00, closed Nov-March. See page 42.

▲**Serbian Orthodox Church and Icon Museum** Active church serving Dubrovnik's Serbian Orthodox community and museum with traditional religious icons. **Hours:** Church-daily 8:00-21:00, Oct-April until 18:00; museum-may be closed for renovation, ask at icon shop near cathedral for status. See page 43.

▲**Rupe Granary and Ethnographic Museum** Good folk museum with tools, jewelry, clothing, and painted eggs above immense underground grain stores. **Hours:** Wed-Mon 9:00-16:00, closed Tue. See page 45.

small entrance **near St. John's Fort** overlooking the Old Port (next to the Maritime Museum).

Crowd Control: Because this is Dubrovnik's top attraction, it's extremely crowded. Your best strategy is to avoid the walls during the times when the cruise ships are in town. If you expect crowds, don't dillydally—enter soon after the 8:00 opening time. Crowds are worst from about 9:30 until 11:00, then decrease ever so slightly. They pick up again in the late afternoon (around 17:00), peaking about an hour before closing time (18:30 in high season). During busy times, your best bet is to hit the walls around 8:00, or just before 17:00 (to avoid both the worst heat and the worst crowds).

Tips: Because your ticket is scanned as you enter, you can't leave and re-enter the wall later; you have to do it all in one go. If you have a Dubrovnik Card—even a multiple-day one—you can only use it once to ascend the walls.

Heat Warning: The walls can get deliriously hot—all that white stone and seawater reflect blazing sunshine something fierce, and there's virtually no shade (except at a few wall-top cafés). It's essential to bring sunscreen, a hat, and water (the Onofrio public fountains are near both the Pile and Ploče entrances). Pace yourself: There are several steep stretches, and you'll be climbing up and down the whole way around. A few shops and cafés along the top of the wall (mostly on the sea side) sell water and other drinks, but it's cheaper to bring what you'll need with you. Particularly on the hottest days (commonly in July-Aug), the walls are best avoided anytime between about 9:00 and 16:00—those first-aid workers you'll see stationed near the entry points aren't just hanging out for fun. If you have trouble with the heat, save the walls for a cloudy day. In that hazy light, the red roof tiles seem more vivid, since they're not washed out by glaring sunshine.

Background: There have been walls here almost as long as there's been a Dubrovnik. As with virtually all fortifications on the Croatian Coast, these walls were beefed up in the 15th century, when the Ottoman navy became a threat. Around the perimeter are several substantial forts, with walls rounded so that cannonballs would glance off harmlessly. These stout forts intimidated would-be invaders during the Republic of Dubrovnik's Golden Age, and protected residents during the 1991-1992 siege.

❷ Self-Guided Tour: It's perfectly fine to just wander the walls and snap photos like crazy as you go. And trying to hew too closely to guided commentary kind of misses the point of being high above the Dubrovnik rooftops. But this brief tour should help give you bearings to what you're seeing, as you read Dubrovnik's unique and illustrious history into its street plan.

Part 1—Ploče Gate to Pile Gate: Begin by ascending near the **Ploče Gate** (go through the gate under the Bell Tower, walk along the stoutly walled passageway between the port and the Dominican Monastery, and look for the wall entrance on your right). Buy your ticket, head up, turn left, and start walking counterclockwise. After climbing some stairs, you'll walk with Mount Srđ and the cable car on your right. After passing the roofline of the Dominican Monastery's cloister on the left, you're walking above what was the poorest part of medieval Dubrovnik, the domain of the craftsmen—with narrow, stepped lanes that had shops on the ground floor and humble dwellings up above. Peering down all of the tight lanes, look for the many little stone ledges sticking out next to windows. These were used to hang banners during the city's Golden Age.

As you walk, keep an eye on the different-colored **rooftops** for an illustration of the damage Dubrovnik sustained during the 1991-1992 siege. It's easy to see that nearly two-thirds of Du-

DUBROVNIK

brovnik's roofs were replaced after the bombings (notice the new, bright-orange tiles—and how some buildings salvaged the old tiles, but have 20th-century ones underneath). The pristine-seeming Old Town was rebuilt using exactly the same materials and methods with which it was originally constructed.

The path you're on alternates between straight stretches and stairs; as

you walk you're rewarded with higher and higher views. Nearing the summit, you pass a juice bar (you can use the WCs if you buy a drink). At the very top, enjoy the best possible view of the Old Town—you can see the rooftops, churches, and the sea. Stuck behind a traffic jam of selfie sticks, ponder the increasing narcissism of our age...then snap a selfie to post to Instagram. For an even better view, it's worth hiking up 63 crowded stone stairs to the top of **Minčeta Tower.** From either viewpoint, observe the valley-like shape of Dubrovnik. It's easy to imagine how it began as two towns—one where you are now, and the other on the hilly island with the church spires across the way—originally separated by a seawater canal. Notice the relatively regular, grid-like pattern of houses on this side, and the more higgledy-piggledy arrangement on the far side (a visual clue that the far side is older).

The **sports court** at your feet is a reminder that Dubrovnik is a living city. (Anyone can play here—B.Y.O. ball.) Underneath the sports court are the remains of a medieval foundry—the centerpiece of Dubrovnik's least-known museum. To learn how the casting process worked in the 16th century, visit the **Foundry Museum** later, after you've descended the walls (see listing, later).

While around 1,500 people currently reside within these walls, that number used to be much higher. Nowadays, renting out your house to tourists is far more lucrative than living there yourself. And life is much easier in the suburbs—imagine the challenges that come with living in such a steep medieval townscape well into the 21st century. Delivery trucks rumble up and down the Stradun early each morning, and you'll see hardworking young men delivering goods on hand carts throughout the day.

Looking up at the fortress atop **Mount Srđ**—seemingly custom-made for keeping an eye on a large swathe of coastline—the strategic position of Dubrovnik is clear. Independent Dubrovnik was not just this walled city, but an entire region.

Now continue downhill (you've earned it), noticing views on your right of the bustling Pile Gate area and the Fort of St. Lawrence (we'll reach better views of both of these soon). You'll pass an overpriced shop (with a pay-to-view movie about the war). And then, as the wall walk levels off, you'll pass an exit (on the left); if you're bushed and ready to head back to town, you can leave here—but once you leave, you can't reenter on the same ticket, and some of the best views lie ahead. It's much better to carry on straight for part 2.

Part 2—Pile Gate to Old Port: This is the most crowded section, where many people enter—be patient. While you're waiting, pause to enjoy the full frontal view of the **Stradun,** barreling right at you. In the Middle Ages, merchants lined this drag, and before that, this was a canal. At your feet is Onofrio's Big Fountain, which supplied water to a thirsty town. From here, you can see a wide range of church steeples representing the cosmopolitan makeup of a thriving medieval trade town (from left to right): Dominican, Franciscan (near you), the town Bell Tower, St. Blaise's (the round dome—hard to see from here), Serbian Orthodox (twin domed steeples), Cathedral, and (high on the hill) Jesuit St. Ignatius. Sit and watch the river of humanity, flowing  constantly up and down one of Europe's finest main streets. Now do a 180 for a good view of the Pile Gate chaos, with a steady stream of buses lumbering up and down the hill, tethering the Old Town to Port Gruž and the Lapad resort zone.

Carry on through the guard tower and along the wall, climbing uphill again. Looking to the wall ahead of you, notice that—after we passed along a straighter, lower stretch—this wall is scampering up a mighty foundation of solid rock. We've left the canal that once separated the two parts of Dubrovnik, and now we're ascending what used to be a separate, very steep, rocky island. This stretch tickles *Game of Thrones* fantasies—many King's Landing scenes were filmed along here.

Climbing higher and looking to your left, into town, you'll see that this area is still damaged—not from the 1991-1992 siege, but from the 1667 earthquake. Notice that, unlike the extremely dense construction on the poorer far side of town, this area has more breathing space and larger gardens. Originally this was also densely populated, but after the quake, rather than rebuild, the wealthy folks who lived here decided to maximize green space. Grates cover the openings to old wells and grain stores that once supplied homes here—essential for surviving a siege.

As the walkway summits and levels out, you reach a drink stand. On the right are stunning views of the **Fort of St. Lawrence,** which worked in concert with these stout walls to make Dubrovnik virtually impenetrable. (That fort is also climbable, and covered by the same ticket as the walls.)

Past the drink stand, you'll stroll past local residents' backyards, peering into their inviting gardens and checking the status of their drying laundry. Farther  along, at the picturesque little turret, is a popular juice bar and an ice-cream stand. Looking outside the wall, you'll spot tables and umbrellas clinging to the rocks at the base of the wall. This is the recommended Cold Drinks "Buža" II, the best spot in town for a scenic drink. (You can't enter from atop the wall—you'll have to wait until later.) On the horizon is the isle of Lokrum and—often—cruise ships at anchor, sending passengers to and fro on tenders. After passing Buža, look down on the left to see another sports court, wedged between the walls—the best they can do in this vertical town.

Soon you'll see the *other* Buža (nicknamed "Little Buža"); just above it, notice the little statue of St. Blaise, Dubrovnik's patron, enjoying some shade under the turret.

Rounding the bend over Little Buža, look left to see the facade of the Jesuit St. Ignatius Church. Notice that the homes in this area are much larger. These are aristocratic palaces—VIPs wanted to live as close as possible to the Cathedral and Rector's Palace, which are just below—and this also happens to be the oldest part of town, where "Ragusa" was born on a steep offshore island.

Continue around the wall, passing two more snack bars (the second is more elaborate, with a better menu, more shade, and pay WCs). Behind the second snack bar are more quake-ruined houses. Eventually you pop out at a high plateau, where *The City Walls— Continuation* signs lead down to the next part. From here you could drop down to the exit (though the final stretch of our wall walk is a snap—at the fork, go right, through the hole in the wall). In the little plant-filled square at the bottom of the next staircase is a sweet cat hospice, with a donation box for feeding some homeless feline residents.

Part 3—Old Port to Ploče Gate: At the start of the next stretch, you'll come to the entrance of the **Maritime Museum.** If you have a museum ticket or Dubrovnik Pass, here's a chance to escape the sun, use a clean WC, and learn about Dubrovnik's 2,500-year seafaring past (see description, later).

Next, walk along the top of the wall overlooking the **Old Port.** Imagine how this heavily fortified little harbor (facing away from Dubrovnik's historic foes, the Venetians) was busy with trade in the Middle Ages. Today it's still the economic lifeline for town—watch the steady stream of cruise-ship tenders injecting dose after dose of tourist cash. The Old Port is so charming partly because they prohibit huge, glitzy yachts from mooring here. All of the boats here must be under a certain size, and belong to locals—humble fishing and pleasure craft.

After circling your way to the middle of the port, immediately above the main pier, the path turns sharply left and heads straight for the Bell Tower—with a good glimpse of the bell ringers, Maro and Baro. Continuing, you'll look down into the inner passage that insulated the wall from the town center. On the sea side, look for the outdoor tables of the unsigned **360°**, a cocktail bar/restaurant catering to high rollers. Gussied-up jet-set diners enjoy coming here for good but extremely expensive designer fare.

Just past 360°, you'll come face to face with the vertical walls of the Dominican Church before finding the stairs back down to where you started this wall walk. Nice work. Now head on down and reward yourself with an ice-cream cone...and some shade.

The "Other" Wall Climb: Your ticket for the City Walls also includes the Fort of St. Lawrence just outside the Old Town (valid same day only; fort described on page 17). If you've already bought a 50-kn ticket there, show it when buying your main wall ticket and you'll pay only the difference.

NEAR THE PILE GATE
▲Franciscan Monastery Museum
(Franjevački Samostan-Muzej)
In the Middle Ages, Dubrovnik's monasteries flourished. As a part of their charity work, the monks at this monastery took on the responsibility of serving as pharmacists for the community. Visiting here today, you'll stroll through a delightful cloister and walk through a one-room museum with an old pharmacy.

Cost and Hours: 30 kn, daily 9:00-18:00, Nov-March until 14:00, Placa 2, tel. 020/321-410.

Visiting the Museum: Enter through the gap between the small church and the big monastery. Just inside the door (before the ticket-seller), a century-old **pharmacy** still serves residents. Notice the antique jars, advertisements (including one of the first known aspirin ads), and other vintage pharmacist gear. By keeping this open, the monastery maintains one of the world's oldest continually operating pharmacies.

Turn left and explore the peaceful, sun-dappled **cloister,** walking clockwise. Examine the capitals at the tops of the 60

Romanesque-Gothic double pillars. Each one is different. Notice that some parts of the portals inside the courtyard are made with a lighter-colored stone—these had to be repaired after being hit during the 1991-1992 siege. The damaged 19th-century frescoes along the tops of the walls depict the life of St. Francis, who supposedly visited Dubrovnik in the early 13th century. If you look closely, in a few panels you may see two layers of (different) scenes; beneath the 19th-century frescoes, restorers have found even more precious fragments of some early-18th-century paintings; where possible, these are also being resurrected.

In the far corner stands the monastery's original medieval **pharmacy.** The Franciscans opened this pharmacy in 1317, and it's been in continual operation ever since.

On display are jars, pots, and other medieval pharmacists' tools. Notice the display of old pharmacists' books from the 16th, 17th, and 18th centuries—expertise imported from as far away as Venice, Frankfurt, Amsterdam, and Bologna. The sick would come to get their medicine at the little window (on the left side), which limited contact with the pharmacist and reduced the risk of passing on disease. On the right wall, look for the glass case marked *venena*—where poisons were locked away and carefully doled out, with a record of who had what.

Around the room, you'll also find some relics, old manuscripts, and a detailed painting of early-17th-century Dubrovnik. In the painting, notice that at the top of Mount Srđ—the highly strategic locale where Napoleon built a fortress that was key during the 1991 siege (see "The Siege of Dubrovnik" sidebar, earlier)—is a chapel. Though Dubrovnik was always heavily fortified, they avoided putting a fortress on the mountaintop—fearing it might seem overly provocative to the Ottoman Empire that surrounded them, and upon whose favor they depended for their autonomy.

Leaving the museum room, turn left and walk to the end of this corridor. Look up to see a tomb with a privileged position, affixed high on the wall. The **Gučetić-Gozze** family donated vast sums to help rebuild the monastery after the devastating 1667 earthquake. As thanks, the Franciscans helped them get just that much closer to God when they passed on, offering them this final resting place that was elevated...in every sense.

NEAR LUŽA SQUARE

These sights are at the far end of the Stradun (nearest the Old Port). As you stand on Luža Square facing the Bell Tower, the Rector's Palace and cathedral are up the wide street called Pred Dvorom to the right, and the Dominican Monastery Museum is through the gate by the Bell Tower and to the left.

▲Rector's Palace (Knežev Dvor)

In the Middle Ages, the Republic of Dubrovnik was ruled by a rector (similar to a Venetian doge), who was elected by the nobility. To prevent any one person from becoming too powerful, the rector's term was limited to one month. Most  rectors were in their 50s—near the end of the average life span and when they were less likely to shake things up. During his term, a rector lived upstairs in this palace. Because it's been plundered twice (most recently by Napoleon's forces, who stole all the furniture), this empty-feeling museum isn't as interesting as most other European palaces. What little you'll see was donated by local aristocrats to flesh out the pathetically empty complex. The palace collection (with paid admission and good English explanations) is skippable, but it does offer a glimpse of Dubrovnik in its glory days. The palace's exterior and courtyard are viewable at no charge.

Cost and Hours: 80 kn, covered by 120-kn "nine museum ticket" and by Dubrovnik Card; daily 9:00-18:00, Nov-April until 16:00; 5-kn English booklet, Pred Dvorom 3, tel. 020/322-096.

Visiting the Palace: The **exterior** is decorated in the Gothic-Renaissance mix (with particularly finely carved capitals) that was so common in Dubrovnik before the 1667 earthquake. Above the entrance is the message *Obliti privatorum publica curate*—loosely translated, "Forget your personal affairs and concern yourself with the affairs of state." This was a bold statement in a feudal era before democracy, when aristocrats were preoccupied exclusively with their self-interests. (It also feels tragically relevant today.)

Standing at the main door, get a free look at the palace's impressive **courtyard**—a venue for the Summer Festival, hosting music groups ranging from the local symphony to the Vienna Boys' Choir. During Dubrovnik's Golden Age, this courtyard was open to the public. People would wander in and out—gossiping, washing their laundry in the fountain (on the left), and bringing food to family members imprisoned in the cells. In the courtyard stands the only secular statue created during the centuries-long Republic. Dubrovnik republicans, mindful of the dangers of hero-worship, didn't believe that any one citizen should be singled out. They made only one exception—for Miho Pracat (a.k.a. Michaeli Prazatto), a rich citizen who donated vast sums to charity and willed a fleet of ships to the city. But notice that Pracat's statue is displayed in here, behind closed doors, not out in public.

If you pay to go **inside,** you'll find good English explanations posted throughout. Start on the ground floor, where you'll ramble through a few rooms of dull paintings, and then go into the green-stucco courtroom (with explanations of the Republic's unique judiciary system, and portraits and bios of some of its key politicians). Next, you'll see one of the palace's highlights: the original bronze bell-ringers from the town Bell Tower (Maro and Baro). Like antique robots (from the Renaissance,

1477-1478), these eerily lifelike sculptures could pivot at the waist to ring the bell. Nearby you'll see stonework that used to decorate city buildings. Farther along, massive iron chests (including a few with elaborate locking mechanisms) are displayed inside some old prison cells, which supposedly were placed within earshot of the rector's quarters, so he would hear the moans of the prisoners... and stay honest. Leaving the prison, you'll enter the courtyard described earlier, where you can get a better look at the Pracat statue.

On the mezzanine level (stairs near the main entrance, above the prison—notice the "hand" rails), you'll find a decent display of furniture, beautiful 18th-century sedans used to tote around V.I.R.s (Very Important Ragusans), a wimpy gun exhibit, votive offerings (mostly silver), an 18th-century coin collection (with magnifying glasses to make out the detail), and an interesting painting of "Ragusa" in the early 17th century—back when its stout walls were surrounded by a moat.

Head back down to the courtyard and ascend the grand stairway to the upper floor (with more "hand" rails). Upstairs, you'll explore old apartments that serve as a painting gallery. The only vaguely authentic room is the red room in the corner, decorated more or less as it was in 1500, when it was the rector's office. Mihajlo Hamzić's exquisite *Baptism of Christ* painting, inspired by Italian painter Andrea Mantegna, is an early Renaissance work from the "Dubrovnik School" (see "Dominican Monastery Museum" listing, later). This area also often displays temporary exhibits.

Back in the courtyard, you can go up the smaller stairs to the Domus Christi collection of old pharmacist tools and pots (well-explained in English).

Handy WCs are just off the courtyard next to the shop, through which you'll exit.

▲Cathedral (Katedrala)

Dubrovnik's original 12th-century cathedral was funded largely by the English King Richard the Lionheart. On his way back from the Third Crusade, Richard was shipwrecked nearby. He promised God that if he survived, he'd build a church on the spot where he landed—which happened to be on Lokrum Island, just offshore. At Dubrovnik's request, Richard agreed to build his token of thanks inside the city instead. It was the finest Romanesque church on the  Adriatic...before it was destroyed by the 1667 earthquake. This version is 18th-century Roman Baroque.

Cost and Hours: Church-free, open daily 8:00-17:00; treasury-20 kn, generally open same hours as church; both have shorter hours off-season.

Visiting the Cathedral: Inside, you'll find a painting from the school of Titian *(Assumption of the Virgin)* over the stark contemporary altar.

Behind the altar is a quirky treasury *(riznica)* packed with 187 relics (pay and enter to the right of the altar). Examining the treasury collection, notice that there are three locks on the treasury door—the stuff in here was so valuable, three different VIPs (the rector, the bishop, and a local aristocrat) had to agree before it could be opened. On the table near the door are several of St. Blaise's body parts (pieces of his arm, skull, and leg—all encased in gold and silver). In the middle of the wall directly opposite the door, look for the crucifix with a piece of the True Cross. On a dig in Jerusalem, St. Helen (Emperor Constantine's mother) discovered what she believed to be the cross that Jesus was crucified on. It was brought to Constantinople, and the Byzantine czars doled out pieces of it to Balkan kings. Note the folding three-paneled altar painting (underneath the cross). Dubrovnik ambassadors packed this on road trips (such as their annual trip to pay off the Ottomans) so they could worship wherever they traveled.

On the right side of the room, the silver casket supposedly holds the actual swaddling clothes of the Baby Jesus. Dubrovnik bishops secretly passed these clothes down from generation to generation...until a nun got wind of it and told the whole town. Pieces of the cloth were cut off to miraculously heal the sick, especially new mothers recovering from a difficult birth. No matter how often it was cut, the cloth always went back to its original form. Then someone tried to use it on the wife of a Bosnian king. Since she was Muslim, it couldn't help her, and it never worked again. True or not, this legend hints at the prickly relationships between faiths (not to mention the male chauvinism) here in the Balkans.

▲Dominican Monastery Museum (Dominikanski Samostan-Muzej)

You'll find many of Dubrovnik's art treasures—paintings, altarpieces, and manuscripts—gathered around the peaceful Dominican Monastery cloister inside the Ploče Gate.

Cost and Hours: 30 kn, daily 9:00-18:00, Nov-March until 17:00, art buffs enjoy the 50-kn English book.

Visiting the Museum: As you climb the **stairs** up to the monastery, notice that the spindles supporting the railing are solid up until about two feet above the ground. This was to provide a modicum of modesty to ladies on their way to church—and to prevent creeps down below from looking up their skirts.

Buy your ticket, then turn left and work your way clockwise around the cloister. The room in the far corner contains paintings from the **"Dubrovnik School,"** the Republic's circa-1500 answer to the art boom in Florence and Venice. Though the 1667 earthquake destroyed most of these paintings, about a dozen survive, and five of those are in this room. Just inside the door, don't miss the triptych by Nikola Božidarović with St. Blaise holding a detailed model of 16th-century Dubrovnik (left panel)—the most famous depiction of Dubrovnik's favorite saint. You'll also see reliquaries shaped like the hands and feet that they hold.

Continuing around the courtyard, duck into the next room.

DUBROVNIK

At the far end of the room is a painting by **Titian** depicting St. Blaise, Mary Magdalene, and the donor who financed this work.

At the next corner of the courtyard is the entrance to the striking **church** at the heart of this still-active monastery. (The church may be closed, or its art removed for renovation.) If it's open, step inside and face the altar. The interior is decorated with modern stained glass, a fine 13th-century stone pulpit that survived the earthquake (reminding visitors of the intellectual approach to scripture that characterized the Dominicans), and a precious 14th-century Paolo Veneziano crucifix hanging in the arch above the altar. Perhaps the finest piece of art in the church is the *Miracle of St. Dominic,* showing the founder of the order bringing a child back to life (to the left as you face the main altar). Behind the altar, find the

Vukovar Cross, embedded with panels painted by different artists from the Croatian school of Naive Art—offering an enticing taste of this unique and fascinating style. It was painted in the Realist style (late 19th century) by Vlaho Bukovac.

NEAR THE OLD PORT (STARA LUKA)

The picturesque Old Port, carefully nestled behind St. John's Fort, faces away from what was Dubrovnik's biggest threat, the Venetians. At the port, you can haggle with captains selling excursions

to nearby towns and islands (described in the next chapter) and watch cruise-ship passengers coming and going on their tenders. The long seaside building across the bay on the left is the Lazareti, once the medieval quarantine house. In those days, all visitors were locked in here for 40 days before entering town. A bench-lined harborside walk leads around the fort to a breakwater, providing a peaceful perch. From the breakwater, rocky beaches curl around the outside of the wall.

Maritime Museum (Pomorski Muzej)

In the 15th century, when Venice's nautical dominance was peaking, Dubrovnik emerged as another maritime power and the Mediterranean's leading shipbuilding center. The Dubrovnik-built "argosy" boat (from "Ragusa," an early name for the city) was the Cadillac of ships, even mentioned by Shakespeare. This worthwhile museum, built into Dubrovnik's walls, fits in tidily with a wall walk. It traces the long history of Dubrovnik's most important industry with contracts, maps, paintings, navigational devices, and models—all well-described in English. The main floor takes you through the 18th century, and the easy-to-miss upstairs covers the 19th and 20th centuries.

Cost and Hours: Covered by 120-kn "nine museum ticket" and by Dubrovnik Card; hours flex on demand—usually Tue-Sun 9:00-18:00, Nov-Feb until 16:00, closed Mon year-round; 5-kn English booklet or elaborate 60-kn book, good WCs at entry, upstairs in St. John's Fort, at far/south end of Old Port, tel. 020/323-904.

Aquarium (Akvarij)
Dubrovnik's aquarium, housed in the cavernous St. John's Fort, is an old-school place, with 31 tanks on one floor. A visit here allows you a close look at the local marine life and provides a cool refuge from the midday heat.

Cost and Hours: 60 kn, kids-20 kn, daily July-Aug 9:00-21:00, progressively shorter hours off-season until 9:00-16:00 Nov-March, English descriptions, ground floor of St. John's Fort, enter from Old Port, tel. 020/323-978.

BETWEEN THE STRADUN AND THE MAINLAND
The first two museums are a few steps off the main promenade toward the mainland.

▲Synagogue Museum (Sinagoga-Muzej)
When the Jews were forced out of Spain in 1492, a steady stream of them passed through here en route to today's Turkey. Finding Dubrovnik to be a flourishing and relatively tolerant city, many stayed. Žudioska ulica ("Jewish Street"), just inside the Ploče Gate, became the ghetto in 1546. It was walled at one end and had a gate (which would be locked at night) at the other end. Today, the same street is home to the second-oldest continuously functioning synagogue in Europe (after Prague's), which contains Croatia's only Jewish museum. The top floor houses the synagogue itself. Notice the lattice windows that separated the women from the men (in accordance with Orthodox Jewish tradition). Below that, a small museum with good English descriptions gives meaning to the various Torahs (including a 14th-century one from Spain) and other items—such as the written orders *(naredba)* from Nazi-era Yugoslavia, stating that Jews were to identify their shops as Jewish-owned and wear armbands. (The Ustaše—the Nazi puppet government in Croatia—interned and executed not only Jews and Roma,

but also Serbs and other people they considered undesirable; see page 147.) Of Croatia's 24,000 Jews, only 4,000 survived the Holocaust. Today Croatia has about 2,000 Jews, including a dozen Jewish families who call Dubrovnik home.

Cost and Hours: 40 kn; daily 9:00-21:00; mid-Nov-April Mon-Fri 10:00-13:00, closed Sat-Sun; 15-kn English booklet (unnecessary), Žudioska ulica 5, tel. 020/321-204.

▲War Photo Limited

If the tragic story of wartime Dubrovnik has you in a pensive mood, drop by this excellent gallery with images of warfare from around the world. The brainchild of Kiwi-turned-Croatian photojournalist Wade Goddard, this thought-provoking museum attempts to show the ugly reality of war through raw, often disturbing photographs taken in the field. Use the loaner guide to understand the well-displayed images on two floors; a small permanent exhibit (on the top floor) captures the Yugoslav Wars through photography and video footage. Each summer, the gallery also houses various temporary exhibits. Note that the focus is not solely on Dubrovnik, but on war anywhere and everywhere.

Cost and Hours: 50 kn; May-Sept daily 10:00-22:00; April and Oct Wed-Mon until 16:00, closed Tue; closed Nov-March; Antuninska 6, tel. 020/322-166, www.warphotoltd.com.

▲Foundry Museum (a.k.a. Gornji Ugao Tower)

This easy-to-miss sight, tucked high up below the City Walls' tallest tower, offers a fascinating glimpse at a medieval foundry that was established here in 1545. Used for the production of cannonballs and gunpowder (essential elements of an independent ministate), the foundry was intentionally located at the very top of town—still barely within the walls, but a safe distance from most residents. Damaged in the great 1667 quake, it was buried under a garbage dump and then under a playground, until it was finally excavated in 2008.

Cost and Hours: 30 kn, daily 10:00-17:00, closed Nov-March, last entrance one hour before closing.

Getting There: You'll enter the complex through the base of the Minčeta Tower, at the top (northernmost) point of the Old Town (follow any of the stepped lanes all the way up to the landward side of town, turn left, and walk along the inside of the wall until you can't walk anymore). Đivo may be hanging out nearby, hoping to snare passing tourists.

Visiting the Foundry: Enthusiastic Đivo (JEE-voh) gives 30-minute tours of the complex. First, you'll walk through the inside of Minčeta Tower, including two levels of casements. Then you'll walk along a private little inner stretch of the City Wall. And finally, you'll explore the foundry's foundations, including its four furnaces, molds for church bells and gigantic cannonballs, and a pile of original casting sand (a volcanic material imported from Italy, essential for the working of any foundry). You'll find out how aqueducts powered the foundry's equipment (harnessing water as it flowed past on its way down to Onofrio's Big Fountain), and see a few of the original items that were cast here, such as buckles, keys, needles, horseshoes, and musket shot.

BETWEEN THE STRADUN AND THE SEA
▲Serbian Orthodox Church and Icon Museum
(Srpska Pravoslavna Crkva i Muzej Ikona)
Round out your look at Dubrovnik's major faiths (Catholic, Jewish, and Orthodox) with a visit to this house of worship—one

of the most convenient places in Croatia to learn about Orthodox Christianity. Remember that people from the former Yugoslavia who follow the Orthodox faith are, by definition, ethnic Serbs. With all the hard feelings about the Yugoslav Wars, this church serves as an important reminder that not all Serbs are bloodthirsty killers.

Dubrovnik never had a very large Serb population (an Orthodox church wasn't even allowed inside the town walls until the mid-19th century). During the Yugoslav Wars, most Serbs fled, created new lives for themselves elsewhere, and saw little reason to return. But some old-timers remain, and Dubrovnik's dwindling, aging Orthodox population is still served by this **church.** The candles stuck in the sand (to prevent fire outbreaks) represent prayers: The ones at knee level are for the deceased, while the ones higher up are for the living. The gentleman selling candles encourages you to buy and light one, regardless of your faith, so long as you do so with the proper intentions and reverence. To better appreciate this church, read "The Serbian Orthodox Church" sidebar.

Cost and Hours: Free but donations accepted; daily 8:00-21:00, Oct-April until 18:00, liturgy Sun 10:00-11:00; Od Puča.

Nearby: A few doors down (at Od Puča 8) is the **Icon Museum,** which may be closed for renovation—ask at the icon shop next door to the cathedral entrance. When open, this small collection features 78 different icons (stylized paintings of saints, generally on a golden background—a common feature of Orthodox churches) from the 15th through the 19th centuries, all identified in English. In the library—crammed with old shelves holding some 12,000

The Serbian Orthodox Church

The emphasis of this book is on the Catholic areas of the former Yugoslavia, but don't overlook the rich diversity of faiths in this region. Dubrovnik's Serbian Orthodox church, as well as Orthodox churches in Kotor (in Montenegro), Sarajevo, and Ljubljana offer invaluable opportunities to learn about a faith that's often unfamiliar to American visitors (see those chapters for details).

Orthodox churches carry on the earliest traditions of the Christian faith. Orthodox and Catholic Christianity came from the same roots, so the oldest surviving early-Christian churches (such as the stave churches of Norway) have many of the same features as today's Orthodox churches.

Notice that there are no pews. Worshippers stand through the service, as a sign of respect (though some older parishioners sit along the walls). Women stand on the left side, men on the right (equal distance from the altar—to represent that all are equal before God). The Orthodox Church uses essentially the same Bible as Catholics, but it's written in the Cyrillic alphabet, which you'll see displayed around any Orthodox church. Following Old Testament Judeo-Christian tradition, the Bible is kept on the altar behind the iconostasis, the big screen in the middle of the room covered with curtains and icons (golden paintings of saints), which separates the material world from the spiritual one. At certain times during the service, the curtains or doors are opened so the congregation can see the Holy Book.

Orthodox icons are not intended to be lifelike. Packed with intricate symbolism, and cast against a shimmering golden background, they're meant to remind viewers of the metaphysical nature of Jesus and the saints rather than of their physical form, which is considered irrelevant. You'll almost never see a statue, which is thought to overemphasize the physical world...and, to Orthodox people, feels a little too close to violating the commandment, "Thou shalt not worship graven images." Orthodox services generally involve chanting (a dialogue that goes back and forth between the priest and the congregation), and the church is filled with the evocative aroma of incense.

The incense, chanting, icons, and standing up are all intended to heighten the experience of worship. While many Catholic and Protestant services tend to be more of a theoretical and rote consideration of religious issues, Orthodox services are about creating a religious experience. Each of these elements does its part to help the worshipper transcend the physical world and join in communion with the spiritual one.

books—look for the astonishingly detailed calendar, with portraits of hundreds of saints.

▲Rupe Granary and Ethnographic Museum (Etnografski Muzej Rupe)

This huge, 16th-century building was Dubrovnik's biggest granary, and today houses the best folk museum I've seen in Croatia. *Rupe* means "holes"—and it's worth the price of entry just to peer down into these 15 cavernous underground grain stores, designed to maintain the perfect temperature to preserve the seeds (63 degrees Fahrenheit). Look down through the hefty grates on the main floor. When the grain had to be dried, it was moved upstairs—where today you'll find a surprisingly well-presented Ethnographic Museum covering Dubrovnik's many traditions and festivals, and displaying tools, jewelry, clothing, instruments, painted eggs, and other folk artifacts from its colorful history. English explanations are scant; it's worth investing 5 kn for the booklet at the entry. The museum hides several blocks uphill from the main promenade, toward the sea (climb up Široka—the widest side street from the Stradun—which becomes Od Domina on the way to the museum).

Cost and Hours: Covered by 120-kn "nine museum ticket" and by Dubrovnik Card; Wed-Mon 9:00-16:00, closed Tue; Od Rupa 3, tel. 020/323-013.

ABOVE DUBROVNIK
▲▲▲Mount Srđ

After adding Dubrovnik to his holdings, Napoleon built a fortress atop the hill behind the Old Town to keep an eye on his new sub-

jects (in 1810). During the city's 20th-century tourism heyday, a cable car was built to effortlessly whisk visitors to the top so they could enjoy the fine views from the fortress and the giant cross nearby. Then, when war broke out in the 1990s, Mount Srđ (pronounced like "surge") became a crucial link in the defense of Dubrovnik— the only high land that locals were able to hold. The fortress was shelled and damaged, and the cross and cable car were destroyed. Minefields and unexploded ordnance left the hilltop a dangerous no-man's land. But more recently, the mountain's fortunes have reversed. The landmines have been removed, and in 2010, the cable car was rebuilt to once again connect Dubrovnik's Old Town to its mountaintop. Visitors head to the top both for the spectacular sweeping views and to ponder the exhibits in a ragtag museum about the war.

Warning: While this area has officially been cleared of landmines, nervous locals remind visitors that this was once a war zone. Be sure to stay on clearly defined paths and roads.

Expect Changes: International developers have plans to build a luxury golf resort on the mountain plateau behind Mount Srđ. You may see construction and, while it likely won't affect the cable car, it may eventually take over the fort and museum.

Getting to the Top: The **cable car** is easily the best option for reaching the summit of Mount Srđ (140 kn round-trip, 85 kn one-way, kunas or credit cards only—no euros; at least 2/hour—generally departing at :00 and :30 past each hour, more frequent with demand, 3-minute ride; daily from 9:00, June-Aug until 24:00, Sept until 22:00, May until 21:00, April and Oct until 20:00, Feb-March and Nov until 17:00, Dec-Jan until 16:00; doesn't run in Bora wind or heavy rain, last ascent 30 minutes before closing, tel. 020/325-393, www.dubrovnikcablecar.com). The lower station is just above the Buža Gate at the top of the Old Town (from the main drag, huff all the way to the top of Boškovićeva, exit through gate, and climb uphill one block, then look right). You may see travel agencies selling tickets elsewhere in town, but there's no advantage to buying them anywhere but here. The line you may see at the cable-car station is not to buy tickets, but to actually ride up. For tips on avoiding a long wait, see below.

If you have a **car,** it's possible to drive up—though the road can be crowded. From the high road above the Old Town, watch for the turnoff to *Bosanka,* which leads you to that village, then up to the fortress and cross—follow signs for *Srđ* (it's twisty but not far—figure a 20-minute drive from the Old Town area). If you're coming south from the Old Town, once you reach the main road above, you'll have to turn left and backtrack a bit to reach the *Bosanka* turnoff. For **hikers,** a switchback trail (used to supply the fortress during the siege) connects the Old Town to the mountaintop—but it's very steep and provides minimal shade. (If your knees are solid and it's not too hot, you could ride the cable car up, then hike down.)

Crowd-Beating Tips: The cable car has a limited capacity, and lines can get long when several cruise ships are in town. If you come during peak times, you may have to wait to board a cable car. Cruise passengers tend to come here first thing upon disembarking, so it can be extremely crowded around 9:30-11:00 and stay busy through the morning. On a busy day, it's best avoided entirely in the morning. Things may quiet down in the mid- to late afternoon. But then there's another rush before sunset—which is, understandably, the most popular time to ascend. Be warned that the line to go back down the cable car stacks up as soon as the sunset ends (see "Sunset Tips," later).

Mountaintop: From the top cable-car station, head up the stairs to the panoramic terrace. The bird's-eye **view** is truly spectacular, looking straight down to the street plan of Dubrovnik's Old Town. From this lofty perch, you can see north to the Dal-

matian islands (the Elaphite archipelago, Mljet, Korčula, and beyond); south to Montenegro; and east into Bosnia-Herzegovina. Gazing upon those looming mountains that define the border with Bosnia-Herzegovina—which, centuries ago, was also the frontier of the huge and powerful Ottoman Empire—you can appreciate how impressive it was that stubborn little Dubrovnik managed to remain independent for so much of its history.

The **cross** was always an important symbol in this very Catholic town. After it was destroyed in the siege, a temporary wooden

one was erected to encourage the townspeople who were waiting out the siege below. During a visit in 2003, Pope John Paul II blessed the rubble from the old cross; those fragments are now being used in the foundations of the city's newest churches. Nearby stands a huge red, white, and blue flagpole—the colors of the Croatian flag.

To reach the museum in the old fortress, walk behind the cable-car station along the rocky red soil toward the gigantic antenna.

Fort and Museum: The Napoleonic-era Fort Imperial (Tvrđava Imperijal) houses the **Dubrovnik During the Homeland War (1991-1995) Museum** (30 kn, daily 9:00-22:00, Oct-April until 18:00). While interesting (and occupying an important location, where the Dubrovnik Defenders burrowed in to fight for their city), the museum's descriptions are rabble-rousing and one-sided ("Serbian and Montenegrin aggression"). Still, it offers an insightful look at the conflict.

The hallway on the right as you enter leads to a changing photo exhibition showing slices of life during the siege. The hallway on the left has the permanent exhibits, where photos, documents, and artifacts tell the story (with English descriptions) of the overarching war with Yugoslavia and how the people defended this fortress. The descriptions are too dense and tactical for casual visitors, but you'll see lots of photos and some actual items used in the fighting: primitive, rusty rifles (some dating from World War II) that the Croatians used for their improvised defense, and piles of spent mortar shells and other projectiles that Yugoslav forces hurled at the fortress and the city. Look for the wire-guided Russian rockets. After being launched at their target, the rockets would burrow into a wall, waiting to be detonated once their operators saw the opportunity for maximum destruction. The tattered Croatian flag seems soaked in local patriotism. A video screen shows breathless international news reports from the front line during the bombing.

After seeing the exhibit, climb up a few flights of stairs to the **rooftop** for the view. The giant communications tower overhead flew the Croatian flag during the war, to inspire the besieged residents below. You might see some charred trees around here—these were claimed not by the war, but more recently, by forest fires. (Fear of landmines and other explosives prevented locals from fighting the wildfires as aggressively as they might otherwise, making these fires more dangerous than ever.)

Sunset Tips: Mount Srđ is a popular vantage point for enjoying the sunset over the Dalmatian islands. There are two viewpoints at the cable-car station: one at the cabin level and another upstairs. Another good vantage point is from near the cross (where some people scramble down onto the dangerously steep, rocky slope below). But, if you're going to tour the museum at the fort anyway, consider timing your visit to be on its rooftop for sunset. It tends to be less crowded and has fine views over the islands. The only disadvantage is that you're farther away from the cable car—and as soon as the sun sets, the line back down begins to form. While the line moves quickly, you may be in for a bit of a wait. Be warned that, up on the arid and breezy mountaintop, the temperature can drop quickly once the sun sets (bring a sweater).

Eating: Boasting undoubtedly the best view in Dubrovnik, **$$$$ Restaurant Panorama** has drop-dead astonishing views over the rooftops of the Old Town and to the most beautiful parts of three different countries. While there's glassed-in seating inside, in good weather I'd exit the building to find the outdoor terrace— the Old Town floats just under your nose. Prices are high, but you can dine affordably if you stick to basic pasta dishes. If riding the cable car late in the day, this is a great place for a breezy dinner; it's often cooler up here than down in the Old Town, and the views can't be beat. There's a rush on tables just after sunset; if you're planning to be here around that time, it's smart to reserve a table ahead of time (open same hours as cable car, tel. 020/312-664).

Activities in Dubrovnik

Swimming and Sunbathing

If the weather's good and you've had enough of museums, spend a sunny afternoon at the beach. There are no sandy beaches on the mainland near Dubrovnik, but there are lots of suitable pebbly options, plus several concrete perches.

The easiest and most atmospheric place to take a dip is right off the **Old Town.** From the Old Port and its breakwater, uneven steps clinging to the outside of the wall lead to a series of great sunbathing and swimming coves (and even a showerhead sticking out of the town wall). Another delightful rocky beach hangs onto the outside of the Old Town's wall (at the bar called Cold Drinks "Buža" I; for more on this bar, and how to find it, see "Entertainment in Dubrovnik," later).

A more convenient—and crowded—public beach is **Banje,** just outside the Ploče Gate, east of the Old Town. This public beach (watched over by an upscale bar/restaurant/lounge) is ideal for sunbathing and wading, with a spectacular backdrop of Dubrovnik's Old Town. To reach the beach, leave the Old Town through the Ploče Gate, walk about five minutes gradually uphill on the main road, then watch for the staircase marked *Banje Beach* (while the stairs pass through the bar, it is public access). The bar itself is slick and swanky, serving pricey food and drink. You can also rent a very expensive sun bed, but it's much more affordable to bring your own towel and find a comfy patch of sand. Pay showers are nearby.

My favorite hidden beach—**St. Jakob**—takes a lot longer to reach, but if you're up for the hike, it's worth it to escape the crowds. Figure about a 25-minute walk (each way) from the Old Town. Go through the Ploče Gate at the east end of the Old Town, and walk along the street called Frana Supila as it climbs uphill above the waterfront. At Hotel Argentina, take the right

(downhill) fork and keep going on Vlaha Bukovca. Eventually you'll reach the small church of St. Jakob. You'll see the beach—in a cozy protected cove—far below. Curl around behind the church and keep an eye out for stairs going down on the right. Unfortunately, these stairs are effectively unmarked, so it might take some trial and error to find the right ones. (If you reach the rusted-white gateway of the old communist-era open-air theater, you've gone too far.) Hike down the very steep stairs to the gentle cove, which has rentable chairs and a small restaurant for drinks (and a WC). Enjoy the pebbly beach and faraway views of Dubrovnik's Old Town. In peak season, water taxis may be ferrying beachgoers between this beach and the Old Port, offering an easier trip (around 30 kn one-way).

Other, even more distant beaches are worth considering. If you're staying at—or visiting—the resort-y zone of **Lapad Bay,** you'll find a fine beach there (near Hotel Kompas).

Locals prefer to swim on **Lokrum Island,** because there are (relatively) fewer tourists there. While there are no sandy or even pebbly beaches, there are several rocky ones, with ladders to lower yourself gingerly into the water. As the rocks here can be particularly jagged, you'll want to wear good water shoes, and beware of uneven footing (both underwater, and on your way to the ladders). For details on taking a boat to Lokrum, see the next chapter.

Finally, for the best sandy beach in this part of Croatia, you'll have to take a boat to the island of Lopud, then hike (or ride a golf cart) across the spine of the island to the gorgeous **Šunj Beach.** Making an all-day trek out here (by public ferry) is worth doing only if you're desperate for a long, lingering day at the beach. If you're cruising the Elaphite Islands, you'll likely stop on Lopud for two or three hours—enough time for a quick dip at Šunj. For more on Lopud and Šunj Beach, see the next chapter.

Sea Kayaking

Paddling a sleek kayak around the outside of Dubrovnik's imposing walls is a memorable experience. Several outfits in town offer half-day tours (most options 250-350 kn); popular itineraries include loops along the City Walls, to secluded beaches, and around Lokrum Island; many include a break for snorkeling (they provide goggles), and some are timed to catch the sunset while bobbing in the Adriatic. Well-established companies include **Adriatic Kayak Tours** (www.adriatickayaktours.com), **Outdoor Croatia** (www.outdoorcroatia.com), **Adria Adventure** (www.kayakingcroatia.com), and **Adventure Dubrovnik** (www.adventuredubrovnik.com)—but new companies pop up all the time...check online or look for fliers locally.

Shopping in Dubrovnik

Most souvenirs sold in Dubrovnik—from lavender sachets to plaster models of the Old Town—are pretty tacky. Whatever you buy, prices are much higher along the Stradun than on the side streets.

A classy alternative to the knickknacks is a type of local jewelry called *Konavoske puce* ("Konavle buttons"). Sold as earrings,

pendants, and rings, these distinctive and fashionable filigree-style pieces consist of a sphere with several small posts. Though they're sold around town, it's least expensive to buy them on Od Puča street, which runs parallel to the Stradun two blocks toward the sea (near the Serbian Orthodox Church). The high concentration of jewelers along this lane keeps prices reasonable. You'll find the "buttons" in various sizes, in both silver (affordable) and gold (pricey).

You'll also see lots of jewelry made from red coral, which can only be legally gathered in small amounts from two small islands in northern Dalmatia. If you see a particularly large chunk of coral, it's likely imported. To know what you're getting, shop at an actual jeweler instead of a souvenir shop.

Gift-Shop Chains: Several gift shops in Dubrovnik (with additional branches throughout Dalmatia) hawk fun, if sometimes made-in-China, items. Look for these chains, which are a bit classier than the many no-name shops around town: **Aqua** sells pleasant nautical-themed gifts, blue-and-white-striped sailor shirts, and other gear. **Bonbonnière Kraš** is Croatia's leading chocolatier, selling a wide array of tasty candies. **Uje** has artisan olive oils and other boutiquey edibles.

Classy Gifts: A shop called **Life According to KAWA,** just outside the Ploče Gate, is a great place to browse for characteristic, hipster-aesthetic local souvenirs and handicrafts. They've got everything from artisanal sea salt and jewelry, to ceramics and Dubrovnik-themed ironic T-shirts. They also stock a fridge full of local microbrews and some carefully selected local wines and foods (daily 9:00-24:00 in peak season, until 22:00 in shoulder season, Hvarska 2, tel. 020/696-958).

Entertainment in Dubrovnik

MUSICAL EVENTS

Dubrovnik annually hosts a full schedule of events for its Summer Festival (July 10-Aug 25, www.dubrovnik-festival.hr), which is quickly followed by its Late Summer Festival. But the town also works hard to offer traditional music outside of festival time. The Cultural Information Desk, inside the Sloboda theater lobby at the bottom of the Bell Tower on Luža Square, is a good source of information on events (open long hours daily). For the latest on any of these festivals and concerts, check the events listings in *The Best in Dubrovnik* guide, or ask the TI.

Here are a few good choices:

Spirited **Lindo folk-music** concerts are performed for tourists twice weekly in the Lazareti (former medieval quarantine building), just outside the Ploče Gate (100 kn, usually Tue and Fri at 21:30, www.lindjo.hr).

The **Dubrovnik Symphony Orchestra** performs crowd-pleasing classics twice weekly in summer (and once weekly through winter)—usually at the Rector's Palace in good weather, or the Dominican Monastery in bad weather (100-400 kn, typically at 21:00, www.dso.hr).

Various historic **churches** around town host touristy but enjoyable concerts (generally 100 kn, each venue hosts about 3/week at 21:00, mobile 098-244-264). Venues include St. Savior, just inside the Pile Gate; the simpler Domina Church, just up Od Domina street from the Stradun; and the little Rosario Church near the Dominican Monastery at the Ploče Gate.

Also consider the folk dancing and market each Sunday morning at Čilipi, a small town near the airport (see the next chapter). Dubrovnik-based companies offer excursions that include transportation there and back.

NIGHTLIFE

Dubrovnik's Old Town is one big, romantic parade of relaxed and happy people out strolling. The main drag is brightly lit and packed with shops, cafés, and bars, all open late. This is a fun scene. And if you walk away from the crowds or out on the port, you'll be alone with the magic of the Pearl of the Adriatic. Everything feels—and is—very safe after dark.

If you're looking for a memorable bar after dark, consider these:

▲▲▲Drinks with a View

Cold Drinks "Buža" offers, without a doubt, the most scenic spot for a drink. Perched on a cliff above the sea, clinging like a barnacle to the outside of the City Walls, this is a peaceful, shaded getaway from the bustle of the Old Town...the perfect place to watch cruise

ships disappear into the horizon. *Buža* means "hole in the wall"—and that's exactly what you'll have to go through to reach these places. There are two different Bužas, both open every day in summer from 9:00 until the wee hours (closed in bad weather and off-season; both have drinks for around 40-50 kn). **Buža II** (nicknamed "Big Buža") is the older and more appealing of the pair. Filled with mellow tourists and bartenders pouring wine and beer into plastic cups, Buža II comes with castaway views and Frank Sinatra ambience. When the seats fill up—as often happens around sunset— you can order a drink at the bar and walk down the stairs to enjoy it "on the rocks"...literally. **Buža I**—also called Mala (Small) Buža— is mellower, plays hip or edgy rather than romantic music, and has concrete stairs leading down to a beach on the rocks below. While lacking Buža II's shade, Buža I is less claustrophobic and often a bit less crowded, making it a viable alternative.

Getting There: Both Bužas are well away from the bustle of the main drag, along the seaward wall. To reach them from the cathedral area, hike up the grand staircase to St. Ignatius' Church, then go left to find the lane that runs along the inside of the wall. To find the classic Buža II, head right along the lane and look for the *Cold Drinks* sign pointing to a literal hole in the wall. For the hipper Buža I, go left along the same lane, and locate the hole in the wall with the *No Toples No Nudist* graffiti.

Cocktails and People-Watching

Bunićeva Poljana, the little square tucked behind the cathedral, is jammed with tables from a half-dozen different cafés, which fill with tourists and locals each evening. Live jazz is provided nightly by **Jazz Caffè Troubadour,** but as their drink prices are outlandish, most people prefer to sit at a nearby place...you can hear the music just as well from there (or from anywhere in this part of the Old Town, for that matter).

Nonenina, a few steps in front of the cathedral on Pred Dvorom, is an outdoor lounge with a fine vantage point for people-watching (daily 9:00-late, across from Rector's Palace).

The Gaffe Irish Pub, with a chummy, pubby interior and a small courtyard, is a rollicking spot to drain a pint and watch some rugby (Miha Pracata 4, mobile 098-196-2149, see listing under "Eating in Dubrovnik," later).

Restaurant Klarisa, tucked in a tight back corner of the Old Town (behind St. Claire's Convent, just up Garište ulica from Onofrio's Fountain), has live jazz each night outside. You can pay for an overpriced meal or drink, or just loiter and enjoy (Poljana Paska Miličevića 4, tel. 020/413-100).

D'Vino Wine Bar is an ideal place to nurse a drink while learning about Croatian wine, nibbling local tapas, and socializing; for details, see full listing under "Eating in Dubrovnik," later. **Glam Café,** just across the street, has a similar vibe and stocks a nice assortment of local microbrews.

Nightclubs

Several places are near or just beyond the Ploče Gate at the east end of town. Head under the Bell Tower, then up the street past the Dominican Monastery. You'll pass the hole-in-the-wall entrance (right) for the snobby, upscale **360°** cocktail bar (www.360dubrovnik.com). Then, after crossing the bridge, look (on the left) for the entrance to **Revelin**—a dance club that fills one of the city wall's fortress towers (www.clubrevelin.com). Then head out and up the street until you reach **Banje Beach,** a bar/lounge/dance club overlooking one of the city's most scenic beaches (www.banjebeach.com). Note that some of these bars and clubs are more exclusive and may charge admission on weekends.

MOVIES

The Old Town has a variety of movie theaters showing American blockbusters (usually in English with Croatian subtitles, unless the film's animated or for kids; for the schedule, see www.kinematografi.org). Two modern cinemas in town have comfortable seating and show current movies: the **Sloboda,** right under the Bell Tower on Luža Square (open outside of the summer outdoor movie season—see next); and **Visia,** just inside the Pile Gate (year-round).

In good summer weather, head for the fun outdoor **Jadran** cinema, where you can lick ice cream (B.Y.O.) while you watch a movie with a Dubrovnik-mountaintop backdrop. This is a cheap, casual, and very Croatian scene, where people smoke and chat, and the neighbors sit in their windowsills to watch the movie (most nights late June-mid-Sept, shows begin shortly after sundown; in the Old Town near the Pile Gate). Another outdoor movie venue, **Slavica,** is farther out of town, on the road leading away from the Pile Gate.

Sleeping in Dubrovnik

You basically have two options in Dubrovnik: a centrally located room in a private home *(soba);* or a resort hotel on a distant beach, a bus ride away from the Old Town. Dubrovnik hotels are generally a rotten value, and you'll have to commute into your sightseeing on crowded buses. For this reason, I heavily favor a central *soba*.

No matter where you stay, prices are much higher mid-June through mid-September, and highest in July and August. Reserve well ahead for these peak times.

SOBE (PRIVATE ROOMS): A DUBROVNIK SPECIALTY

In Dubrovnik, you'll almost always do better with a *soba* or apartment than with a hotel. Before you choose, carefully read the information on page 206. All of my favorite *sobe* are run by friendly English-speaking Croatians and are inside or within easy walking distance of the Old Town.

All of my listings are air-conditioned and come with private facilities, and most have kitchenettes. A few are in family homes, but you can be as anonymous as you like. These *sobe* accept cash only (no credit cards), and you're on your own for breakfast—I've listed some suggestions later, under "Eating in Dubrovnik."

My four long-time, personal favorites here are Dubrovnik Gardens, Jadranka Benussi, Karmen Apartments, and Villa Ragusa. These all enjoy conscientious management, a fine location, and good value for the price. Early birds will want to book these ahead. But if they're full (which often happens), I've also listed several almost-as-good options.

To search from home, you can use the regular booking sites (such as Airbnb or Booking.com)—but if you want to book one of the places I've listed here, **please book direct** (by sending them an email), which saves both you and your host money. These hosts respond to email quickly, and many will offer you a discounted rate if you book direct. Another good place to search is www. dubrovnikapartmentsource.com, run by an American couple and offering a range of carefully selected, well-described accommodations.

In the Old Town, Above the Stradun Promenade

These options are located at the top of town, high above the Stradun, just far enough away from nighttime noise. The first three are within a few steps of each other, along a little block dubbed by some "Rickova ulica." If you don't mind the very steep hike up, you'll find this area to be a handy home base. When one of these places is full, they work together to find space for you. The last two listings are a few blocks over, just as nice, and equally steep. Because all of these hosts live off-site, be sure to let them know when you'll arrive so they can let you in.

$$ Villa Ragusa offers a good value in the Old Town. Pero Carević renovated a 600-year-old house at the top of town. The five comfortable, modern rooms come with wooden beams and antique furniture. There are three doubles with bathrooms (including a top-floor room with rooftop views over the Old Town for no extra charge—request when you reserve) and two singles that share a bathroom (extra for breakfast at an atmospheric café just down the stairs, Žudioska ulica 15, mobile 098-765-634, www.villaragusadubrovnik. com, villa.ragusa@du.t-com.hr).

$$ Apartments Paviša, next door to Villa Ragusa and run by Pero Paviša, has three good, older-feeling rooms at a higher price (RS%, Žudioska ulica 19, mobile 098-427-399, www.apartmentspavisa.com, pero. pavisa@gmail.com). Pero also rents two more rooms in the Viktorija neighborhood, about a 20-minute mostly uphill walk east of the Old Town. While it's a long-but-scenic walk into town, the views from these apartments are spectacular (same prices and contact as in-town rooms, Frana Supila 59, bus stop nearby).

$$ Ivana and Anita Raič are sisters renting three simple, well-priced apartments with kitchenettes and modern, stylish, pastel flourishes (Žudioska ulica 16, Ivana's mobile 098-996-0858, Anita's mobile 099-592-1568, www.apartments-raic.com, ivanaraic@gmail.com).

$$$ Apartments Martecchini has three units lower down, closer to the main drag (Kovačka 2, mobile 095-587-6036, www. apartmentsmartecchini.com, cizek1981@gmail.com, Petra).

$ Plaza Apartments, run by Lidija and Maro Matić, rents three well-appointed, heavily perfumed apartments on a plant-filled lane—the steepest and most appealing stretch of stairs leading up from the Stradun. Lidija's sweet personality is reflected in the cheerful rooms, which are a great value if you don't mind the hike (RS%, all apartments have kitchenettes and laundry machines, climb the stairs past Dolce Vita gelato shop to Nalješkovićeva 22, tel. 020/321-493, mobile 091-517-7048, lidydu@yahoo.com).

$ Minerva Apartments has three cozy, budget-priced units a block over, near the top of a similar lane, in the home of Dubravka Vidosavljević-Vučić (laundry machine, Antuninska 14, mobile 091-252-9677, duvivu@gmail.com).

In the Old Town, near the Cathedral and St. John's Fort

The following places are south of the Stradun, mostly clustering around the cathedral and St. John's Fort, at the end of the Old Port. To find the Karmen and Zijadić apartments from the cathedral, walk toward the big fort tower along the inside of the wall (follow signs for *akvarji*); for Dubrovnik Gardens, climb up the grand staircase to the Jesuit St. Ignatius Church.

$$$$ Fresh Sheets Kathedral, well-run by Canadian-Croatian couple Jon and Sanja, rents six bright, stylish, modern rooms in an ideally located building—next door to the cathedral and squeezed between two of Dubrovnik's most happening squares (better for those who enjoy being out late). Three of the rooms have shared bathrooms, and all have views over interesting squares and landmarks in the heart of the Old Town. While pricey, the hospitality, well-appointed rooms, and great location can make it worthwhile (Bunićeva Poljana 6, mobile 091-896-7509, www.freshsheetskathedral.com, stay@freshsheetskathedral.com).

$$$ Karmen Apartments are well-run by a Brit named Marc and his Croatian wife Silva, who offer four welcoming apartments just inside the big fort. While a bit pricey, the apartments are roomy, well-equipped, and homey-feeling, each with a bathroom and kitchen. The decor is eclectic but tasteful, drawing from Marc and Silva's extensive art collection; the stairwell has a virtual mini museum of historic Dubrovnik maps and documents (RS%, near the aquarium at Bandureva 1, tel. 020/323-433, mobile 098-619-282, www.karmendu.com, mvanbloe@gmail.com).

$$ Dubrovnik Gardens, conscientiously run by Roberto and his mother Marija (also recommended tour guides—see "Tours in Dubrovnik," earlier), is unique and a top value. From the big square in front of the Jesuit St. Ignatius Church, you'll let yourself in through a hidden door to reach a rare private garden—a peaceful oasis smack-dab in the heart of the bustling city. Two units have their own exclusive slice of the garden: a cozy freestanding cottage (can work for a family of up to 4); and an elegant, bright, spacious, artistically appointed studio apartment. Each unit has full access to its own garden, where you can even order food from the neighboring restaurant (the recommended Kopun)...very cool, particularly in a city with virtually no green space. They also have a bigger, antique-furnished, two-room apartment (garden views but no access, up several flights of stairs, sleeps up to 4; all units have kitchenette, mobile 091-541-6637, www.dubrovnikgardens.com, dubrovnikgardens@gmail.com).

$$ Apartments Placa (PLAH-tsah; not to be confused with Plaza Apartments, described earlier) is run by Tonči (TOHN-chee). He rents three apartments with some antique furnishings and some modern, overlooking the market square in the heart of the Old Town. You might get some early-morning noise from the market set-up, but the double-paned windows help, and the location is wonderfully central. Since Tonči lives elsewhere, clearly communicate your arrival time (Gundulićeva

DUBROVNIK

Old Town Hotels & Restaurants

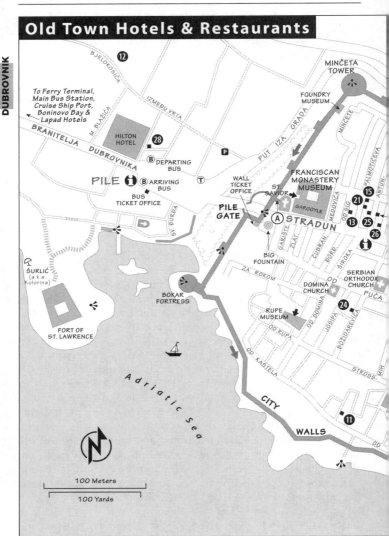

BJELOKOSIĆA ⑫

MINČETA TOWER

To Ferry Terminal, Main Bus Station, Cruise Ship Port, Boninovo Bay & Lapad Hotels

IZMEĐU VRTA

FOUNDRY MUSEUM

BRANITELJA

M. BLAŽIĆA

HILTON HOTEL

DUBROVNIKA

㉘

Ⓑ DEPARTING BUS

Ⓟ

Ⓣ

PUT IZA GRADA

MINČETE

PILE Ⓘ Ⓑ ARRIVING BUS

FRANCISCAN MONASTERY MUSEUM

PALMOTIĆEVA

BUS TICKET OFFICE

SV. ĐURĐA

WALL TICKET OFFICE

ST. SAVIOR

OD SIG

⑮ ㉑

ANTUN-

PILE GATE

Ⓐ STRADUN

GARGOYLE

⑬ ㉕

MEDOVIĆA

㉖

Ⓘ

ŠURLIĆ (a.k.a. Kolorina)

BIG FOUNTAIN

GARIŠTE ZLAT.

ZA ROKOM

ĆURRAN BORR.

SIROKA

BOKAR FORTRESS

DOMINA CHURCH

OD DOMINA

SERBIAN ORTHODOX CHURCH

PUČA

RUPE MUSEUM

㉔

FORT OF ST. LAWRENCE

OD RUPA

JOSIPA

BOŽIDAREVIĆA

A d r i a t i c   S e a

OD KAŠTELA

CITY

STROSS.

MIH

Ⓝ

WALLS

⑪

OD

100 Meters

100 Yards

Accommodations

1. Villa Ragusa & Apartments Paviša
2. Raič Apartments
3. Apartments Martecchini
4. Plaza Apartments
5. Minerva Apartments
6. Fresh Sheets Kathedral B&B
7. Karmen Apartments
8. Dubrovnik Gardens
9. Apartments Placa
10. Renata Zijadić Rooms & Cogito Coffee
11. City Walls Hostel
12. To Benussi Rooms
13. Hotel Stari Grad
14. To Viktorija Apartments, Hotel Excelsior & Grand Villa Argentina

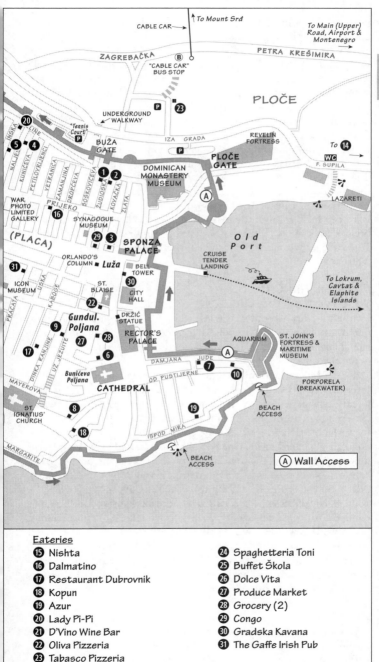

Eateries

15 Nishta
16 Dalmatino
17 Restaurant Dubrovnik
18 Kopun
19 Azur
20 Lady Pi-Pi
21 D'Vino Wine Bar
22 Oliva Pizzeria
23 Tabasco Pizzeria
24 Spaghetteria Toni
25 Buffet Škola
26 Dolce Vita
27 Produce Market
28 Grocery (2)
29 Congo
30 Gradska Kavana
31 The Gaffe Irish Pub

poljana 5, mobile 091-721-9202, www.dubrovnik-online.net/apartments_placa, tonci.korculanin@du.t-com.hr).

$ Renata Zijadić offers three older but well-located rooms with slanting floors. She rents an affordable, older, simple double with an ornate cabinet and no views, and two overpriced apartments that are worth considering if you're in a pinch or would like a great view over the Old Port (follow signs for wall access and walk up the steps marked *ulica Stajeva* going over the street to find Stajeva 1; mobile 095-532-3505, www.dubrovnik-online.net/house_renata, renatadubrovnik@yahoo.com).

¢ City Walls Hostel is a good budget option in the Old Town. The 18 bunks (two 6-bed dorms, one 4-bed dorm, and a double room) sit above a tight common area. Located at the very top of Dubrovnik just inside the City Walls, this bright and cheery place is a steep hike up from the main drag (closed Nov-March, includes breakfast, lockers, kitchenette, Svetog Šimuna 15, mobile 091-799-2086, www.citywallshostel.com, citywallshostel@gmail.com, Marijana).

Outside Pile Gate,
Just West of the Old Town

While the area in front of the Pile Gate is a congested tourist hub, one of my favorite Dubrovnik lodgings sits high on the hill above the chaos, offering a warm welcome to travelers hardy enough to make the hike.

$$$ Jadranka Benussi rents two apartments in a quiet, traffic-free neighborhood. Her delightful stony-chic home, complete with a leafy terrace, is a steep 10-minute hike above the Old Town—close enough to be convenient, but far enough to take you away from the bustle and into a calm residential zone. Jadranka speaks good English, enjoys visiting with her guests, and gives her place a modern Croatian class unusual for a *soba*. This is one of your most comfortable home bases in Dubrovnik, if you don't mind the walk (kitchenettes, Miha Klaića 10, tel. 020/429-339, mobile 098-928-1300, www.dubrovnik-benussi.com, jadranka@dubrovnik-benussi.com). To find Jadranka's house, first go to the big Hilton Hotel just outside the Pile Gate. Walk up the little stepped lane called Marijana Blažića at the upper-left corner of the Hilton cul-de-sac. When that lane dead-ends, go left up ulica Don Iva Bjelokosića (more steps) until you see a little church on the left. Jadranka's house is just before this church.

HOTELS

If you must stay in a hotel, you have only a few good options. There are just two hotels inside the City Walls—and one of them charges $500 a night (Pucić Palace, www.thepucicpalace.com). Any big, resort-style hotel within walking distance of the Old Town will run you at least €200. These inflated prices drive most visitors to Boninovo Bay or the Lapad Peninsula, a bus ride west of the Old Town. The following are good choices for those who don't mind spending a lot on big-hotel amenities.

$$$$ Hotel Stari Grad knows it's the only real hotel option inside the Old Town—and charges accordingly. It has eight extremely stylish rooms a half-block off the Old Town's main drag. The rooftop breakfast terrace enjoys an amazing view over orange tiles (air-con, lots of stairs with no elevator, Od Sigurate 4, tel. 020/322-244, www.hotelstarigrad.com, info@hotelstarigrad.com).

$$$$ Adriatic Luxury Hotels is a chain with several plush hotels near Dubrovnik. Location-wise, the most enticing are **Hotel Excelsior** (Frana Supila 12) and **Grand Villa Argentina** (Frana Supila 14)—which are a scenic 10-minute walk outside the Ploče Gate, east of the Old Town—as well as the **Hotel Bellevue** (on Boninovo Bay, a short bus ride or long walk west of the Old Town; see "Greater Dubrovnik" map, earlier). For top-of-the-top luxury lodgings without regard for the price tag, browse their options at www.adriaticluxuryhotels.com.

Eating in Dubrovnik

Dubrovnik's restaurant scene is hit-or-miss. Many places are in business only to extract money from people who are passing through on a cruise ship. However, I've carefully selected the following gems, which are better established and more likely to treat you like a return customer. All of my recommendations are in or very near the atmospheric Old Town. Anywhere you dine, breezy outdoor seating is a no-brainer, and scrawny, adorable kittens beg for table scraps. In general, seafood restaurants are good only at seafood; if you want pasta, go to a pasta place.

$$ Nishta ("Nothing"), featuring a short menu of delicious vegan-fusion cuisine with Asian, Indian, and Mexican flair, offers a welcome change of pace from the Dalmatian seafood-pasta-pizza rut. Busy Swiss owner/chef Gildas cooks, while his wife Ruža and their staff cheerfully serve a steady stream of return diners. This tiny place—which has been a reliably delicious and improbably affordable crowd-pleaser for years—has just a few cramped indoor and outdoor tables. Even if you're a carnivore, it's worth a visit; reserve the day ahead in peak season (Mon-Sat 11:30-22:00, closed

Sun and Jan-Feb, on the restaurant-clogged Prijeko street—near the Pile Gate end of the street, tel. 020/322-088).

$$$ Dalmatino offers some of the best traditional Dalmatian cooking in the city, presented with modern class. This is quality food at prices that, while not cheap, won't blow your budget. While there are only a few outdoor tables tucked along the alley, the dining room is spacious and sophisticated, but not stuffy. This is a rare Dubrovnik eatery that's open year-round—a good sign (daily 11:00-23:00, also on the Prijeko "restaurant row" at #15, tel. 020/323-070, http://dalmatino-dubrovnik.com, Robert).

$$$$ Restaurant Dubrovnik, well-regarded for its Dalmatian and international cuisine, is the place for a fine-dining experience without blowing your entire budget. And in good weather, the setting is gorgeous: Their expansive terrace is tucked deep in the Old Town, under floodlit old houses and drying laundry (though when they close the roof in bad weather, it loses much of its appeal). If you're going to splurge, this is worth serious consideration. Reserve ahead (daily 12:00-23:00, Marojice Kaboge 5, mobile 099-258-5871, www.restorandubrovnik.com).

$$$$ Kopun just feels special, with an off-the-beaten-path setting on a gravelly square facing the Jesuit St. Ignatius Church. They serve up regional specialties (mostly seafood) with a touch of class. Several dishes make use of the restaurant's namesake, *kopun*—a rooster that's castrated young and plumps up (daily 11:00-23:00, Poljana Ruđera Boškovića 7, tel. 020/323-969, www.restaurantkopun.com).

$$$ Azur, tucked near the Buža bars just inside the City Walls, offers a break from the standard regional fare. The menu presents Mediterranean cuisine with an Asian twist (for example, swordfish in a black curry sauce). Owner Vedran has created a hit with discerning locals and travelers alike with careful preparation and service. Book ahead for an outside table (daily 11:00-24:00, Pobijana 10, tel. 020/324-806).

$$$ Lady Pi-Pi, named for a comical, anatomically correct, and slightly off-putting statue out front, sits high above town, barely inside the wall. The clientele skews a bit younger, and many of the tasty dishes are prepared over an open grill. Several tables overlook the rooftops of Dubrovnik, but these fill up fast, and no reservations are possible—come early or be prepared to line up. The non-view tables, on a stony, vine-strewn terrace, are nice but nothing special (daily 9:00-22:30, closed Oct-April and in bad weather, Peline b.b., tel. 020/321-288).

Wine Bar with Food: Just a few steps off the main drag, **$$$ D'Vino Wine Bar** has a relaxed atmosphere and a smart, easygoing approach to Croatian wines. Run by gregarious Aussie-Croat Sasha and his capable staff (including Anita and Toni), this cozy bar encourages you to slow down and really be on vacation. Their user-friendly menu of more than 60 wines by the glass highlights small producers with helpful descriptions of each wine. The various three-taste flights make a good introduction to Croatian wines, and they can do full-blown tastings in their on-site tasting room (customized to your schedule and interests—ask). Their tasty appetizers—cheese-and-meat and *antipasti* plates—pair perfectly with the wines and can easily add up to a tasty lunch or dinner; the smoked duck or swordfish plates go well with the reds. Sit in the get-to-know-your-neighbor interior or linger at the sidewalk tables. And if you're in a rush and just want a takeaway coffee, they've got you covered there, too. Reservations are smart if you'll be here during dining hours—after about 18:00 (daily 10:30-late, Palmotićeva 4a, tel. 020/321-130, www.dvino.net). Sasha takes wine lovers on all-day wine tours to the Pelješac Peninsula (see the next chapter for more on this region) and frequently comes up with fun new activities for travelers—check their website or drop in and ask for the latest. If you'll be in the Lapad resort area, check their website to see if their new wine shop there is open.

Pizza: Dubrovnik seems to have a pizzeria on every corner. Little separates the various options—just look for a menu and outdoor seating option that appeals to you. **$$ Oliva Pizzeria,** just behind St. Blaise's Church, puts out consistently good food (Lučarica 5, daily 10:00-24:00, tel. 020/324-594); around the side is a handy takeout window selling affordable slices. Close to the Old Town, but just far away to be frequented mostly by locals, **$$ Tabasco Pizzeria** is tucked at the corner of the parking lot beneath the cable-car station. Unpretentious and affordable, this is the place to come if the pizza is more important than the setting—though the outdoor terrace does have views of the City Walls...over a sea of parked cars (daily 9:00-23:00, Hvarska 48A, tel. 020/429-595). A few other lowbrow places (good for diners on a budget) line Hvarska downhill from here.

Pasta: $$ Spaghetteria Toni is nothing fancy; it's just a reliable old standby that offers good pastas (including a few creative choices) at reasonable prices. Choose between the cozy 10-table interior or the long alley filled with outdoor tables (daily in summer 11:00-23:00, closed Sun in winter, closed Jan, Nikole Božidarevića 14, tel. 020/323-134).

Sandwiches: Just a few steps off the Stradun, **$ Buffet Škola** is a rare bit of preglitz Dubrovnik, serving takeaway or sit-down sandwiches on homemade bread. Squeeze into the hole-in-the-wall interior, or sit at one of the outdoor tables (skip the overpriced ham-and-cheese boards, daily 8:00-22:00, Antuninska 1, tel. 020/321-096).

Ice Cream: Dubrovnik has lots of great *sladoled*, but locals swear by the stuff at **Dolce Vita.** In addition to good ice cream, they have tasty crêpes (daily 9:00-24:00, a half-block off the Stradun at Nalješkovićeva 1A, tel. 020/321-666).

The Old Town's "Restaurant Row," Prijeko Street: The street called Prijeko, a block toward the mainland from the Stradun promenade, is lined with outdoor, tourist-oriented eateries— each one with a huckster out front trying to lure in diners. Don't be sucked into this vortex of mediocre food at inflated prices. The only places worth seeking out here are Nishta and Dalmatino (both described earlier), which distinguish themselves with a long track record of quality cooking. Still, it can be fun to take a stroll along here—the atmosphere is lively, and the sales pitches are entertainingly desperate.

Picnic Tips: Dubrovnik's lack of great restaurant options makes it a perfect place to picnic. You can shop for fresh fruits and veggies at the open-air produce market (each morning near the cathedral, on the square called Gundulićeva Poljana). Supplement your picnic with basic supplies from **Konzum grocery store** (one location on the market square near the produce vendors, another near the bus stop just outside Pile Gate, both open Mon-Sat 8:00-22:00, Sun until 21:00). Good picnic spots include the shaded benches overlooking the Old Port; the Porporela breakwater (beyond the Old Port and fort—comes with a swimming area, sunny no-shade benches, and views of Lokrum Island); and the green, welcoming park in what was the moat just under the Pile Gate entry to the Old Town.

Premade Gourmet Picnics: Canadian expat Alex runs **$$$$ Piknik Dubrovnik,** which can hand you a high-end, readymade picnic in an insulated backpack, with plenty of tips on where to enjoy it. While it's not cheap, it's a hit with adventurous foodies (around 600 kn/2 people, arrange at least 24 hours in advance, mobile 098-175-1103, www.piknikdubrovnik.com, piknikdubrovnik@gmail.com).

Gourmet Coffee: If you're craving something a notch above the standard *bijela kava,* head for **Cogito Coffee**—an artisanal coffee shop (part of a Zagreb-based chain), tucked under a little tunnel near the bottom of the Maritime Museum stairs, near the Old Port (daily 9:00-19:00, Pustijerne 1).

BREAKFAST

If you're sleeping in a *soba,* you'll likely be on your own for breakfast. Fortunately, you have plenty of cafés and pastry shops to choose from, and your host probably has a favorite he or she can recommend. For something substantial, several restaurants in inviting locations serve up eggy breakfasts for around 65 kn. Choose a fine perch along the Stradun and pay a bit too much for the privilege of watching the town wake up and the cruise passengers file in (**Congo,** at Placa 6, opens before anyone else at 7:00—handy if you're departing early). Locals who meet along here each morning—catching up with their friends as they stroll by—call this their low-tech version of "Facebook." Another scenic perch is just around the corner: **Gradska Kavana,** tucked between the Bell Tower and Rector's Palace (served daily 8:00-11:30, Pred Dvorom 1). **D'Vino Wine Bar** (described earlier) has a short but appealing menu of more interesting breakfast options, and a shady alley to hang out in (served daily 8:00-11:00). And if you'd like an even wider menu of affordably priced breakfast options—in a less atmospheric setting—try **The Gaffe Irish Pub** (served daily 9:00-11:00, Miha Pracata 4—for location see "Old Town Hotels & Restaurants" map, earlier, tel. 020/640-152).

Dubrovnik Connections

While ferries and catamarans have traditionally used Dubrovnik's Port Gruž (a bus ride away from the Old Town), a planned redevelopment could relocate some or all boats to the far end of the port, under the big bridge. Ask locally for the latest.

By Catamaran: Speedy catamarans connect Dubrovnik to points north. As these are operated by three different companies—and the schedules tend to change from year to year—it's important to check all three websites to fully understand your options: Krilo (www.krilo.hr), Jadrolinija (www.jadrolinija.hr), and Nona Ana (www.gv-line.hr). You can buy tickets on each of these websites, which you should do at least a day or two ahead (or longer) at very busy times. Boats sell out. (Note that Jadrolinija requires you to buy tickets in person, at Port Gruž, for same-day departures.)

Catamarans take about 1.5 hours to **Mljet National Park** (use the Polače or Pomena docks—not Sobra), 2 hours to **Korčula,** 3 hours to **Hvar,** and 4-5 hours to **Split.**

The **Krilo** catamaran runs twice each afternoon through the summer to Korčula and Split; en route, one of these stops at Pomena on Mljet, and the other stops at Hvar (2/day mid-June-mid-Sept, 1/day late May-mid-June and mid-Sept-early Oct, 3-4/week spring and fall, none Nov-late April). The **Jadrolinija** catamaran departs in the early morning and stops at Korčula, Hvar, and Split (mid-June-mid-Sept). The **Nona Ana** has a shorter season (June-Sept) and doesn't reach as far north, departing each morning for Polače on Mljet Island; in July and August, it sometimes continues to Korčula (4/week, 2.5 hours). In winter (Oct-May), the boat goes only to Šipan (one of the Elaphite Islands near Dubrovnik) and Sobra (on Mljet, but far from the national park).

By Bus to: Split (1-2/hour, less off-season, 4.5 hours), **Korčula**

(summer: 2/day generally around 9:00 and 15:00, may also be a later bus 2/week in summer, 3.5 hours; off-season: 1/day at 15:00), **Rijeka** (5/day, 13 hours), **Zagreb** (15/day, overnight options, 10 hours), **Kotor** in Montenegro (8/day in summer, less off-season, 2-2.5 hours—or can take much longer due to border delays), **Mostar** (5/day in summer, less off-season, 3-4 hours), **Sarajevo** (1-2/day, 6 hours; includes a night bus in summer only at 22:30), **Pula** and **Rovinj** (1/day overnight departing at 15:30, 15 hours to Pula, 16 hours to Rovinj). As usual, schedules are subject to change— confirm locally before making the trip to the bus station. You can check schedules and buy tickets at www.getbybus.com. For additional bus information, check www.libertasdubrovnik.com or call 060-305-070 (a pricey toll line, but worth it).

By Plane: To quickly connect remote Dubrovnik with the rest of your trip, consider a cheap flight. For information on Dubrovnik's airport, see "Arrival in Dubrovnik: By Plane," earlier.

By Car: For tips on driving along the Dalmatian Coast between Dubrovnik and Split, see page 86.

Can I Get to Greece from Dubrovnik? Your best bet is to fly. There are direct flights to Athens on Aegean and Croatia Airlines. Even though Croatia and Greece are nearly neighbors, no direct boats connect them, and the overland connection is extremely long and rugged.

What About Italy? Flying is the easiest option, though there are only a few direct flights (to Rome, Venice, Naples, and Milan; airlines include Croatia Airlines, Volotea, EasyJet, and Vueling). You can take a direct night boat from Dubrovnik to Bari, or head to Split for more boat connections. The overland connection is too long (figure 5 hours to Split, then 5 hours to Zagreb, then 7 hours to Venice).

NEAR DUBROVNIK

Excursions from Dubrovnik's Old Port • Cavtat • Trsteno Arboretum • Pelješac Peninsula • Mljet National Park

The longer you linger, the clearer it becomes: Dubrovnik isn't just a town, it's an entire region. Stretching up and down the glimmering Dalmatian Coast from Dubrovnik are a variety of worthwhile getaways.

Just offshore from the city's Old Town—and accessible via scenic boat trip from its historic port—are enticing islands and villages, where time stands still for lazy vacationers: the playground islet of Lokrum and the archipelago of the Elaphite Islands. The serene resort town of Cavtat, just south of Dubrovnik, has some of the best art treasures of this part of Dalmatia (including a stunning mausoleum designed by Ivan Meštrović). Nearby, the medieval canals and waterwheels of the Konavoski Dvori area offer a welcome and refreshing escape from sun-baked coastal towns.

To the north is a lush arboretum called Trsteno, with a playful fountain, a 600-year-old aqueduct, a villa, a chapel...and, of course, plants galore. Poking into the Adriatic is the vineyard-covered Pelješac Peninsula, where friendly vintners are eager to impress you with their wines, and where the mighty little town of Ston lures you to climb its sprawling fortifications. And out at sea is the sparsely populated island called Mljet, a third of which is carefully protected as one of Croatia's most appealing national parks, where you can hike, bike, kayak, and swim to your heart's content. Best of all, there's no better place to "come home to" than Dubrovnik—after a busy day exploring the coastline, strolling the Stradun to unwind is particularly sweet.

Dubrovnik Day Trips at a Glance

The international excursions to Bosnia-Herzegovina and Montenegro—which are worth considering for overnight stops—are covered in their own chapters.

In Bosnia-Herzegovina

▲▲▲Mostar The side-trip with the highest degree of cultural hairiness—but, for many, also the greatest reward—lies to the east, in Bosnia-Herzegovina. With its iconic Old Bridge, intriguing glimpse of European Muslim lifestyles, and still-vivid examples of war damage, Mostar is unforgettable. Allow a full day or more (best reached by bus or car).

Međugorje Devout Catholics may want to consider a trip to this pilgrimage site in Bosnia-Herzegovina, with a holy hill that some believe is visited regularly by an apparition of the Virgin Mary. Allow a full day or more (car or bus).

In Montenegro

▲▲The Bay of Kotor For rugged coastal scenery that rivals anything in Croatia, head south of the border to Montenegro. The Bay of Kotor is a dramatic, fjord-like inlet crowned by the historic town of Kotor, with twisty Old World lanes, one of Europe's best town walls, and oodles of atmosphere. Allow a full day or more (car or bus).

The Montenegrin Interior A visit to Montenegro's scruffy but historic former capital, Cetinje, comes with a twisty drive up a mountain road and across a desolate, forgotten-feeling plateau. Allow a few hours' side-trip from Kotor (car).

Budva Riviera Montenegro's best stretch of sandy beaches isn't worth a special trip, but it's a fun excuse for a drive if you've got extra time to kill. The highlight is the famous resort peninsula of Sveti Stefan. Allow a few hours' side-trip from Kotor (car).

On the Mainland near Dubrovnik

▲Cavtat A charming resort/beach town, unassuming Cavtat

holds a pair of wonderful and very local art experiences: an elaborate mausoleum designed by
the sculptor Ivan Meštrović,
and the house and museum
of Cavtat-born modern painter Vlaho Bukovac. Allow a
few hours (boat or bus).

▲**Pelješac Peninsula** This
long, narrow, scenic spit of
land—between the main
coastal road and Korčula Island—is a favorite of wine lovers, who
can joyride through its vineyards and sample its product (or just
enjoy the beautiful scenery). Allow a half-day to a full day (car).

▲**Trsteno Arboretum** Plant lovers will enjoy this surprisingly engaging botanical garden just outside Dubrovnik, punctuated by
a classical-style fountain and aqueduct. Allow a half-day (bus or
car).

Konavoski Dvori This rugged, forested landscape of ancient canals and still-spinning waterwheels is a refreshing spot for a countryside meal. Allow a few hours (car).

Ston A small town with giant fortifications, Ston (on the Pelješac
Peninsula) is worth a short stop to scramble up its extensive walls.
Allow an hour (car or bus).

Off the Coast of Dubrovnik
▲**Mljet National Park** While this largely undeveloped island is
time-consuming to reach from Dubrovnik, Mljet offers an opportunity to romp on a pristine island without tacky tourist towns.
This is for serious nature lovers eager to get away from civilization
to hike, swim, and kayak. Allow a full day (boat).

Lokrum Island The most convenient excursion from Dubrovnik,
this little island—just a short hop offshore from the Old Port—is
a good chance to get away from (some of) the tourists. Allow a
few hours (boat).

Elaphite Islands This inviting archipelago offers a variety of island experiences without straying too far from Dubrovnik. With
more time, Korčula (for a small town) or Mljet (for a back-to-nature experience) are better, but the "Elafiti" are more convenient.
Allow a half-day to a full day (boat).

PLANNING YOUR TIME

Give yourself at least two nights (one full day) to experience Dubrovnik itself. But if you can spare the time, set up in Dubrovnik for several nights and use your extra days for some of the excursions described in this chapter. (This also gives you the luxury of keeping an eye on the weather reports and saving the most weather-dependent activities for the sunniest days.) For suggestions on how much time to allow per destination, see the "Dubrovnik Day Trips at a Glance" sidebar. Use a map to strategically line up these attractions—for example, you can easily do Trsteno, Ston, and the Pelješac Peninsula on a drive between Dubrovnik and Korčula, while Cavtat pairs nicely with a trip to the airport or Montenegro.

I've listed day trips in this chapter in order of ease from Dubrovnik—the farther down the list, the more difficult to reach

(Montenegro and Mostar, the most time-consuming, are covered in their own chapters).

GETTING THERE

Cavtat and the Elaphite Islands are easy to reach by private **excursion boat** from Dubrovnik's Old Port; Cavtat also works by bus. A **city-run boat** links the Old Port to nearby Lokrum. **Public ferries** connect Dubrovnik's Port Gruž to the Elaphite Islands (the most appealing is Lopud). The other destinations are farther afield, best reached by **boat** (Mljet) or by **car** or **bus** (Montenegro, Mostar, Trsteno, Pelješac Peninsula).

I've listed public transportation options for each, but consider **renting a car** for the day. Or you can splurge for your own **private driver** (see page 16); to make it more affordable, rally other travelers to accompany you and split the cost.

Alternatively, a variety of travel agencies in Dubrovnik offer **guided excursions** (by bus and/or boat) to nearby destinations. Popular itineraries include everything mentioned in this chapter, plus Korčula and others. While these excursions can be a convenient way to see otherwise difficult-to-reach destinations, the quality can be hit-or-miss. The biggest companies are efficient mass-tourism machines—you'll be jammed into buses and boats until every seat is filled, and the guides typically do their spiel (mostly a memorized script) in several languages. Smaller outfits offer a more casual experience with more personal attention, but lack the polish of the big players. Since this scene is constantly evolving, check online reviews, look around for fliers, and ask locals for tips. (Be aware that many small travel agencies simply sell seats on the big companies' trips.)

Excursions from Dubrovnik's Old Port

At Dubrovnik's salty Old Port, captains set up tiny booths to hawk touristy boat trips. It's fun to chat with them, page through their sun-faded photo albums, and see if they can sell you on a short cruise. In addition to the islands noted below, you can also take a boat from the Old Port to **Cavtat** (described later).

PANORAMA CRUISE
The basic option is a 50-minute "panorama cruise" out on the water and back again (75 kn, departures about every hour). You'll loop around the City Walls—which offer a unique view on Dubrovnik's stout defenses—and do a circuit around Lokrum Island as well. Understandably, these cruises are most popular at or shortly before sunset.

You could just hop on whichever boat is departing next, but I enjoy the **Sv. Ivan,** a cargo boat dating from 1878. Prowling its decks and leaning back against rope railings just feels right in this seafaring town. They also offer a 20 percent discount to readers of this book (60 kn for 50-minute panorama cruise; look for their desk among the many sales kiosks at the Old Port, mobile 098-427-177, www.dubrovnik-panoramacruise.com).

LOKRUM ISLAND

This island, a protected natural area just offshore from the Old Town, provides a handy escape from the city. When the Old Town just gets too jam-packed with tourists, locals hop a boat out here for some peace and quiet. They call it the "Island of Love," because it offers many secluded spots popular with courting couples. The main attractions here are hiking (on shaded paths that curl up, over, and around the thickly wooded island) and bathing (on jagged, rocky beaches—many of which are designated nude beaches).

NEAR DUBROVNIK

Getting There: Lokrum is reachable only by an official city-run boat, which departs twice hourly from the end of the pier in Dubrovnik's Old Port. The hefty boat ticket price also includes your admission to the island (120 kn round-trip, 15-minute crossing, runs daily mid-June-Aug 9:00-20:00, shorter hours in shoulder season, stops running Nov-March).

Visiting the Island: From the Lokrum boat dock, walk up to the pink building—the visitors center—to buy a map of the island. Continuing up, you'll reach a fork: To head across the narrow middle of the island, continue straight ahead, where you'll find a monastery-turned-Habsburg-palace. This building is gradually being converted into a free museum. Already in place are exhibits on Richard the Lionheart and his historical connections to this island (he was shipwrecked on his way back from the Third Crusade and landed safely on Lokrum), and on *Game of Thrones*. You'll see "behind the scenes" footage from filming in the Dubrovnik area, and you can pose for photographs with an Iron Throne. Additional exhibits may be completed by the time you visit. (For more *GOT*-related sights, see the sidebar on page 14.)

Nearby is a small botanical garden. Just beyond this area, uneven rocks lead to ladders where you can ease yourself into the sea. There's also a small lake (fed by an underwater canal from the sea) called the "Dead Sea" (Mrtvo More) that's suitable for swimming.

Another option from the boat dock is to hook left and curl around the cove to the island's most popular beach, on the Bay of Portoč, that's famous for its nude sunbathing. If you'd like to (carefully) subject skin that's never seen the sun to those burning rays, follow the *FKK* signs from the boat dock for about five minutes to the slabs of waterfront rock, where naturists feel right at home. Continuing past this beach, you can work your way up and over to the other side of the island (on very rocky trails).

For an even more serious hike, head right from the boat dock for the two-hour hike that goes all the way around the island, and consider a detour to its highest point (at 315 feet above sea level), capped by Fort Royal, an old Austro-Hungarian military fortification.

You can bring your own picnic, but you'll also find a few cafés and restaurants scattered around the island, mostly along the main path from the boat dock to the monastery complex. The island also has WCs and showers for swimmers.

ELAPHITE ISLANDS (ELAFITI)

This 13-island archipelago, just north of Dubrovnik, is popular among day-trippers because it allows you to hit three different islands in a single day: Koločep, Lopud, and Šipan. These "Deer Islands" (supposedly named for their shape—though I don't see it) are a bit overhyped and can't hold a candle to some of the more distant Dalmatian islands, such as Mljet, Korčula, and Hvar. But they're a decent choice if you need a break from Dubrovnik's crowds and want a lazy day cruising Dalmatia. Along the way, you'll discover fishing ports, shady forests, inviting beaches, and forgotten escape mansions of old Dubrovnik aristocracy. The two smaller islands (Koločep and Lopud) are traffic-free, making them a restful backwater getaway. While there's little to actually see on each island, each church, beach, and walking path is well-signed, making it easy to just wander. Bring decent footwear for hiking uneven trails, and pack along swimwear. Each island has some sort of beach relatively near the boat dock; on a hot day, you could just wear your swimsuit on the boat and make a point to take a dip at each stop.

Getting There: The easiest way to cruise the Elafiti is to buy an excursion at Dubrovnik's Old Port, which usually includes a "fish picnic" cooked up by the captain as you cruise (about 250 kn with lunch, several boats depart daily around 10:30-11:00, return around 15:45-19:30; so they can be sure to buy enough food, companies prefer you to reserve and pay a 50-kn deposit the day before). For a bigger and more memorable ship—and a more corporate experience—you can pay a bit more to go on the *Karaka* or the *Sirena*, modern replicas of the traditional cargo ships once built here in Dubrovnik (advertised along with the others at the Old Port).

Regardless of which company you go with, you generally spend about two to three hours on Lopud and about an hour each on Koločep and Šipan, with about 2.5 hours on the boat. To get to the Elaphite Islands without a tour (on a cheap ferry), you'll sail from Dubrovnik's less convenient Port Gruž.

Koločep

The nearest island to Dubrovnik, and the sleepiest, Koločep's harbor arcs away from its boat dock. Walking around it, you'll quickly reach a small main square with al fresco cafés spilling out onto the seawall; beyond that is a sandy beach in front of a hotel, with rentable chairs. Near the boat dock, well-signed steps lead up into the hills, passing several small churches and Koločep's little museum of ecclesiastical art (the only museum I saw on the Elafiti).

On a short visit, you'll barely have time to stroll the harbor; if your excursion leaves you here a bit longer, consider a low-impact **hike** over the spine of the island to the village of Gornje Čelo, on the opposite side (about 1.5 miles away). You'll climb up stairs past an old guard tower, pass a pink stucco church near a cemetery, then follow the narrow path between high stone walls and past olive groves. You'll wind down to a little port town with an inviting beach; looping around to Placet takes you to a wall of dramatic cliffs. *Donje Čelo* signs lead you back to your boat.

▲Lopud

The main attraction of the Elaphite Islands, Lopud feels like a humbler Cavtat without all the great art. But Lopud's trump card is its fine beaches, especially Šunj—one of the nicest beaches in southern Dalmatia (a long hike or short golf-cart ride from the main boat dock). Lopud feels bigger, more vital, and more inviting than the other two islands. Most excursions give it far more time than Koločep or Šipan; it's also accessible by public ferry, and may be worth considering for an all-day beach getaway.

Your boat docks near the stout Franciscan monastery, which pokes out into the sea, dominating the townscape. From there, a picturesque promenade winds past several beaches (sand, then pebbles, then sand) and the entrance to a lush garden, before stretching all the way to a luxury hotel. Near the boat dock, you'll find a **TI** (Obala Iva Kuljevana 12, tel. 020/759-086).

For beach bums, the main attraction on Lopud is at the other end of the island: **Šunj Beach.** This gorgeous, shallow, sandy beach—hemmed in on both sides by forested cliffs—splays serenely between beach bars and ritzy yachts that drop anchor to take a dip. The almost entirely sandy floor and gentle incline makes this beach ideal for waders and families. The

catch is that it takes a bit of effort to reach: It's a moderately strenuous 1.5-mile walk over the scraggly spine of the island. Otherwise, golf carts zip arriving tourists over to the beach for a small fee. To find the golf carts, follow the promenade as far as the abandoned Grand Hotel, then head inland (on a drab, poorly maintained concrete trail), following signs for *Šunj Beach*. From here, you can either flag down a golf cart or continue to hike the rest of the way. Given its distance from the main boat dock, it's not worth attempting to visit Šunj if you're on Lopud for less than two hours.

Šipan

By far the biggest island (at just over six square miles), and the northernmost, Šipan has two different port towns. Your ship will

most likely use the one facing Lopud, called Suđurad (named for the local patron saint, George). Suđurad's harbor is watched over by the fortified, castle-like 16th-century villa of a local aristocrat. A beach beckons just across the bay from the boat dock. Next to the harbor, the small Church of St. George—with a large covered porch—has a vivid fresco over the altar of George slaying the dragon while being watched over by two other locally revered saints, Blaise (Dubrovnik's protector) and Nicholas (the patron saint of sailors).

If you need an excuse for a short hike, head from the harbor straight up the street away from the water, following signs for the Church of Sv. Duh (Holy Spirit). After passing through a humble residential zone, you'll arrive at a stout, fortress-like church, with raw-stone walls. If it's open, poke inside to see the rough-and-tumble interior. The stairs to the right of the altar lead up to the rooftop, where you can see the large, fertile valley that sits in the middle of this island. If you're tempted to ring the bell, resist—locals ring it only when a member of the local community dies.

South of Dubrovnik

A variety of worthwhile stopovers line up along the main road south of Dubrovnik, toward the border with Montenegro, in the region called Konavle.

Cavtat

This sleepy resort town—filling a wooded peninsula just 12 miles to the south, and rated ▲—offers a milder alternative to bustling Dubrovnik. With its strategic location sheltered inside a nearly 360-degree bay, this settlement was thriving long before there was a Dubrovnik. The Greeks called it Epidaurus, while the Romans called it Epidaurum—but these days, it's Cavtat (TSAV-taht). The town is best known as a handy spot to find a room when Dubrovnik's booked up. But even those suffering from beach-resort fatigue will enjoy a side-trip to Cavtat, which is home to two gems of Croatian art: a breathtaking hilltop mausoleum by the great Croatian sculptor Ivan Meštrović, and the former home-turned-museum of the Cavtat-born, early-20th-century painter Vlaho Bukovac.

GETTING TO CAVTAT

Boats to Cavtat leave about hourly from Dubrovnik's Old Port (100 kn round-trip, about 45 minutes each way, hourly return boats from Cavtat). The boat deposits you right along Cavtat's main seafront promenade.

You can also reach Cavtat by public **bus** #10, which leaves from Dubrovnik's main bus station and also stops at the "cable car" bus stop above the Old Town (1-2/hour, 30-40 minutes, 25 kn). The bus brings you to Cavtat's parking lot (described next). Returning by bus from Cavtat, hop off at the Dubrovnik bus stop that's along the main road high above the Old Town—about a 5- to 10-minute walk down into town. (Note that the bus to or from Cavtat does *not* stop at Dubrovnik's Pile Gate.)

For variety, consider going to Cavtat by boat (buy a one-way ticket), then returning by bus.

Drivers find Cavtat an easy detour when heading to points south, including Montenegro or the airport; the town is well-signed off the main road. The big parking lot is at the back of Cavtat's peninsula, just around the corner from the main part of town and seafront promenade.

Orientation to Cavtat

Cavtat is set within an idyllic, horseshoe-shaped harbor hemmed in by a pair of peninsulas. Tucked around the back side of the peninsula is the parking lot and **TI** (Zidine 6, tel. 020/479-025, www.tzcavtat-konavle.hr). Cavtat is basically a one-street town, but that street is a fine pedestrian promenade running along the harbor, with a few narrow lanes winding steeply up into the hill. Capping the hill above town is a cemetery with the Meštrović mausoleum.

Sights in Cavtat

Waterfront Wander

Strolling along Cavtat's waterfront, you'll be immersed in a wrap-around bay and surrounded by Europeans vacationing well. At

the near end of the promenade, notice the big water polo court roped off in the bay; Cavtat and Dubrovnik are the birthing ground for many of the core players of the Croatian national water-polo team. Across the street is **St. Nicholas Church,** with a humble, dull interior (though hanging high in the altar area are Vlaho Bukovac's paintings of the four evangelists). About halfway along the drag, at the little square called Trg Tuđmana, one of the narrow lanes leading up the hill (appropriately named Bukovčeva) takes you to the fine **Vlaho Bukovac House** (described below). At the end of the main waterfront area is the **Church of Our Lady of the Snows,** commemorating a freak—and seemingly miraculous—midsummer snowstorm in ancient Roman times, believed to have been a sign sent by the Virgin Mary. Inside, above the altar, is a Vlaho Bukovac painting (from 1909) of Mary and the Baby Jesus watching over Cavtat.

Climbing the steep steps up to the right of the church leads you up to Ivan Meštrović's **Račić Mausoleum** (described later). With more time, consider continuing around the peninsula to its pointy tip for distant views of Dubrovnik's Old Town. This is one of the favorite spots in this area for watching the sunset. (If you continue all the way around the point, in about 20 minutes you'll wind up back at the parking lot at the start of town.)

▲Vlaho Bukovac House (Kuća Bukovac)

One of the joys of travel is learning about locally beloved artists who are little known outside their homelands. Cavtat proudly introduces you to native son Vlaho Bukovac (1855-1922), who grew up in this very house and went on to become the most important Croatian painter of the modern period. Bukovac moved to New York City with his uncle at age 11, beginning a life of great adventure. After a brief career as a sailor (traveling to Peru and San Francisco), he trained as an artist in Paris, then in Zagreb. For his last 20 years, Bukovac spent his summers in Prague and his winters here in Cavtat.

Cost and Hours: 30 kn; Tue-Sat 9:00-18:00, Sun until 14:00, closed Mon; Bukovčeva 5, tel. 020/478-646, www.kuca-bukovac.hr.

Visiting the Museum: Touring the collection (with good English explanations), you'll get to know Bukovac's life and his works. Bukovac's paintings are mostly realistic (in accordance with his formal Salon training in Paris), but shimmer with a hint of Post-Impressionism; his later works echo the slinky Art Nouveau Slavic pride of the Czech painter Alfons Mucha, who was Bukovac's contemporary.

From the ground floor (with temporary exhibits), head up to find old furniture, early sketches, and portraits of Bukovac and

his family. The top floor houses one big atelier room filled with canvases from various periods, allowing you to survey his impressive artistic development with a sweep of the head. Look for the painting of his children's disembodied heads hanging on the wall—macabre but strangely tender. Throughout the house are murals painted by Bukovac in his early days, offering a glimpse of a burgeoning artist who would go on to make Cavtat very proud.

▲▲Račić Family Mausoleum (Mauzolej Obitelji Račić)

This harmonious masterwork of Croatia's greatest artist is the gem of Cavtat, and worth ▲▲▲ to fans of Ivan Meštrović's powerful sculptures.

Cost and Hours: 20 kn, Mon-Sat 10:00-17:00, closed Sun and Nov-March.

Getting There: Capping the hill above town, it's a steep 10-minute walk from the Cavtat waterfront. From the Church of Our Lady of Snows at the far end of the waterfront, climb up the stairs (following *mauzolej* signs). You can also wrap all the way around the fine waterfront promenade, to the back of the peninsula, and climb the stairs up near the restaurant and rocky beach.

Visiting the Mausoleum: Over the course of one tragic year, all four members of the wealthy Račić family—father, mother, son, daughter—died in the 1918-19 Flu Pandemic. From 1920 to 1922, in accordance with their will, Ivan Meštrović was commissioned to craft their final resting place. He used the opportunity to create a cohesive meditation on Christian faith and death, made entirely of brilliant white stone from the island of Brač.

As you enter, take a moment to appreciate how the interior ponders birth, life, and death. The four inner walls of the octagonal hall hold the tombs of the departed; above each tomb, an angel lovingly carries their souls up to heaven—spiriting them into a cupola studded with angel heads. The floor has symbols for the four evangelists: Matthew (angel), Mark (lion), Luke (bull), and John (eagle). The chapel to the left holds a crucifix; to the right, an altar to St. Rok (the patron saint of illness, to whom the chapel is dedicated—the dog licking the wound in his leg is his symbol). Straight ahead is an altar with Mary holding the Baby Jesus above a relief of the Lamb of God, and below that, Jesus' body being taken down from the cross. Flanking this altar, notice the bases of the twisting candelabras: alternating angels, with agonized and mournful expressions, look down to honor the dead.

The chapel rewards those who linger over the details, such as the bronze doors, with four saints, Glagolitic inscriptions, and the 12 Apostles. The saints chosen for this door preach both ecumenism and Yugoslav unity: Cyril and Methodius (the Byzantine missionaries who first brought Christianity to this region), along with a Catholic bishop (Bishop Gregory of Nin) and an Orthodox saint (St. Sava). Taken together, the mausoleum is an astonishing display of talent, especially considering it was Meštrović's first architectural work.

Nearby: The mausoleum sits in the middle of a tranquil cemetery that's still used for the funerals of Cavtat residents. As you exit the mausoleum, bear left into the cemetery and look for five communal graves for the poor—with smaller markers and flower pots lined up along large plinths. Also in this cemetery is the grave of the artist Vlaho Bukovac.

IN THE COUNTRYSIDE NEAR CAVTAT
Čilipi

This nearby village—five miles from Cavtat and the namesake for Dubrovnik's airport—hosts a Sunday-morning folk festival through the summer (Easter-Oct, starting at 9:00). There's a special Mass at the church, an open-air market, and—starting at

11:15—a costumed folk-dancing show (tel. 020/771-007, www. cilipifolklor.hr).

Konavoski Dvori

The rugged terrain stretching south of Dubrovnik, toward the Montenegrin border, huddles under steep limestone peaks—a sure recipe for lots of rushing water. This area's name—Konavle—comes from the ancient Roman word for "channels." And since antiquity, these foothills have been a popular place for settlement and for primitive industry, with canals, aqueducts, and spinning millwheels designed to harness the constant flow of high-mountain runoff. Today, a short detour from the main highway takes you to Konavoski Dvori ("the Palaces of Konavle"), where you can stroll through a well-preserved network of medieval canals and even step into a reconstructed 400-year-old mill (open sporadically).

As the road passes through Gruda (about 18 miles, or 30 minutes, south of Dubrovnik), turn off and head up into the village of Ljuta (whose name means "Angry," for the fierce flow of the river by the same name). The steep, wooded terrain is laced with nature trails that follow gurgling canals—handy for a pre- or post-meal wander. The main reason most people come here is for a meal at one of two destination restaurants: the traditional, unpretentious **$$$ Konoba Vinica Monković** (mobile 099-215-2459, www. konobavinica.com) and the fancier, more elaborate complex of **$$$$ Restaurant Konavoski Dvori** (huge terraces, trout ponds, tel. 020/791-039, www.esculaprestaurants.com). At either place (both open long hours daily in good weather, closed off-season), it's smart to reserve in advance for an outdoor table, along the gurgling canals. Most locals come here for a *peka* meal—meat slow-simmered under a copper baking lid covered in glowing coals—which should also be requested when you book your table. While not worth the trip alone, this experience works well with a visit to Cavtat or Montenegro, and offers an opportunity to escape the crowds and heat of Dubrovnik's Old Town and spend some time in the cool and refreshing countryside.

North of Dubrovnik

These attractions are on or near the northbound highway from Dubrovnik, on the way to Split or Mostar. (For more ideas along the back roads toward Mostar, see page 183.)

NEAR DUBROVNIK

Trsteno Arboretum

Take a stroll through the shaded, relaxing botanical garden in Trsteno (worth ▲), just up the coast from Dubrovnik. Nongardeners may find it a bit dull, but Trsteno is a horticulturalist's heaven.

Cost and Hours: 40 kn, daily 7:00-19:00, Nov-April 8:00-16:00, tel. 020/751-019.

Getting There: Trsteno is best reached by car, particularly if you're taking your time driving to Dubrovnik from the north (the main coastal road goes through the town of Trsteno, right past the well-marked arboretum). You also have two bus options from Dubrovnik (20-30 minutes). Any long-distance northbound bus can drop you in Trsteno—ask about the next bus at the main station. Alternatively, the slower local buses #12 and #15 also reach Trsteno. Coming back from Trsteno to Dubrovnik is trickier: Wait at the bus stop with the glass canopy by the park entrance and wave down any Dubrovnik-bound bus that passes (at least hourly).

Visiting the Arboretum: Spread over 63 acres on a bluff overlooking the sea, this arboretum features hundreds of different Mediterranean, Asian, and American plants (each one labeled in six languages, including English). The whole complex is laced with easy footpaths and sprinkled with fun attractions—a column-studded Renaissance Garden, a desolate villa, a little chapel, an old mill and olive-oil press, and a seaview pavilion. *Game of Thrones* fans will recognize it as the backdrop of many park-set scenes at King's Landing.

As you wander, the world melts away and you're alone with the sounds of nature: wind, water, birds, and frogs. The garden's centerpiece is the whimsical 18th-century Neptune Fountain,

featuring the god of the sea flanked by water-spouting nymphs and fishes as he holds court over a goldfish-stocked, lily-padded pond. Circling around behind the fountain, you'll discover that it's fed by an impressive 230-foot-long aqueduct that was built in the 15th century.

Nearby: On the waterfront below the arboretum, next to the little village harbor, you'll see the shell of a once-grand 18th-century **palace,** which was damaged during the siege of Dubrovnik and is now abandoned. It's still owned by the government, but investors are lining up for a chance to buy this prime real estate—possibly the most desirable ruin in Croatia.

Pelješac Peninsula

North of Trsteno, the skinny, 55-mile-long Pelješac (PEHL-yeh-shahts) Peninsula—practically an honorary island, and rated ▲—splits off from the Croatian coastline as if about to drift away to Italy. (The far tip of Pelješac comes within a stone's throw of Korčula Island.) This sparsely populated peninsula, famous for its rugged terrain—and the grapes that thrive here—is worth a detour for wine lovers. But its heavily fortified town of Ston, just a short side-trip from the main coastal road, merits a stretch-your-legs visit for anyone. Notice that if you're connecting from Korčula to anywhere else in Croatia by car, you'll probably be taking the ferry to the Pelješac Peninsula anyway; consider slowing down to sample a few wines, to scramble up the walls at Ston, or to have a meal at Mali Ston.

Getting There: Buses between Dubrovnik and Korčula traverse the Pelješac Peninsula, but drivers have the option of stopping where they like (such as at Ston or a winery). Some public buses also stop at Ston.

STON

The town of Ston, at the base of the peninsula, is the gateway to Pelješac. This "Great Wall of Croatia" town is famous for the im-

pressive wall that climbs up the mountain behind it (about a half-mile encloses the town itself, while another three miles clamber up the hillsides). The unassuming town was heavily fortified (starting in 1333) for two reasons: to defend its strategic location, where mountains and bays create a bottleneck along the road from Dubrovnik to Pelješac, near the Republic of Dubrovnik's northern boundary; and to protect its impressive salt pans, which still produce the mineral. Filling a low-lying plain that sprawls in front of Ston's doorstep, these pans provided Dubrovnik with much of its wealth, back in the days when salt was worth more than its weight in gold. The pans would be flooded with saltwater, then sealed and left to evaporate—leaving the salt easy to harvest.

Today, the sleepy town—with more than its share of outdoor cafés and restaurants—is notable only for the chance to scramble

A Bridge Too Far?

As you drive along the coast between Split and Dubrovnik, you may be surprised to reach a border checkpoint for Bosnia-Herzegovina at the resort town of Neum. How is it that Bosnia wound up with its very own five-and-a-half-mile stretch of the Dalmatian Coast?

During the heyday of the Republic of Dubrovnik, the city's leaders granted this land to the Ottoman Empire to provide a buffer between Dubrovnik's holdings and the Republic of Venice, to the north. (They knew the Venetians would never dare to enter the territory of the Ottomans, their feared enemy.) Later, as the borders of Europe were being redrawn in modern times, Bosnia retained possession of this strip of land.

For years, coastal Bosnians and their Croatian neighbors have coexisted, albeit with a bit of friction. Prices for hotel rooms, groceries, and other staples are slightly cheaper in Neum, whose rest stops lure tourist buses with low prices and generous bus-driver kickbacks. Visitors are inconvenienced by having to go through a passport checkpoint as they enter Bosnia and again, just a few minutes later, as they exit Bosnia. On busy days, lines can back up at this border—have your passport and rental car's "green card" (proof of insurance) ready. Beyond the red tape, Croatians are irritated by Neum merchants underselling Croatian alternatives nearby.

As Croatia extends its expressway southward, the most logical approach would be a route through Bosnia to Dubrovnik. But some Croatian politicians have been looking for a way to avoid Neum altogether. One solution is to build a 1.5-mile-long bridge from just north of Neum to the Pelješac Peninsula, then rejoin the coastal road back in Croatia, just south of Neum—effectively bypassing Bosnian territory. It's a very expensive way to avoid a tiny strip of land, and environmentalists worry about the impact the bridge will have on the ecosystem around Mali Ston. Because of the proposed bridge's popularity with a certain segment of the voting population, talk about the bridge always escalates just before election season...then tapers off afterwards with nothing officially decided. Will the Bosnian bypass ever be built? Stay tuned.

up its massive **fortifications** (park your car in the big lot, then cross the street into town and look right; the entrance to the walls is in the big tower). These walls are undergoing an extensive restoration, and the long, skinny strip running over the ridge to the town of Mali Ston (described next) is already complete. For a short wall experience, you can just do a circle around the stout lower

walls (about 30 minutes); for a more serious hike, you can climb all the way up and over to Mali Ston (figure an hour or more). Be warned that the walls can be blazing hot—with all that glistening limestone reflecting heat—and there's virtually no shade (50 kn to enter walls regardless of how far you walk, daily June-Sept 8:00-19:00, shorter hours off-season).

Other than the walls, there's not much to do in Ston. The town's deserted feel is a result of a devastating 1996 earthquake, from which Ston is still rebuilding. But there are several inviting cafés for a lazy drink and various places to grab a sandwich or pizza slice. If you want a serious sit-down meal, skip Ston's mediocre offerings and head over to Mali Ston instead.

Eating near Ston, in Mali Ston: From Ston, the walls scamper over a ridge to its little sister, the bayside village of Mali Ston ("Small Ston"). Surrounded by a similar, but smaller, fortified wall, Mali Ston is known for its many mussel and oyster farms, and for its good restaurants. A local favorite is **$$$$ Kapetanova Kuća,** a memorable place with a fine location on Mali Ston's waterfront. Celebrity chef Lidija Kralj prides herself on her unpretentious but delicious food, made with fresh produce from the restaurant's own garden. For dessert, her bizarre *makaruli*—macaroni cake—is tastier than it sounds (daily 9:00-23:00, tel. 020/754-264).

Near the entrance to Kapetanova Kuća's parking lot, look for the simple **oyster shack/souvenir kiosk,** where local women sell fresh oysters and mussels from the adjacent bay and Pelješac wine decanted into plastic water bottles—all for cheap.

PELJEŠAC WINE COUNTRY

Farther along, the sparsely developed Pelješac Peninsula is blanketed with vineyards. Wine is the draw here, and a variety of vintners open their doors for passing visitors to sample their products. While it's a bit distant from Dubrovnik (about a two-hour drive to the heart of the wine-producing area), it's a worthwhile pilgrimage for wine lovers—or even just wine likers—and an easy stop-off for those driving from Korčula. Pelješac is an overlooked gem, and feels like a throwback to an age when wine tastings were relaxed, chatty, and fun, rather than corporate and rushed.

Tours of Pelješac: To really do the peninsula justice, consider hiring a guide to take you for a spin around Pelješac. **Sasha Lušić,** who runs the D'Vino Wine Bar in Dubrovnik, is a gregarious Aussie-Croat. He prides himself on taking you to a wide variety of vintners, who represent the best of what's happening here. Sasha's tours, which flex from day to day based on his customers' interests and stamina, can go late into the evening (other options include cheaper half-day tours to areas closer to Dubrovnik—prices depend on what's included—and traditional *peka* lunch or sunset seaside dinner; you might get one of his well-trained associates, www.dvino.net, sasha@dvino.net). Other Dubrovnik-based drivers also do good wine tours (which include several other worthwhile, scenic stops), including **Petar Vlašić** (see page 16).

❍ Self-Guided Driving Tour

I've arranged this tour in the order you'll come from the tip of Pelješac (Orebić, just across the channel from Korčula). Even if you're doing it from Dubrovnik, begin by driving all the way to the village of Potomje (you can skip the section between there and Orebić) and visit the wineries on your way back (since there's just one road, you'll have to backtrack regardless). I've included a detour to some of Croatia's finest (and largely undiscovered) vineyards.

If you're crossing from Korčula Island, you'll begin the tour in **Orebić**. It's basically one main road from here back to Ston (where you'll meet up with the main coastal road to Dubrovnik or Split), so you can't really get lost—though we will make an off-the-beaten-path vineyard detour.

Follow the main road (toward Dubrovnik and Split) up, up, up for about 15 minutes to a dramatic **viewpoint** (there's a pullout on the right with benches—watch for the giant wine bottle) looking back toward Korčula. The jagged cliffs to your left are the Pelješac Peninsula (where we're about to drive), and the island poking out to the left is Mljet National Park. Straight ahead is Korčula, and behind that, the island of Lastovo. On a clear day, you can almost see to Italy. Below you and to the right, you can see some vineyards in the **Postup** area; to the left (not quite visible from here) are the vineyards of **Dingač**. These are the two best wine-growing regions of Pelješac: Both areas are steeply angled, so they catch a maximum amount of sun, which creates very sweet grapes that produce high-alcohol, very dark (actually called "black" in Croatian) wine with strong legs (or, as Croatians call them, "tears"). The rugged, rocky limestone provides natural irrigation (since water can flow freely through it), and the high winds here keep off bugs and other pests. It all adds up to extremely healthy vines; because disease is rare, pesticides are not needed.

Continuing along the road, you'll crest the hill and pass the turnoff for Trpanj (where ferries connect to the mainland); soon after, watch on the left for the **Peninsula Wine Bar.** Owned by local vintners Boris and Baldo, and run by Toni, this place feels like a glorified truck stop. But it's ideal for one-stop shoppers who want to learn about and try wine from a variety of producers. They usually have about 60 wines available. You can sample wine by the taste (look for tasting flights listed on the chalkboard), by the glass

Sampling Pelješac Wines

Most Pelješac wines are made with *plavac mali* ("little blue") grapes, a distant relative of California zinfandel (they're called "son of zinfandel") and Italian *primitivo*. These wines are usually quite "big," with lots of tannins and high alcohol content (thank the warm climate for that).

Reds from the *plavac mali* grape are the real draw here, even though they account for just a third of the production (most are whites, with a few rosés). Winery staff enjoy explaining that this small area has three entirely different terroirs. The flat, easy-to-harvest Potomje valley produces cheaper, lower-quality wines; bottles are generally labeled simply with the type of grape (for example, *plavac mali*). Just over the mountains are the steep, sea-facing, sun-drenched Dingač and Postup areas (Dingač wines, a notch up in quality, tend to have more finesse than the coarser Postup wines). Bottles from these areas are usually labeled with the region rather than the grape.

Some vintners are starting to blend the *plavac mali* grape with other red grapes, like cabernet franc, merlot, and marselan, which creates a softer, less robust wine.

(most about 25 kn), or by the bottle (most around 50 kn). Tastings are free if you buy a few bottles. They also offer tastings of local olive oil and grappa (daily 9:00-23:00, closed Nov-March, tel. 020/742-503, www.peninsula.hr).

After the wine bar, you'll drop down into a **plateau** surrounded by cliffs. The vines you'll see in this so-called "continental" area are the same *plavac mali* grapes as in Postup and Dingač, but they receive less sun and are less sweet. Notice that many of the vines appear to be almost wild; these are older vineyards, which aren't irrigated, so they must let the vines grow this way to help them survive the hot summer months. This method maximizes yield but reduces quality. Newer vineyards are irrigated and use guide wires, and generally look more manicured.

Soon you'll arrive in the village of **Potomje,** which is at the center of this important wine-growing area and makes a perfect stop for wine tasting. Four wineries here welcome visitors and offer a helpful introduction to Pelješac wines; taken together, they deliver a good range in experience, from mom-and-pop to state-of-the-art: Matković, Madirazza, Matuško, and Violić.

Violić is an appealingly Back Door experience, and worth saving for last. All are staffed by friendly English speakers who are eager to introduce you to their wines; while the tastings are free, it's good form to buy a bottle or two. (If you want a more elaborate tasting with food pairings or for a small group, call ahead.) Unless otherwise noted, these places open around 8:00-20:00, but close earlier in shoulder season and are generally closed in winter (Nov-March—but call ahead and they may be able to open for you, cash only). Most wineries also have various brandies to try (including *travarica*, an herb-infused brandy).

Start your tasting at the beginning of town on the right, where you can pull into the small tasting room of **Vina Matković.** The gentle owner, Željka, can pour you a sample of their well-balanced and reasonably priced wines (reds only, don't miss her blend with marselan grapes, June-Oct daily 9:00-21:00, call ahead at other times, mobile 091-211-1230, www.vinamatkovic.com).

Next, near the far end of town, look for the big, pink building of the **Madirazza** winery. Notice the roses that line the vineyards—like a canary in a coal mine, these are more quickly affected by disease than the vines, offering an early-warning system in the event of an unwanted infestation. Madirazza's oaky, fairly acidic wines cost 50-100 kn per bottle, or more for reserve bottles (mobile 098-212-163, www.dingac.hr, Mina).

Across the main road from Madirazza's parking lot is a smaller road (marked with *Matuško* and *Tunel Dingač* signs) leading to the **Matuško** winery. This handsome winery sports a library-like tasting room and makes finer, less coarse wines than Madirazza's. The range of wines available to taste is exceptional (including a chardonnay and tasty rosé—although red is what they do best and most). If you ask nicely, you can visit the sprawling network of atmospheric cellars where tour groups sip wines between aging barrels (30-130-kn bottles, more for reserve bottles, good place for a WC stop, tel. 020/742-393, mobile 098-428-676 www.matusko-vina.hr).

Backtrack to the road that leads to the tunnel. As you face the entrance to the tunnel, turn left, following *Boris Violić* signs to the unassuming **Violić** family home and winery. Offering a good contrast to the polished and more mainstream-feeling wineries described above, chatty Boris Violić-Matuško and his charming wife Marine invite passing visitors to slow down and enjoy some home-style hospitality. In addition to sampling their wines (four reds and two whites made the "old-fashioned" way, 30-150-kn bottles), consider buying some brandy, olive oil, or their delicious grandma-made treats (Potomje 6, mobile 091-575-4422).

When you're ready to move on, look for the **tunnel** through the mountain marked *Tunel Dingač,* with the picture of a donkey. Before this tunnel was dug, beasts of burden trod surefootedly up and over this mountain to carry the grapes from Dingač, on the far side, to this village. The donkey remains a symbol of this wine-growing region. In the 1970s, this tunnel was built to make everyone's lives easier. Take advantage of it by driving through the mountain and into another world.

Popping out at the sea, you're in the heart of the **Dingač** vineyards. Turn left (toward *Borak*) and drive on the one-lane road

above all those vines, with a green and jagged waterline that looks almost Celtic. (Drive carefully: While it's a paved road, it's narrow, with a very steep shoulder.) Croatia's best reds are lovingly raised right here, soaking up ample sunshine as they struggle against a very rocky soil (ideal for wine grapes). Locals explain that these grapes are bathed in sunlight from every angle—not just the sun above, but the reflection of those rays from both the sea and the white soil. Dingač never freezes (unlike the valley), and rainfall runs off immediately through its porous limestone soil, making these plants very disease-resistant. By the time they are harvested, Dingač grapes are withered by the sun—halfway to raisins, packed with sugar, and ideal for producing top-quality and highly alcoholic wines. At the fork, continue down to the right, toward *Dingač/Borak;* at the next fork, when the Borak road turns sharply down and to the right, keep going straight onto the smaller road.

As you drive, keep enjoying dramatic views of Mljet Island. When you enter an area of trees, look across the harbor to see

a building perched on a cliff over the water—that's our next stop. Soon you'll come to the village of Trstenik; at the T-intersection, make a sharp right turn, then turn left to pass along its little waterfront. At the far end of town, on the way up the hill, turn into the parking lot for the **Grgić** winery. Perhaps the best-known and best-regarded Croatian vintner, Mike Grgić's facility is less appealing than the others we've visited, and you have to pay for the tasting (30 kn)...but the fame of the wine may be worth it for some. This place is surprisingly humble. Keeping things simple,

Grgić does a white wine (*pošip*, with grapes grown on Korčula but produced here) and a red wine; breaking with convention, he names his red simply *plavac mali* partly to help promote this largely unknown and underappreciated grape. He also sells wines from his California winery, Grgich Hills, at or below their California prices (daily 9:00-17:00, tel. 020/748-090, www.grgic-vina.com).

If you're ready for a meal, overlooking this same cove is **$$$ D'Oro Bar & Grill,** a casual harborfront eatery with high-quality Dalmatian cuisine and fine views (daily 8:00-24:00, closed Dec-March, Kraj 23 in Trstenik, mobile 098-327-404).

Exiting the Grgić winery, turn right (uphill) and twist up to the main road, where you'll turn right, toward Ston. Cresting the hill, you'll see the other side of the peninsula and the channel separating it from the mainland—as if to emphasize the narrowness of this spit of land. From here, you'll continue straight along all the way to Ston. You may be tempted by the *vino* signs in **Janjina,** but these are aimed mainly at Croatians buying table wine in bulk— 100 liters at a time.

Leaving Janjina, keep following signs for *Ston* and *Dubrovnik.* You'll twist down and follow the **Bay of Ston,** which is famous for its shellfish production. Here where the Neretva River (which runs under Mostar's Old Bridge) empties into the sea, conditions are perfect for cultivating mussels, oysters, and clams. (You'll spot many such farms out in the bay—look for the areas roped off with buoys.) The road climbs up once more, passing the aptly named Bella Vista viewpoint café (which overlooks the dock for the ferry to the national park on Mljet Island), before continuing into the walled town of **Ston.**

Leaving Ston, turn right (toward Dubrovnik) once you hit the main road; from here, it's about an hour back into town. En route, watch out for the speed traps at the towns of Doli and Orešac.

Mljet National Park

Carefully protected against modern development, the island hide-away of Mljet National Park (rated ▲) offers a unique back-to-nature escape. With ample opportunities for hiking, swimming, biking, and kayaking—and without a nightclub, tacky T-shirt, or concrete "beach" in sight—Mljet (muhl-YAYT) is appreciated by active, outdoorsy travelers looking to escape some of the crowds and find their own pristine corner of Dalmatia.

Though Mljet Island is one of Dalmatia's largest, it has fewer than 1,500 residents. Nearly three-quarters of the island is cov-

ered in forest, leaving it remarkably untamed. Aside from its beautiful national park, Mljet has inspired some of the most memorable tales of the Croatian coast—the poet Homer, his protagonist Ulysses, and the Apostle Paul all spent time here...or so the locals love to boast.

PLANNING YOUR TIME

While back-to-nature travelers invest an overnight here, it's perfectly doable to visit Mljet as a day trip—most logically from either Dubrovnik or Korčula. In summer, this can be done by public catamaran: on the Nona Ana from Dubrovnik to Polače, or on the Krilo from Korčula to Pomena. At other times—or from other home bases—you may find it easier to sign up for a package excursion. Excursion prices may not include the hefty park entry—if comparison-shopping, be clear on this before you choose.

No matter how you arrive, one day is plenty to get a nice taste of Mljet. The three best experiences are: the **boat trip to the Island of St. Mary;** the **bike ride around the Great Lake** (allow about 1 hour, plus photo and swimming stops); and **swimming at the Small Bridge,** or at your choice of secluded cove around either of the park's two lakes.

Hikers can also do the easy walk around the Small Lake or the more strenuous summit to the park's highest point, Montokuc.

If you enjoy **kayaking,** the Great Lake is a good place to do it. And if you have your own snorkeling gear (no rentals on the island), the coral reef near Soline (where the Great Lake meets the Adriatic) is a popular spot.

These activities can be done in any order. However, it can be smart to do the boat ride to the island first; that way, once back on the mainland, you'll know exactly how much time you have left to bike, swim, hike, or kayak before heading back to your boat.

Mljet en Route from Korčula to Dubrovnik: In summer, when the catamarans are running at full schedule, it's possible to squeeze the national park into this journey: Ride the morning Krilo from Korčula to Pomena, and find somewhere to stow your bag (see "Helpful Hints," later); spend the day enjoying the park; head back to Pomena to get your bag and ride the shuttle to Polače; take the Nona Ana to Dubrovnik in time for a late dinner. As the catamaran schedule is always in flux, carefully confirm this will work; the Korčula TI is helpful in sorting out the logistics. This can also be done in reverse: Take the morning Nona Ana catamaran

NEAR DUBROVNIK

from Dubrovnik to Polače, ride a taxi over to Pomena to drop your bag at the hotel, and take the Krilo to Korčula in the late afternoon.

Off-Season Visits: Be warned that everything here is very seasonal and weather-dependent, so visiting outside of peak season (June-Sept) will come with some frustration (and the park is officially closed Nov-Feb). However, locals say that off-season visitors particularly enjoy the island's many orchids, which bloom only outside of summer.

Orientation to Mljet

The island of Mljet is long (23 miles) and skinny (less than two miles wide). The national park occupies the western third of the island. You're likely to reach Mljet via one of three port towns: **Polače** (POH-lah-cheh) and **Pomena** (POH-meh-nah) are the main entry points into the national park, while **Sobra** (SOH-brah) is much less convenient (a 35-minute drive across the island from the park). The Nona Ana catamaran from Dubrovnik puts in at both Polače and Sobra; the Krilo catamaran and most excursions use Pomena; and car ferries to the mainland use Sobra. While drivers on Mljet find some enjoyable activities outside the park, day-trippers should simply ignore the rest of the island and focus on the national park.

Polače and Pomena flank the heart of the national park—a pair of adjoining "lakes" (actually large saltwater lagoons fed by canals from the Adriatic) called **Great Lake** (Veliko Jezero) and **Small Lake** (Malo Jezero). These two bodies of water meet at the aptly named **Small Bridge** (Mali Most), where you can rent kayaks and bikes. A 15-minute walk or five-minute pedal along the Great Lake from the Small Bridge brings you to **Pristanište** (meaning, roughly, "transit hub"), which is connected by shuttle bus to Polače. In the middle of the Great Lake sits the **Island of St. Mary,** which is served by national park shuttle boats (included in your ticket) from both the Small Bridge and Pristanište. Everything's well-signed, and it's hard to get lost if you use the free orientation map that comes with your ticket. But if you want to do some serious hiking, you can invest in a detailed park map (available at the entry kiosks).

Beyond Pomena and Polače, the national park has a few small settlements. **Babine Kuće** is on the lakeside path, between the Small Bridge and Pristanište; **Soline,** a lonely fishing village, sits along the channel where the Great Lake connects to the sea; and the cliff-climbing town of **Govedari** is home to many of the people who work at the park, but is not interesting to tourists.

Cost and Hours: To enter the park, you'll pay an entrance fee of 125 kn (June-Sept) or 70 kn in shoulder season. This includes access to the park's trails and beaches, plus the boat to the Island of St. Mary and the shuttle bus from Polače to Pristanište. The park is open daily June-mid-Sept 7:00-21:00, until 19:00 in shoulder season, and closed Nov-Feb.

TOURIST INFORMATION

The **national park ticket kiosks,** where you buy your ticket, can help you plan your day (tel. 020/744-041, www.np-mljet.hr). The only **official TI** is in Polače, across from where the Nona Ana catamaran docks (tel. 020/744-186). The island's lone hotel, the **Hotel Odisej** in Pomena, also acts as a tourist information point (tel. 020/362-111). The island's general-information website is www.mljet.hr.

ARRIVAL IN MLJET

At Polače (on the catamaran from Dubrovnik): Exit to the right, pass the TI, and walk a few minutes up (through some scant ruins of what, at one time, was the third largest Roman palace in Croatia) to the blue national park kiosk. Here you can buy your entry ticket and catch a minibus to the Pristanište transit hub at the Great Lake (coordinated with boat arrival). If the line for the shuttle bus is too long—not uncommon on busy mornings—ask them to point you to the old Roman trail that leads about 30 minutes through the woods to Pristanište, where you can hop on the hourly boat to the Island of St. Mary.

At Pomena (on the catamaran from Korčula, or an excursion): Exit the boat to the left (passing Hotel Odisej), hike uphill, and look for the national park kiosk on your left. Buy your ticket here, then continue up past some restaurants and grocery stores (last chance to stock up on water and snacks). Just after you leave town, a stepped path on your right leads through the woods to the Small Lake, about a 10-minute walk. When you reach the lake, turn left and follow the shore another five minutes to the Small Bridge. Use the Small Bridge as a home base for the rest of your day.

Note that there's no official bus between Polače and Pomena, but Hotel Odisej operates a handy and comfortable shuttle to coincide with the Dubrovnik catamaran (45 kn one-way; not covered by park ticket). The island also has some minibus-taxis (tel. 098-505-654). A low-capacity "tourist train" (just a big golf cart) occasionally loops around the Great Lake, but it's too small to be practical.

At Sobra: If you come on a car ferry into Sobra, it's about a 35-minute drive on twisty roads to reach the Polače/Pomena tourist hub. If you're not bringing a car to Mljet, don't get off the boat in Sobra—there are no convenient bus connections to the national park, and a taxi will run you around 350 kn. In a pinch, there's typically an afternoon speedboat connecting Polače and Sobra.

Returning to Your Boat: At the end of the day, Dubrovnik-bound boats depart from Polače. If you're in the Small Bridge area, you have two choices: The easiest is to walk to Pomena and pay for the shuttle to Polače (just a few minutes in an air-conditioned van, book at Hotel Odisej); or you can walk or ride the boat to Pristanište, then hop on the shuttle bus to Polače from there. If you're hiking up to Montokuc, you can hike from the summit all the way down to Polače.

HELPFUL HINTS

Bike Rental: At both Polače and Pomena, you'll see companies advertising bike rentals, but these places are separated from the Great Lake's beautiful bike path by hilly terrain. Unless you like hills, wait to rent your bike until you reach the Small Bridge.

Kayak Rental: You can rent basic kayaks next to the Small Bridge. Enjoy the calm waters: Motorized boats (beyond the official park boats, and the occasional local's dingy) are not allowed on the lakes.

Bag Storage: Pomena has no official baggage storage, but the Hotel Odisej or the national park ticket kiosk are generally willing to watch your bag for the day...if you ask sweetly.

Eating in the Park: You'll find several small eateries in both **Pomena** and **Polače.** Once at the lakes, you may spot a very basic ice-cream truck at the **Small Bridge** (but nothing else there). The lakefront towns of **Babine Kuće** and **Soline** both have some nice eateries with great views. And the **Island of St. Mary** has the **$$** Restaurant Melita (with a menu of typical Dalmatian dishes) and an adjacent, simpler **$** pizzeria (with basic pizzas and sandwiches).

Services: Because the island has limited access to fresh water, there are no showers for swimmers here...be prepared for a salty ride back to Dubrovnik. The Small Bridge has some pit toilets with no running water, and no formal changing areas for swimmers (wear your swimsuit under your clothes, brave the tight and smelly WCs, or discreetly change under a towel...European-style). The restaurant on the Island of St. Mary has a pay WC (with actual running water). In Pomena, you can discreetly use the bathroom in the lobby of Hotel Odisej.

What to Bring: With so many tempting **swimming** spots in the park, you'll certainly want to bring a swimsuit and towel. If you have **snorkel gear,** this is a good place to use it (you can't rent it on the island). There are a few lunch options on-island (see earlier), but packing a **picnic** gives you more flexibility. With limited refreshment available once inside the park, bring plenty of **water.**

Overnighting on Mljet: This chapter is designed for day-trippers, but if you'd like to spend the night, consider the island's lone hotel. **$$$ Hotel Odisej,** with 157 rooms, sits right on Pomena's waterfront. It's a predictably comfortable home base, with a helpful staff (closed late Oct-late April, tel. 020/362-111, www.adriaticluxuryhotels.com). The park also has a variety of rustic **$** *sobe* **and apartments** in its various villages; some are listed at www.mljet.hr.

Sights at Mljet National Park

▲▲The Lakes

The "Great Lake" and "Small Lake," with shimmering turquoise waters, are saltwater bays—fed by the sea and affected by ocean currents. Scientists love these lakes, which contain various shellfish species unique to Mljet. One of them—the biggest shellfish in the Mediterranean, which grows up to three feet long—is the noble pan shell, which naturally filters the water here, keeping it crystal-clear.

The Tales of Mljet

For a mostly undeveloped island, Mljet has had a surprisingly busy history. Home to Illyrians, Greeks, Romans, Slavs, Venetians, Habsburgs, Yugoslavs, and now Croatians, the island has hosted some interesting visitors (or supposed visitors) that it loves to brag about.

Around the eighth century B.C., the Greek epic poet Homer possibly spent time here. He was so inspired by Mljet that he used it as the setting for one of the adventures of his hero Ulysses (a.k.a. Odysseus). This is the island where Ulysses fell in love with a beautiful nymph named Calypso and shacked up with her in a cave for seven years. Today there's a much-vaunted "Ulysses' Cave" (Odisejeva Spilja), a 40-minute hike below the island's main town, Babino Polje (at the far end of the island—skip it unless you're a Ulysses groupie).

Flash forward nearly a millennium, when a real-life traveler found his way to Mljet. According to the Bible (Acts 28), the Apostle Paul was shipwrecked on an island called "Melita"— likely this one—for three months. While on the island, Paul was bitten by a deadly snake, which he threw into a fire. The natives were amazed that he wasn't affected by the poison, and he proceeded to cure their ailments. This event was long believed to have happened on the similarly named isle of Malta, in the Mediterranean Sea. But more recently, many historians began to believe that Paul was on Mljet. The most convincing argument: Malta never had poisonous snakes. Incidentally, Mljet no longer does, either—the Habsburgs imported an army of Indian mongooses to rid the island of problematic serpents. Because of this historical footnote, people from Mljet are nicknamed "mongooses" by other Croatians.

The heroics continue with today's "mongooses." There have been more than 100 fires on the island in the last 20 years (most caused by lightning, some by careless visitors), but only three have spread and caused significant destruction. That's because the people of Mljet—well aware of the fragility of the island that provides their income—are also a crack volunteer firefighting force, ready to spring into action and save their home at the first wisp of smoke.

Swimmers love the lakes, too. There are two channels where it's fun to see (and swim in) the tidal currents: at the Small Bridge, and at the footbridge (near Soline) where the Great Lake connects to the Adriatic. The most popular and most satisfying place to take a dip is at the little beach near the Small Bridge, with warm water, a

mostly level and only slightly rocky bottom, and—best of all—a narrow channel where you can ride the current between the two lakes. Crossing between them, you'll notice that the Small Lake is always a few degrees warmer than the Great Lake or the sea. Circling either lake, you'll see plenty of other opportunities to lower yourself into the alluring blue.

▲The Island of St. Mary (Sv. Marija)

From the Small Bridge or Pristanište, you can hop on a boat for the 15-minute crossing to the Great Lake's Island of St. Mary (included in park ticket, boats depart about hourly—schedule posted at park entrances and at boat docks). While this island-within-an-island isn't too exciting, it's a fun excuse for a boat ride and an easy hike.

Benedictine monks lived on Mljet starting in the 12th century and founded a monastery on this island. Though the monastery

complex has been modified over the ages, fragments of the original Romanesque structure still survive.

From the boat, turn left and find the stairs up to the tall, austere, limestone church interior, with its gracefully rounded arches, and peek into the adjoining cloister. From there, an easy stepped trail leads up to the top of the island, passing remains of old fortifications, some Roman ruins, and a rugged stone stable with the island's only permanent residents: a handful of donkeys. From the summit, you can hike steeply down the other side—passing more tiny chapels and a miniature cemetery—to reach the inviting promenade at the back of the island, popular with swimmers. The promenade leads back around to the boat dock.

You'll have about an hour to explore between boats, but it only takes half that to see everything. You can relax with an overpriced drink (or meal) at the restaurant by the boat dock or the nearby pizzeria.

▲Biking Around the Great Lake

The Great Lake is surrounded by a mostly paved, mostly level, five-mile path that's enjoyable for a bike ride. You can do the entire loop in about an hour, not counting photo, swimming, or eating stops. The entire lakeshore is nicely manicured, with strategically placed information boards, benches, and places to get in the water. It's all well-signed and the ride is easy—just stay on the main path, which is almost always within sight of the lake.

Rent a bike at the Small Bridge, then head clockwise around

the Great Lake (with the water on your right). You'll curl along the lakeshore, through the charming waterfront village of Babine Kuće (with some appealing restaurants), then climb a little hill and continue around. At about the halfway point, you come to a little footbridge that crosses the channel where the Great Lake meets the sea; you'll need to carry your bike across the bridge to continue the loop (to avoid this, go back around the lake the way you came). Before crossing the footbridge, you can detour (about a half-mile) to the humble fishing village of Soline (with more restaurants); if you continue even farther, you'll come to the popular snorkeling area of the largest coral reef in the Mediterranean Sea. (It's a brown, not-too-striking "pillow coral," making it less exciting than it sounds.)

If you make your way across the footbridge, the rough path curls around a gorgeous bay, overlooking the Island of St. Mary. Continuing on, the path gets better as it takes you back around to the Small Bridge.

Note: The unpaved path around the Small Lake is rough and rocky, making biking there more difficult, but it's a pleasant walk (1.25 miles, about 30 minutes).

Hiking to Montokuc

The most rewarding hike takes you up to the national park's highest point, Montokuc. At 830 feet above sea level, this is a serious hike—skip it unless you're in good shape, and be sure to bring water. There are several trails up, including two along the lakeshore of the Great Lake, one in the village of Soline, and one in Polače. If you're doing this or any other hike, the park map is essential (sold at park entry kiosks and other merchants).

Mljet Connections

By Catamaran: Two convenient passenger catamarans connect Mljet to other major destinations. Schedules can vary from year to year, and both of these boats can sell out in peak season; check the schedules and prebook tickets at one of the websites below.

The **Krilo catamaran,** which uses the dock at Pomena, offers more departures (daily late May-early Oct, 3-4/week spring and fall, none Nov-late April) and more destinations. From Pomena, it heads south (morning only) to Dubrovnik (1.5 hours) and north (afternoon only) to Korčula (1 hour), Hvar (2 hours), and Split (3 hours; www.krilo.hr).

The **Nona Ana catamaran** heads from Polače to Dubrovnik each afternoon in summer (June-Sept, 1.5 hours, www.gv-line.hr). On some days in the peak months of July and August, the Nona Ana also heads north in the morning to Korčula (4/week, 1 hour).

In winter (Oct-May), the boat runs only from Sobra to Dubrovnik, making it pointless for day-trippers to the national park.

By Car Ferry: For drivers, a car ferry connects the town of Prapratno (near the base of the Pelješac Peninsula, not far from Ston) to Sobra on Mljet (for schedules, see www.jadrolinija.hr). Once at Sobra, it's a 35-minute drive to the park.

By Excursion: Many destinations are more conveniently connected to Mljet by excursion than by public transit. While you don't need a guide to enjoy the island, the simple convenience of round-trip transportation makes this worth considering—particularly if the catamarans are booked up.

MONTENEGRO
Crna Gora

MONTENEGRO

The Bay of Kotor • Kotor • The Montenegrin Interior • The Budva Riviera

If Dubrovnik is the grand finale of a Croatian vacation, then Montenegro is the encore. One of Europe's youngest nations awaits you just south of the border, with dramatic scenery, friendly locals proud of their unique land, and a rough-around-the-edges appeal.

Crossing the border (with passport ready—Montenegro is not part of the EU), you know you've left sleek and tidy Croatia for a place that's gritty, raw, and a bit exotic. While Croatia's showpiece Dalmatian Coast avoided the drab, boxy dullness of the Yugoslav era, less affluent Montenegro wasn't so lucky. Between the dramatic cliffs and time-passed villages, you'll drive past grimy, broken-down apartment blocks and some truly unfortunate concrete architecture. Montenegro is also a noticeably poorer country than its northern neighbor.

Historically, Montenegro has been even more of a crossroads of cultures than Croatia. In some ways, there are two Montenegros: the remote, rugged, rustic mountaintop kingdom that feels culturally close to Serbia; and this chapter's focus, the sun-drenched coastline of staggeringly strategic importance that has attracted a steady stream of rulers over the millennia. At one point or another, just about every group you can imagine has planted its flag here—from the usual suspects (Venetians, Austrians, Russian czars) to oddball one-offs (Bulgarian kingdoms, Napoleon's Ljubljana-based Illyrian Provinces). In spite of their schizophrenic lineage, or maybe because of it, Montenegrins have forged a unique cultural identity that defies many of the preconceived notions of the Balkans. Are they like Serbs or Croats? Do they use the Cyrillic or the Roman alphabet? Do they worship the Roman Catholic God or the Eastern Orthodox one? Yes, all of the above.

Since Montenegro gained independence in 2006, its coast has become a powerful magnet for a very specific breed of traveler: multimillionaires from Russia and the Middle East, who have chosen to turn this impressionable, fledgling country—with its gorgeous coastline—into their very own Riviera. The Tivat airport is jammed with charter flights from Moscow, signs along the coast advertise Russian-language radio stations, and an extravagant luxury yacht marina caters to the rich near Tivat (Porto Montenegro, www.portomontenegro.com). And so Montenegro finds itself in an awkward position: trying to cultivate an image as a high-roller luxury paradise, while struggling to upgrade what is—in places— a nearly Third World infrastructure. Glittering new €500-a-night boutique hotels are built, then suffer power and water outages. Lower your expectations, and don't expect a fancy facade and high prices to come with predictable quality.

Still, nothing can mar the natural beauty of Montenegro's mountains, bays, and forests. For a look at the untamed Adriatic,

a spin on the winding road around Montenegro's steep and secluded Bay of Kotor is a must. The area's main town, also called Kotor, has been protected from centuries of would-be invaders by its position at the deepest point of the fjord—and by its imposing town wall, which scrambles in a zigzag line up the mountain behind it. Wander the enjoyably seedy streets of Kotor, drop into some Orthodox churches, and sip a coffee at an al fresco café.

With more time, romantics can corkscrew up into the mountains to sample the Balkans' best smoked ham at Njeguši and visit the remote, original capital of the country at Cetinje, beach bums can head for the Budva Riviera, and celebrity-seekers can daydream about past glories at the striking hotel-peninsula of Sveti Stefan.

GETTING TO MONTENEGRO

This chapter is designed for day-tripping to Montenegro from Dubrovnik; all of the sights are within about a three-hour drive of Dubrovnik, and within about an hour of each other. If you're arriving in Montenegro by cruise (as many visitors do these days), see the "Cruising into Kotor" sidebar, later.

By Car: Driving is the best option, giving you maximum flexibility for sightseeing—but be aware of possible border delays (see "Helpful Hints," later). I've narrated a self-guided driving tour of the Bay of Kotor, and another for the most accessible slice of the

MONTENEGRO

Montenegro Almanac

Official Name: After being part of "Yugoslavia," then "Serbia and Montenegro," it's now the Republic of Montenegro (Republika Crna Gora)—which means "Black Mountain." It might have gotten its name from sailors who saw darkly forested cliffs as they approached, or it may have been named for a mythical mountain in the country's interior.

Snapshot History: Long overshadowed by its Croatian and Serbian neighbors, Montenegro finally achieved independence on June 3, 2006, in a landmark vote to secede from Serbia—its influential and sometimes overbearing "big brother."

Population: Montenegro is home to about 650,000 people. Of these, the vast majority are Eastern Orthodox Christians (45 percent Montenegrins, 29 percent Serbs), with minority groups of Muslims (including Bosniaks and Albanians, about 11 percent total) and Catholics (1 percent).

Area: 5,415 square miles (slightly smaller than Connecticut).

Red Tape: Americans and Canadians need only a passport (no visa required) to enter Montenegro.

Geography: Montenegro is characterized by a rugged, rocky terrain that rises straight up from the Adriatic and almost immediately becomes a steep mountain range. The country has 182 miles of coastline, about a third of which constitutes the Bay of Kotor. The only real city is the dreary capital in the interior, Podgorica (190,000 people). Each of Yugoslavia's six republics had a town called Titograd, and Podgorica was Montenegro's.

Economy: Upon declaring independence in 2006, Montenegro's

Montenegrin interior. Even if you don't have a rental car during your Dubrovnik visit, consider renting one just for the day to visit Montenegro. Perhaps most satisfying—but more pricey—is to hire your own Dubrovnik-based driver to bring you here (my favorites are recommended on page 16). While this is expensive (around €250 for the day), you can try to team up with other travelers to share the cost.

By Bus: Bus service between Dubrovnik and Montenegro is good in the summer (8/day, 2.5 hours or longer with border delays), but decreases off-season. It's possible to day-trip from Dubrovnik to the town of Kotor, but it's a long day on the bus: The first morning bus departs Dubrovnik at 7:00, usually arriving in Kotor between 10:00 and 11:00 (depending on the wait at the border). In summer, there may be additional morning buses, departing at 8:15, 10:00, and/or 11:00—but these can be even more susceptible to border delays. From Kotor, return buses typically depart at 14:40 (reaching Dubrovnik around 17:15) and at 18:00 (arriving in Du-

economy was weak. But the privatization of its economy (including its dominant industry, aluminum) and the aggressive development of its tourist trade (such as soliciting foreign investment—mostly Russian—to build new luxury hotels) have turned things around. In fact, in recent years, Montenegro has had one of the highest foreign investment rates in Europe. Still, it remains a poor place: Montenegro's unemployment rate hovers around 17 percent, and its per-capita GDP is just $16,500.

Currency: Though it's not a member of the European Union, Montenegro uses the euro as its currency: €1 = about $1.20.

Language and Alphabet: The official language is Montenegrin, which is nearly identical to Serbian but predominantly uses "our" Roman alphabet (rather than Cyrillic). Still, you'll see plenty of Cyrillic here—catering to both the country's large Serb minority as well as Russian tourists and investors.

Telephones: Montenegro's country code is 382. When calling from another country, first dial the international access code (00 from Europe, 011 from the US), then 382, then the area code (minus the initial zero), then the number. Note that Montenegro has changed its area codes. If you see the former code for the Bay of Kotor area, 082, you'll have to replace it with the new one: 032.

Flag: It's a red field surrounded by a gold fringe. In the middle is the national seal: a golden, two-headed Byzantine eagle topped with a single crown, holding a scepter in one hand and a ball in the other (symbolizing the balance between church and state). The eagle's body is covered by a shield depicting a lion with one paw raised (representing the resurrected Christ).

MONTENEGRO

brovnik late, around 21:00). Keep in mind that if you ride the bus, you can't stop to explore the sights along the way. As the schedule is always in flux, it's important to confirm times carefully at the Dubrovnik TI or bus station. Sit on the right side of the bus on your way to Montenegro, and the left side on the way home.

It's also possible to take a bus from Montenegro to **Mostar** in Bosnia-Herzegovina; it's a long journey via Trebinje in the mountainous interior (9 hours), or somewhat shorter via Dubrovnik (5.5 hours). For details, see "Kotor Connections," later.

By Excursion: As a last resort, consider taking a package excursion that follows basically the same route covered in this chapter (sold by various travel agencies in Dubrovnik; see page 72).

PLANNING YOUR TIME

Assuming you have your own car, for a straightforward one-day plan, drive to Kotor and back (figure about eight hours, including driving time and sightseeing stops). To extend your time, you can add as much Montenegro as you like. Get an early start (to avoid lines at the border, I'd leave Dubrovnik as early as 7:30). It takes about two hours to drive from Dubrovnik to Kotor (add about 1.5 hours if you stop in Perast for the boat trip out to the island). Kotor is worth two or three hours. From Kotor, you can return directly to Dubrovnik (about 1.5 hours if you use the ferry shortcut—see page 119); or drive another hour up to Njeguši and Cetinje in the Montenegrin interior, or a half-hour to the Budva Riviera (from either place, figure about 2.5-3 hours back to Dubrovnik). To cram everything into one extremely long day, you can do Dubrovnik-Kotor-Cetinje-Budva Riviera-Dubrovnik.

HELPFUL HINTS

Border Delays: The main Croatian-Montenegrin border is at Debeli Brijeg. When it's not busy, this border is relatively straightforward—just stop, have your passport scanned, and show your car's "green card" (proof of insurance). However, there can be long delays here on very busy days—especially on Saturdays in August, and to a lesser degree in July and early September. On the busiest days, the line can be hours long. To avoid wasting time, you have two options: Get an early start (locals suggest reaching the border by 8:00—leaving Dubrovnik around 7:30—to get there ahead of the tour buses); or use the secondary crossing, called Konfin, which is generally less busy (big buses are not allowed at Konfin, but savvy locals know about it, so on the busiest days it can be backed up, too). While the Konfin border might save you time, it's a bit less straightforward (with a few turnoffs rather than a straight shot on the main road), and takes a few more miles. I've narrated a scenic route ("Konfin Border Detour") in my self-guided driving tour, later.

Afternoon Delays: The Debeli Brijeg border crossing can also be severely delayed coming back to Dubrovnik in the afternoon. (Lines are worst in summer around 16:00 or 17:00—when a long chain of excursion buses all head back at the same time.) If this happens, use the secondary (and typically less crowded) Konfin border crossing. To avoid delays, some people like to make their way back to Dubrovnik in the early afternoon, perhaps stopping for dinner in Konavle; others prefer to linger for dinner in Kotor, and come back later, after the lines have thinned out.

Local Guide: While many Dubrovnik-based drivers/guides can bring you to Montenegro, if you really want the Montenegrin perspective, consider hiring a local guide here. I spent a great day learning about this area from **Stefan Đukanović,** a young, energetic, knowledgeable guide who speaks good English and has an infectious enthusiasm for his homeland. Hiring Stefan is a great value. The catch is that he can't come and get you in Dubrovnik, so it works best if you drive yourself to Montenegro and pick him up when you get there. Stefan is also an excellent choice if you're arriving in Kotor by cruise ship (guiding only: €60/half-day, €100/day, extra for driver if going outside of Kotor; several shore excursions possible—contact for details and rates, mobile 069-297-221 or 069-369-994, www.miroandsons.com, djukan@t-com.me).

The Bay of Kotor

With dramatic cliffs rising out of the glimmering Adriatic, ancient towns packed with history and thrilling vistas, an undeveloped ruggedness unlike anything in Croatia, and a twisty road to tie it all together, the Bay of Kotor represents the best of Montenegro. To top it off, it's easy to reach by car from Dubrovnik. (Don't forget your passport.)

Bay of Kotor Driving Tour

The Bay of Kotor (Boka Kotorska—literally the "Mouth of Kotor"; sometimes called "Boka Bay") is Montenegro's most enjoyable and convenient attraction for those based in Dubrovnik. This self-guided day trip—worth ▲▲—narrates the drive from the Croatian border to the town of Kotor, in the Bay of Kotor's deepest corner.

The Montenegrin border is about 40 minutes south of Dubrovnik. Simply follow the main coastal road south (signs to *Ćilipi*), past Cavtat and the airport.

From Dubrovnik to the Border

As you leave Dubrovnik, the jagged cliffs on your left eventually give way to a pastoral countryside called **Konavle** (meaning "canal," recalling how the Romans built aqueducts through this area to supply their settlement at today's Cavtat). This farming region—effectively Dubrovnik's hinterland—was badly damaged during the Yugoslav Wars, when the Yugoslav People's Army invaded from the south, forcing villagers to flee to safety in Dubrovnik. But today it's bouncing back, and is home to many appealing *konobas* (taverns) serving traditional local food. To stop off here (perhaps for dinner at the end of your Montenegro day), see "Konavoski Dvori" on page 81.

Soon after the turnoff for the Bosnian border, on the right, you'll pass **Kupari,** with one of the few buildings in the area that

MONTENEGRO

Cruising into Kotor

With cruise-ship crowds reaching capacity in nearby Dubrovnik, the Montenegrin town of Kotor has emerged as a hugely popular port of call on Mediterranean cruises. If you're one of them, here are some pointers.

Arrival in Kotor by Cruise Ship: It's easy. Ships either dock at or tender to the long pier that juts out directly in front of the Old Town. All passengers are funneled out of the same port gate, with the Old Town straight ahead. As you leave the port gate, look left to find an **ATM** in a freestanding orange kiosk (the main square of the Old Town, less than a five-minute walk away, also has ATMs); and look right to see an official **taxi** stand. (Unscrupulous taxis have been known to camp out near here to commandeer cruise passengers; be sure to use one at an official stand, and with a taxi logo and phone number on the side of the car.)

Exiting the port gate, continue straight ahead with the water on your right. Watch for the crosswalk (on your left, marked with brown *Kotor* sign) over the busy harborfront road, which you can use to get to the square in front of the Old Town, the TI, and the start of my self-guided walk.

Amenities: Free **Wi-Fi** is available near the TI kiosk. The two **pharmacies** in the Old Town are open long hours daily (for locations, see the "Kotor" map, later).

Sightseeing Options: The **Old Town of Kotor** itself is the obvious place to spend your day—though seeing everything, including my self-guided orientation walk and all of the museums—won't take you more than a couple of hours. Add a couple more hours if you're up for the stiff hike to the fortress above town (and maybe another hour or so just to recover). With more time, you may want to venture farther afield. The easiest choice is **Perast,** where you can explore a seaside village and ride a small boat out to one of the islands in the middle of the fjord (for details, see page 115); allow about four hours total for the round-trip to Perast and the island. Public buses connect Kotor town to Perast, or you can spring for a taxi (legitimate cabbies charge €20-25 one-way or €40-50 round-trip, including waiting time; negotiate a fixed price up front). For either of these trips—or to reach other, more distant Montenegrin destinations explained in this chapter—consider hiring a **local guide;** I recommend Stefan Đukanović (see "Helpful Hints," earlier).

Sail-in and Sail-away: Cruisers visiting Kotor are treated to a spectacular sail-in and sail-away, through the fjordlike bay and the narrow Verige Strait. If the weather's good and you enjoy dramatic scenery, this is not a day to sleep in or nap during the sail-away.

still has war damage. Originally Tito's villa, the building later became a vacation home for Yugoslav military officers. Now it's a ruin, awaiting investors.

From Kupari, you'll curl around the picturesque **Bay of Cavtat,** where some of the world's richest people tie up their yachts. Partway along the bay, after the village of Plat, you'll pass (on the left) an electrical plant, which harnesses the power of an underground river to generate more than enough clean energy for the entire city.

After the pleasant resort town of **Cavtat** (described on page 77), then the airport, you have the option of turning off (on the right, toward *Molunat*) to take advantage of the less crowded border crossing at Konfin (described next). Otherwise, just cruise along the main road until you reach the primary Debeli Brijeg border crossing. (If there's a line-up when you arrive, it's easy to backtrack to the alternate crossing: Just after the town of Gruda, follow signs for *Pločice,* then *Vitaljina,* then *Herceg Novi,* joining up with the route described next.)

Optional Konfin Border Detour

If you suspect that there will be long lines at the primary border crossing (in the peak of summer)—or if you simply prefer a longer and more scenic route—consider this uncongested detour via the secondary border, at Konfin. Soon after passing the airport, take the turnoff on the right for *Molunat.* You'll pass through a tranquil, nearly Tuscan landscape of pointy cypresses, vineyards, olive groves, and fig trees. Just before the village of Radovčići, on the right, watch for **Kojan Koral,** a horse farm that has hosted moviestar equines for *Game of Thrones.* They offer horseback rides, ATV safaris, and off-road Segway tours (www.kojankoral.hr).

Farther along, you'll enjoy fine views (on the right) down on the dramatic, elongated peninsula of **Molunat.** Notice that the H-shaped peninsula forms two protected bays. The larger one, facing north (toward Dubrovnik), is used to harbor ships in winter, while the smaller, south-facing one is better in summer.

When the road reaches a T-intersection, turn left for *Dubrovnik* and *Park Prevlaka,* then follow signs right for *Đurinići,* then right again for *Vitaljina.* As you continue on this road—through the villages of Đurinići, Višnjići, and Vitaljina—high on the mountains to your left is the point locals call **Tromeđe** ("Three Borders"), where Croatia, Bosnia-Herzegovina, and Montenegro converge.

Continue straight along this road all the way to the border, following signs for *Herceg Novi* and *GP Konfin.* You'll pass a turnoff on the right for **Park Prevlaka,** an old Austro-Hungarian and Yugoslav army fortress that has been converted into a park; you

MONTENEGRO

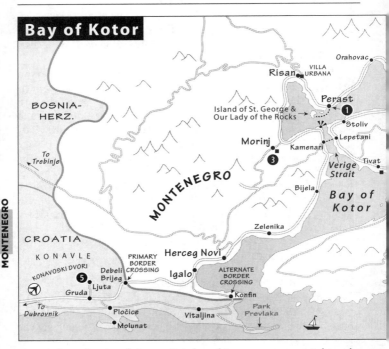

Bay of Kotor

MONTENEGRO

can see it at the tip of the peninsula poking out on your right—the southernmost point in Croatia.

Before long, you'll arrive at the Croatian border post, and then the Montenegrin one. After entering Montenegro, you'll curve along the small bay into Igalo, where you can pick up the self-guided driving tour.

• *From either border, you can make it to Kotor in about an hour without stopping, but with all the diversions en route you should plan for much more time. Navigating on this tour is really simple: It's basically the same road, with no turnoffs, from Dubrovnik to Kotor. First, you'll approach the coast at the town called...*

Igalo

Driving through Igalo, keep an eye out (on the right) for a big concrete hotel called **Institut Dr. Simo Milošević** (no relation to war-criminal Slobodan). This internationally regarded spa is one of the world's premier treatment facilities for arthritis and nerve disorders. Especially popular among Scandinavians, it's capable of hosting more than 1,000 patients at once. Yugoslav President-for-Life Tito had a villa nearby and took treatments here.

• *A couple of miles beyond Igalo, you enter the biggest city you'll see today...*

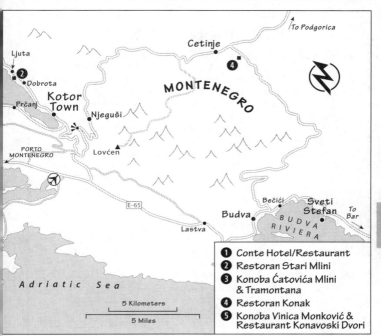

To Podgorica

Cetinje

Ljuta

Dobrota

MONTENEGRO

Kotor Town

Prčanj

Njeguši

PORTO MONTENEGRO

Lovćen

E-65

Bečići

Sveti Stefan

To Bar

Budva

BUDVA RIVIERA

Lastva

Adriatic Sea

5 Kilometers

5 Miles

1 Conte Hotel/Restaurant
2 Restoran Stari Mlini
3 Konoba Ćatovića Mlini & Tramontana
4 Restoran Konak
5 Konoba Vinica Monković & Restaurant Konavoski Dvori

MONTENEGRO

Herceg Novi

The drab economic and industrial capital of the Bay of Kotor, Herceg Novi (with 25,000 people) is hardly the prettiest introduction to this otherwise striking landscape. Herceg Novi flourished during the Habsburg boom of the late 19th century, when a railroad line connected it to Dubrovnik, Sarajevo, and Vienna. Back then, Austrians vacationed here—but more recent development has been decidedly less elegant than the Habsburgs'. While there is a walled Old Town core to Herceg Novi, it's not worth stopping to see; skip the turnoff for the town center, carrying on along the main road toward Budva.

Passing above Herceg Novi's Old Town, keep an eye out on the right for the town's stout 15th-century **fortress,** which was built by the Ottomans—who controlled this area, but never made it deeper into the bay.

Also in Herceg Novi, watch for tropical trees. Locals pride themselves on their particularly mild climate, sheltered by the fjord. Supposedly, "it never drops below 50 degrees Fahrenheit." Town symbols include banana trees and the mimosa flower, which blooms all winter long. Each February, as much of Europe (and most of Montenegro) is under a blanket of snow, Herceg Novi proudly hosts a Mimosa Festival.

MONTENEGRO

The History of Kotor

With evidence of prehistoric settlements dating back to 2500 B.C., the Bay of Kotor has been a prized location for millennia. Its unique bottleneck shape makes the Bay of Kotor the single best natural harbor between Greece and Venice.

One of the earliest known civilizations in Kotor (third century B.C.) was that of the Illyrians, whose Queen Teuta held court here until her lands were conquered by the Romans. After the Roman Empire split in the fourth century A.D., Montenegro straddled the cultural fault line between West (Roman Catholic) and East (Orthodox Christian). As Rome crumbled in the sixth and seventh centuries, the Slavs moved in (some Orthodox, some Catholic).

By the 10th century, Montenegro's Slavs had organized into a sovereign state, affiliated with the Byzantine (Eastern Roman) Empire. Thanks to its protected location, medieval Kotor became a major city of the salt trade. The area further flourished in the 14th century, under the Serbian emperor Dušan the Mighty. Notorious for his aggressive law enforcement—chopping off the hand of a thief, slicing off the nose of a liar—Dušan made the Bay of Kotor a particularly safe place to do business. If a visiting merchant was robbed, the nobleman who controlled that land would be ruthlessly punished. Soon 2,000-horse caravans could pass without a worry along this fjord.

But the Serbian Empire went into steep decline after Dušan. As the Ottomans threatened to invade in the 15th century, Kotor's traders turned to Venice for help. The Venetian Republic would control this bay for the next 450 years, and it was never taken by the Ottomans.

In the late 19th century, when Venice fell to Napoleon, the Bay of Kotor came briefly under the control of France, then Russia, then Austria. With the decline of feudal traditions and trading wealth, the Bay of Kotor entered a period of architectural stagnation—preserving many time-warp towns that travelers appreciate today.

When Montenegro became part of Yugoslavia following World War I, the Serbs (who felt a cultural affinity with the Montenegrins that wasn't always reciprocated) laid claim to the Montenegrin coast as their own little patch of seafront. This Serb connection helped Montenegro avoid the initial violence of the breakup of Yugoslavia. But a few years later, the Montenegrins decided it was time to part ways. For the rest of the story, see the "Montenegro: Birth of a Nation" sidebar, later.

Despite its tropical cachet, however, Herceg Novi is basically a mess. (Don't worry—the drive gets much prettier later on.) Why so much ugliness compared to Croatia? For one thing, Tito viewed Croatia's Dalmatian Coast as a gold mine of hard Western currency—so he was inclined to keep it Old World–charming. But in Montenegro, a heritage of corruption and bribery spurred some unfortunate construction. ("Would five thousand dinars convince you to ignore my new hotel's code violations?") From an architectural point of view, it's a sad irony that gorgeous Dubrovnik was devastated by bombs while the gritty cities of Montenegro survived the war essentially unscathed. Today, Montenegro is encouraging the construction of top-end resort hotels to lure high rollers from around the world (such as James Bond, who came to "Montenegro" to join a poker tournament at the Casino Royale—actually filmed in the Czech Republic). But this new development is poorly regulated, threatening to turn Montenegro into a charmless, concrete Costa del Sol–style vacation zone. Enjoy the Bay of Kotor's pristine areas (which we'll enter soon) while you still can.

• *As you go through Herceg Novi, at the roundabout, follow signs for* Budva, Kotor, *and* Trajekt/Ferry.

After the tunnel, you'll pass through **Zelenika**, *once the end of the line for the Habsburg rail line from Vienna, which first brought tourism to this area.*

You'll carry on through a few more dreary towns. Entertain yourself by gazing across the strait on your right to look for caves burrowed into the cliff face at sea level. These once provided shelter for Yugoslav warships. Also along this cliff, you'll see naval barracks. In **Bijela**, *you'll pass a big industrial shipyard on your right; in addition to the rusty, hardworking ships you'll likely see here, this slip also services luxury yachts—another example of Montenegro's odd juxtaposition of gritty industry and nouveau wealth.*

Eventually, you'll emerge into a more rustic setting. This fjordside road is lined with fishing villages, some now developed as resorts (including a few with severe communist-era touches). Each waterfront house seems to have its own little boat dock sticking out into the glassy water. You'll pass through the town of **Kamenari**, *which has a handy ferry that you could use to shave time off your return trip to Dubrovnik (described at the end of this drive). Two minutes after leaving Kamenari (just after the* Kostanjica *sign), watch for a convenient gravel pullout on the right (likely packed with tour buses, by the small white lighthouse). Pull over to check out the narrowest point of the fjord, the...*

Verige Strait

Any would-be invaders had to pass through this strategic bottleneck to reach the port towns inside the bay. It's narrow enough to carefully monitor (not even a quarter-mile wide), but deep enough

MONTENEGRO

to allow even today's large megaships through (more than 130 feet deep). Because this extremely narrow strait is easy to defend, whoever controlled the inside of the fjord was allowed to thrive virtually unchecked.

Centuries before Christ, the Bay of Kotor was home to the Illyrians—the mysterious ancestors of today's Albanians. In the third century B.C., Illyrian Queen Teuta spanned this strait with an ingenious shipwrecking mechanism to more effectively collect taxes. To this day, many sunken ships litter the bottom of the bay. (Teuta was a little too clever for her own good: Her shrewdness and success attracted the attention of the on-the-rise Romans, who seized most of her holdings.)

In later times, chains were stretched across the bay here to control the entrance (the name "Verige" comes from a Slavic word for "chain"). Later still, the Venetians placed cannons on either side of the strait, with a clear shot at any entering ships. Looking across the wide part of the bay, notice the town of Perast (by the two islands). Perast—where we'll be stopping soon—was also equipped with cannons that could easily reach across the bay. This extensive defense network succeeded in keeping the Ottomans—and any other would-be invaders—out of the bay.

• *Continue driving around the fjord. You'll pass through the village of...*

Morinj

This town is known for two starkly different reasons: First, it's the home of a recommended restaurant with fine food in a gorgeous setting (Konoba Ćatovića Mlini); another, more casual eatery sits nearby (both described later, under "Eating in Kotor"). And second, it was the site of a concentration camp for Croat prisoners captured during the 1991-1992 siege of Dubrovnik. Some 300 civilians from in and near Dubrovnik were forcibly brought here, where they lived in horrifying conditions. After the war, six of the guards from this camp were convicted of war crimes.

• *After going through Morinj and some other small villages, you'll pass through the larger resort town of...*

Risan

Back in Greek times, when the Bay of Kotor was known as *"Sinus Rhizonicus,"* Risan was the leading town of the bay. Later, during the Illyrian Queen Teuta's brief three-year reign, Risan was her capital. Today the town is still home to the scant remains of Teuta's castle (on the hilltop just before town), but it's mostly notable for its giant communist eyesore hotel—named, appropriately enough, Hotel Teuta.

In the town center, historians may want to turn off to the left (at the brown *Roman Mosaics* sign) for a quick look at a few partly intact mosaic floors of the second-century A.D. Roman **Villa Ur-bana** (€2, daily 8:00-20:00). You'll enter through a small modern building to access the large, covered footprint of the villa. Between the knee-high stone walls are mosaics of checkerboards, stylized marine life (including calamari), and—most significant—a small mosaic of reclining Hypnos, the god of dreams.

• *Continue on to Perast. As you approach the town, take the right fork (marked with brown sign) directly down into Perast; or you can first take the left fork to pass above town for sweeping views over the bay, then backtrack down into the town center.*

Perast

Called the "Pearl of Venetian Baroque," little Perast is a handy and scenic spot to stretch your legs and consider a boat trip. In high sea-son (June-mid-Sept), you're required to pay to park near the entrance of town, and then walk 10 level minutes or ride the free shuttle bus into the town center; at other times, you may be allowed to drive along the waterfront road and park for free in front of the church.

Remember that Perast, with its cannons aimed at the Verige Strait across the bay, was an essential link in the Bay of Kotor's fortifications. In exchange for this important duty, Venice re-warded Perast with privileged tax-free status, and the town became extremely wealthy. Ornate mansions proliferated here during its 17th- and 18th-century heyday. But after Venice fell to Napoleon, and the Bay of Kotor's economy changed, Perast's singular defen-sive role disappeared. With no industry, no hinterland, and no natural resources, Perast stagnated—leaving it a virtual open-air museum of Venetian architecture.

Go to the tallest steeple in town, overlooking a long and nar-row harborfront square. Perast is centered on its too-big (and in-complete) **Church of St. Nicholas**—dedicated to the patron saint of fishermen. It was originally designed to extend out into the sea (the old church, still standing, was to be torn down). But Napo-leon's troops came marching in before the builders got that far, so the plans were scuttled—and this massive partial-church was instead simply grafted on to the existing, modest church.

Go inside (free, treasury-€1, sporadic hours, generally daily June-Sept 9:00-19:00, until 14:00 off-season and closed Dec-March except by request—ask locals around the church if someone can let you in, closed during Mass). Beyond the small sanctuary, you'll find a treasury with relics and icons. Look for the priceless crucifix from the school of the 18th-century Venetian artist Giovanni Battista Tiepolo (#1, in the center display case), with Jesus on one side, and Mary and the saints on the other. Beyond the treasury is what was to be the main apse (altar area) of the unfinished massive church (notice it's at a right angle to the altar of the existing smaller church). The rough, unadorned brick walls make it clear

that they didn't get very far. Check out the model of the ambitious but never-built church. The Baroque main altar is by Bernini's student Francesco Cabianca, who lived in this area and was always trying to earn money to pay off his gambling debts. The small room at the end displays old vestments.

You can pay €1 to climb the **church tower** for the view. I'd skip the Town Museum, farther down the waterfront (fills a grand old hall with paintings, furniture, model ships, and other historical bric-a-brac).

Eating in Perast: For a seafront meal, window-shop the restaurants with seating out on the water. **$$$ Conte,** filling a pier in the middle of town, is a classic choice (tel. 032/373-687).

• *Before leaving Perast, take a close look at the two islands just offshore (and consider paying a visit).*

St. George (Sv. Đorđe) and Our Lady of the Rocks (Gospa od Škrpjela)

These twin islands—one natural, the other man-made—come with a fascinating story.

The **Island of St. George** (the smaller, rocky island with trees and a monastery—closed to tourists) was once part of the fortifica-

tion of the Bay of Kotor. Nearby was an underwater reef with a small section poking above the surface. According to legend, two fishermen noticed a strange light emanating from the reef in the early-morning fog. Rowing out to the island, they discovered an icon of Our Lady. They attempted to bring it ashore, but it kept washing back out again to the same spot. Taking this celestial hint, local seamen returning home from a journey began dropping rocks into the bay in this same place. The tradition caught on, more and more villagers dropped in

Montenegro: Birth of a Nation

Montenegro, like Croatia and Slovenia, was one of the six republics that constituted the former Yugoslavia. When these republics began splitting away in the early 1990s, Montenegro—always allied closely with Serbia, and small enough to slip under the radar—decided to remain in the union. When the dust had settled, four of the six republics had seceded, leaving only two united as "Yugoslavia": Serbia and Montenegro.

At first, Montenegrin Prime Minister Milo Đukanović was on friendly terms with Serbia's Slobodan Milošević. But in the late 1990s, as Milošević's political stock plummeted, Montenegro began to inch away from Serbia. Eager to keep its access to the coast (and the many Serbs who lived there), Serbia made concessions that allowed Montenegro to gradually assert its independence. In 1996, Montenegro boldly adopted the German mark as its official currency to bail out of the inflating Yugoslav dinar.

By 2003, the country of Yugoslavia was no more, and the loose union was renamed "Serbia and Montenegro." Thus began a three-year transition period that allowed Montenegro to test the waters of real independence. During this time, Serbia and Montenegro were united only in defense—legislation, taxation, currency, and most governmental functions were separate. And after three years, Montenegro would be allowed to hold a referendum for full independence.

That fateful vote took place on May 21, 2006. In general, ethnic Montenegrins tended to favor independence, while ethnic Serbs wanted to stay united with Serbia. To secede, Montenegro needed 55 percent of the vote. By the slimmest of margins—half a percent, or just 2,300 votes—the pro-independence faction won. On June 3, 2006, Montenegro officially declared independence. (To save face, two days later, Serbia also "declared independence" from Montenegro.)

Today, Montenegrins are excited to have their own little country and enthusiastic about eventually joining the European Union. But many view independence as an epilogue rather than a climax. Shortly after the referendum, I asked a Montenegrin when the countries would officially separate. He chuckled and said, "Three years ago."

rocks of their own, and eventually more than a hundred old ships and other vessels were loaded with stones and intentionally sunk in this spot. And so, over two centuries, an entire island was formed in the middle of the bay.

Flash forward to today's **Our Lady of the Rocks** (the flat island with the dome-topped Catholic church). In the 17th century, locals built this Baroque church on this holy site and filled it with symbols of thanks for answered prayers. Step inside (free entry) to explore the collection: silver votive plaques—many of them with images of ships in storms or battles—given by appreciative sailors who survived; 1,700 silver and gold votive plaques from other grateful worshippers; 68 canvases by local Baroque painter Tripo Kokolja; and a huge collection of dried wedding bouquets given by those who had nothing else to offer (the church is a popular place for weddings). Take a close look at the main altar. That legendary icon, which refused to budge from this spot, still caps the altar today. The faithful squeeze into the very tight space behind the altar, where a hole in the back of the structure lets them reach through and touch the original reef where the icon was found. Give it a try—if you dare.

The adjacent **museum** is an entertaining mishmash of items. The entry price includes a fun little tour by Davorka, Nataša, or Sandra (€1, May-Oct daily 9:00-18:00, off-season opens sporadically with boat arrival—or call ahead to Davorka's mobile 069-621-322). Just inside, study the models of both islands. The artificial one—the one you're on—is shaped vaguely like a boat. The collection comprises a wide range of ancient artifacts, including a glass case displaying fragments dating—staggeringly—from 3500  B.C. (found in the hills just above Perast). There's also a small modern-art gallery with various depictions of the two islands created by artists who came here and were inspired by this place; paintings of ships commissioned by local sailors (notice that most have a saintly image of Mary and the Baby Jesus hovering nearby); and other gifts given through the ages. Upstairs, near the gift shop counter, look for the amazing embroidery made by a local woman who toiled over it for more than 25 years. She used her own hair for the hair of the angels—which you can see fade from brown to gray as she aged (beginning at around 3 o'clock and going clockwise, you'll see the subtle change in color).

Getting There: Boats to Our Lady of the Rocks leave from in front of St. Nicholas' Church in Perast—look for the guys milling around the harborfront with boats ready to go. The going rate is €5/person round-trip, but Zoran (who has the boat with the red awning marked *Taxi Boat Perast*) says he'll charge only €4/person if you show this book. If it's quiet, they'll drop you on the island for about 30 minutes before returning to get you.

• *When you're ready to move on, continue driving around the fjord. After the large town of Orahovac, you'll see part of the bay roped off for a mussel farm; these farms do best when located where mountain rivers spill into the bay. And a hundred or so yards later, you cross a bridge spanning the don't-blink-or-you'll-miss-it...*

Ljuta River

According to locals, this is the "shortest river in the world"—the source is under the cliff just to the left of the bridge, and it meets the sea just to the right. Short as it is, it's hardly a trickle—in fact, its name means "Angry River" for its fierce flow during heavy rains. The river actually courses underground for several miles before emerging here. Like the Karst area south of Ljubljana, this is a karstic landscape—limestone that's honeycombed with underground rivers, caves, and canyons.

• *Immediately after the bridge, look for the turnoff (on the right) to the recommended Restoran Stari Mlini—a tranquil spot for a meal or drink. Fittingly, this "Old Mill" sits right where the river comes tumbling out—the perfect spot to harness that hydropower.*

Continuing along the fjord, as you pass through the town of Dobrota, look across the bay to the village of...

Prčanj

This town is famous as the former home of many centuries' worth of wealthy sea captains. When the Bay of Kotor was part of the Austrian Empire, Emperor Franz Josef came to Prčanj. Upon being greeted by some 50 uniformed ship captains, he marveled that such a collection of seafarers had been imported for his visit...not realizing that every one of them lived nearby.

• *Keep on driving. When you see the giant moat with the town wall, and the smaller wall twisting up the hill above, you'll know you've arrived in **Kotor** (see next page).*

Before leaving Kotor, make a decision about where you want to go next. You have three basic options: Budva Riviera; the mountainous Montenegrin interior; or back to Croatia (see instructions for the third option in the next section).

*Continuing past Kotor's Old Town, you'll follow the edge of the fjord. At the far end of town (and the fjord), you'll come to a roundabout. Bearing left at the roundabout takes you toward the handy tunnel to the **Budva Riviera**—or, along this same road, if you turn right after the cemetery and just before the tunnel, you'll take the extremely twisty road up, up, up into the **Montenegrin interior** (Njeguši and Cetinje).*

Once you're finished in Montenegro, it'll be time to head...

Back to Croatia: Lepetani-Kamenari Ferry Shortcut

When you're ready to return to Dubrovnik, you can go back the way you came. Or, for a quicker route, consider the ferry that cuts across the narrow part of the fjord (between the towns of Lepetani

MONTENEGRO

and Kamenari). On the Kotor side of the bay, the boat departs from the town of Lepetani.

From Kotor, you have two options to reach the ferry: The easiest option is to leave Kotor, bear left at the roundabout at the far end of town, and take the tunnel toward Budva. Once through the tunnel, follow signs into Tivat, and continue straight through Tivat on the main road to reach Lepetani, which is a few miles beyond the end of town. Or, for a more challenging but more scenic route, simply turn right at the roundabout and continue driving on the waterfront road clockwise around the bay (through Prčanj and Stoliv) until you land in Lepetani. But be warned that this road is extremely narrow (one lane, with an Adriatic shoulder) and can be exhausting. However, it also offers grand views back across the fjord at Kotor, Perast, and other picturesque towns you came through earlier.

No matter how you approach, remember that "ferry" is *trajekt* (it's also signed for *Herceg Novi*—the big city across the bay). The boat goes continuously (in slow times, you may have to wait briefly for enough cars to show up), and the crossing takes just four minutes (it takes longer to load and unload all the cars than it does to cross). A small car and its passengers pay €4.50 each way.

On your way back to Dubrovnik after the ferry, if there are long lines at the primary border crossing—or you want a quieter, more scenic return—use the Konfin alternate crossing described earlier: After exiting Igalo, just before the border, take the first left after the Hipermarket and Petrol gas station (following small yellow sign to *Višnjići*)—watch for the turnoff on the left that's marked *granični prijelaz Konfin*. From the Konfin border, follow signs to *Dubrovnik* (on back roads at first, later merging with the main road).

Kotor

Butted up against a steep cliff, cradled by a calm sea, naturally sheltered by its deep-in-the-fjord position, and watched over by an imposing network of fortifications, the town of Kotor is as impressive as it is well-protected. Though it's enjoyed a long and illustrious history, today's Kotor is a time-capsule retreat for travelers seeking an unspoiled Adriatic town.

The ancient town of Catarum—named for the Roman word for "contracted" or "strangled," as the sea is at this point in the gnarled fjord—was first mentioned in the first century A.D. Like the rest of the region, Kotor's next two millennia were layered with history as it came under the control of foreign powers: Illyrians,

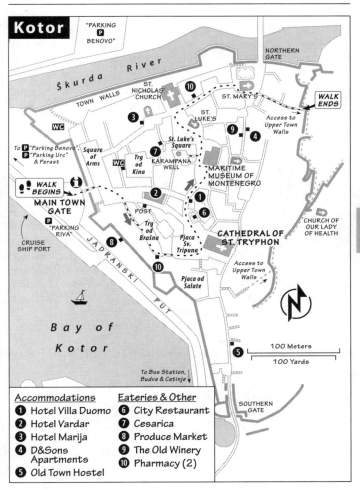

MONTENEGRO

Romans, Serbs, Venetians, Russians, Napoleonic soldiers, Austrians, Tito's Yugoslavia...and now, finally, Montenegrins. Each group left its mark, and Kotor has its share of both Catholic and Orthodox churches.

Through all those centuries, Kotor avoided destruction by warfare. But it was damaged by earthquakes—including the same 1667 quake that leveled Dubrovnik (known here as the "Great Shaking"), as well as a devastating 1979 earthquake from which the city is still cleaning up.

With an extremely inviting Old Town that seems custom-built for aimless strolling, Kotor is an idyllic place to while away a few hours. Though it's sometimes called a "little Dubrovnik," Kotor is more low-key, less ambitious, less historic, flatter, and much smaller than its more famous neighbor. And yet, with its own special spice that's exciting to sample, Kotor is a hard place to tear yourself away from.

Orientation to Kotor

Kotor (or Cattaro in Italian) has a compact Old Town shaped like a triangle. The two sides facing the bay are heavily fortified by a thick wall, and the third side huddles under the cliff face. A meandering defensive wall climbs the mountainside directly behind and above town. While only 3,000 people live within the Old Town walls, greater Kotor has a population of about 12,000.

The Old Town's mazelike street plan is confusing, but it's so small and atmospheric that getting lost is more fun than frustrating. The natives virtually ignore addresses, including the names of streets and squares. Most Old Town addresses are represented simply as "Stari Grad" (Old Town) and a number, useless if you're trying to navigate by streets. To make matters worse, a single square can have several names—so one map labels it Trg od Katedrale (Cathedral Square), while another calls it Pjaca Sv. Tripuna (Piazza of St. Tryphon). My advice: Don't fret about street or square names. Simply navigate with a map and by asking locals for directions. Thanks to the very manageable size of the Old Town, this is easier than it sounds.

TOURIST INFORMATION

The TI is in a kiosk just outside the Old Town's main entrance gate (daily May-Oct 8:00-20:00, Nov-April until 17:00, tel. 032/325-950, www.tokotor.me). Pick up the free map and browse the collection of other brochures. There's a free Wi-Fi hotspot around this kiosk; look for the "TOKOTOR" network.

ARRIVAL IN KOTOR

By Car: Approaching town, you'll first see Kotor's substantial wall, which overlooks a canal. You can park in one of three pay lots, which are all priced around €1/hour: "Parking Riva," along the bay immediately across from the main gate, is the closest to the Old Town and a bit more expensive (to the right just after crossing the bridge by the wall); "Parking Benovo," in the lot across the canal (on the left just before the bridge by the wall—you'll be sent back here if the first lot is full); or "Parking Urc" (a bit farther out and along the water). All three are easily walkable from the Old Town entrance. Be sure you've parked legally, in one of these designated lots; while locals brazenly leave their cars anywhere they like, tourists get towed without remorse.

By Bus: The bus station is about a half-mile (10-minute walk) south of the Old Town. Arriving here, simply exit to the right and walk straight up the road—you'll run into the embankment and town wall.

Sights in Kotor

Because of its tangled alleys and irregular street plan, Kotor feels bigger than it is. But after a few minutes of strolling, you'll discover you're going in circles and realize it's actually very compact. (In fact, aimless wandering is Kotor's single best activity.) As you ramble, keep an eye out for these key attractions. I've listed them roughly in the order of a counterclockwise route through town, beginning outside the main entrance gate.

▲Main Town Gate (Glavna Gradska Vrata)

The wide-open **square** fronting the bay and waterfront marina now welcomes visitors. But for centuries, its purpose was exactly the opposite. As the primary point of entry into this heavily fortified town, it was the last line of defense. Before the embankment was built, the water came directly to this door, and there was only room for one ship to tie up at a time. If a ship got this far (through the gauntlet we saw back at the Verige Strait), it was carefully examined here again to levy taxes before its passengers could disembark. This double-checkpoint was designed to foil pirates who might fly the flag of a friend to get through the strait, only to launch a surprise attack once here. (The pirates' primary booty wasn't silver or gold, but men—kidnapped for ransom, or, if ransom wasn't paid, as slaves to row on ships.)

Check out the pinkish **gate** itself. The oldest parts of this gate date from 1555. It once featured a Venetian lion, then the double-headed eagle of the Habsburg Empire. But today, most of the symbolism touts Tito's communism (notice the stars and the old Yugoslav national seal at the top). The big date (November 21, 1944) commemorates this area's liberation from the Nazis by Tito's homegrown Partisan Army. The Tito quote *(tuđe nećemo svoje nedamo)* means, roughly, "Don't take what's ours, and we won't take what's yours"—a typically provocative statement in these troubled Balkans.

• *Notice the **TI** in the kiosk just to the left of the gate. Then go through the gate into town. You'll emerge into the...*

Square of Arms (Trg od Oržja)

Do a quick spin-tour of the square, which is ringed with artifacts of the city's complex history. Looking to the left, you'll see a long building lined with cafés. This was once the palace of the rector, who ruled Kotor on behalf of Venice. Princes could watch the action from their long balcony overlooking the square, which served as the town's living room. Later, the palace became the Kotor Town Hall. Beyond the long building, two other buildings poke out into the square (on either side of the lane

leading out of the square). The one on the right is the Venetian arsenal, the square's namesake. The one on the left is the "French Theater," named for its purpose during the time this area was under Napoleon's control. Directly across from the gate you just came through, you'll see the town's Bell Tower, one of Kotor's symbols. The odd triangular structure at its base was once the town pillory, where wrongdoers would be chained and subjected to public ridicule of the rudest kind imaginable. In the little recessed square just right of that, you'll spot the recommended, copper-roofed Hotel Vardar. Handy ATMs around this square dispense euros.

• *Walk down the long part of the square directly ahead of where you entered (toward Hotel Vardar). Take the broad lane angling off to the right (paved with red-and-white-striped tiles), which leads past mansions of Kotor's medieval big shots. Cross a square (Trg od Brašna) and turn left down the little lane at its end. After one short block, you'll hit Pjaca Sv. Tripuna (a.k.a. Trg od Katedrale), home to the...*

▲Cathedral of St. Tryphon (Katedrala Sv. Tripuna)

Even though most of today's Kotorians are Orthodox, Kotor's most significant church is Catholic. According to legend, in 809, Venetian merchants were sailing up the coast from Nicea (in today's Turkey) with the relics of St. Tryphon—a third-century martyr and today's patron saint of gardeners. A storm hit as they approached the Bay of Kotor, so they took shelter here. Every time they tried to leave, the weather worsened...so they finally got the message that St. Tryphon's remains should remain in Kotor.

Cost and Hours: €2.50, daily June-Sept 9:00-19:00, April-May and Oct 9:00-18:00, Nov-March 9:00-15:00, Mass on Sun at 10:00.

Visiting the Cathedral: Take in the cathedral's **exterior.** The church has been rebuilt after four different earthquakes—most extensively after the 1667 quake, when it achieved its current

Renaissance-Baroque blend. That earthquake, which also contributed to Dubrovnik's current appearance, destroyed three-quarters of Kotor's buildings. A fire swept the city, and all of the dead bodies attracted rats (and with them, the plague)—a particularly dark chapter in Kotor's history.

Why are the two **towers** different? There are plenty of legends, but the most likely answer is that restorers working after 1667 simply ran out of money before they finished the second one. Notice the Church of Our Lady of Health way up on the hill above this church—built in thanks to God by survivors of the plague (it also serves as part of the town fortifications—described later).

Within the cathedral, the **nave** of the church is marginally interesting, with stout columns; surviving Byzantine-style frescoes under the arches—all that's left of paintings that once covered the church; and a fine 15th-century silver-and-gold altar covered by a delicate canopy.

But the best part is the **reliquary** upstairs. Find the stairs at the rear and walk up to the chapel. Behind the Baroque altar (by Bernini's student Francesco Cabianca, whose work we saw in Perast) and the screen are 48 different relics. In the center is St. Tryphon—his bones are in a silver casket, and his head is in the golden chalice next to it. In the small room up the stairs, examine the fascinating icon of the Madonna and Child from the 15th century (it's in a freestanding wooden frame with a crucified Jesus on the other side; to find it, you may have to look around back or rotate the frame). The painting exemplifies this town's position as a bridge between Western and Eastern Christianity: The faces, more lifelike, are Western-style (Catholic) Gothic; the stiff, elongated bodies are more Eastern (Orthodox) and Byzantine-style. From here, take a slow walk around the upper gallery of the church to see its displays of relics (such as arms and feet covered in silver), paintings, vestments, and other ecclesiastical items.

• *Exit the church, veer right, and exit the square on the street near the recommended City Restaurant, marked by trees. In a block, you'll wind up on a little square that's home to the...*

Maritime Museum of Montenegro (Pomorski Muzej Crne Gore)

Like so many Adriatic towns, Kotor's livelihood is tied to the sea. This humble museum covers three floors and explores that important heritage. As you climb the stairway, notice the evocative maps and etchings of old Kotor. Portraits of salty swashbucklers, traditional costumes, and 98 coats of arms representing aristocratic families who have lived here (ringing the main room upstairs) are all reminders of the richness of Kotor's history. You'll see a display of rifles and swords (some with fun ornamental decorations illustrating the art of killing) and lots of model ships. The museum is housed in the Gregorina Palace, one of dozens of aristocratic mansions that dot the Old Town—yet another reminder of the historically high concentration of wealth and power in this little settlement.

Cost and Hours: €4, includes English audioguide; July-Aug Mon-Sat 9:00-20:00, closes earlier off-season, Sun 9:00-13:00 year-round; on Trg Grgurina, tel. 032/304-720, www.museummaritimum.com.

• *Turn right out of the museum, and make a right again on the first lane. After 10 yards, you'll pass a well on your left called the...*

Karampana

This well served as Kotor's only public faucet until the early 20th century. As such, it was also the top place in town for gossip, like the office water cooler. It's said that if your name was mentioned here, you knew you had arrived. Today, though the chatter is no longer raging on this square, the town's gossip magazine is called *Karampana*. While the pump still works (swing the pendulum once and keep it there), it's sometimes disconnected to prevent tourists from swinging it back and forth too aggressively.

• *Continue straight past the well into the next square...*

▲St. Luke's Square (Trg Svetog Luke)

There are two Serbian Orthodox churches on this pretty square, each with the typical Orthodox church features: a squat design, narrow windows, and portly domes. Little **St. Luke's Church** (Crkva Sv. Luka), in the middle of the square, dates from the 12th century. Locals debate long and hard as to whether St. Luke's was originally built as a Catholic church or an Orthodox one. (Although it "looks" Orthodox, it was constructed at a time when even Catholic churches were built in the Orthodox style.) Regardless of its origin, during the Venetian era the church did double duty as a house of worship for both. These days, it's decidedly Orthodox. Step into the humble interior (free, daily May-Oct 10:00-20:00, Nov-April 8:00-13:00 & 17:00-19:00).

The bigger and much newer **St. Nicholas' Church** (Crkva Sv. Nikola), was built in 1909—because of its Neo-Byzantine design, it has similarly spherical domes and slitlike windows (free, same hours as St. Luke's).

Before entering, notice how the Orthodox crosses on the steeples of St. Nicholas' Church differ from the cross seen in Roman

Catholic churches (known as a Latin cross). In addition to the standard cross-bar, Orthodox crosses often also have a second, smaller crossbar near the top (representing the *I.N.R.I.* plaque that was displayed above Jesus' head). Sometimes Orthodox crosses also feature a third, angled crossbar at the bottom. Many believe that rather than being nailed directly to the cross, Jesus' feet were nailed to a crossbar like this one to prolong his suffering. The slanted angle represents Jesus' forgiveness of the thief crucified to his right (the side that's pointing up)...and suggests where the unrepentant thief on his left ended up.

Stepping into these (or any other Orthodox) churches, you'll immediately notice some key differences from Catholic church-

es: no pews (worshippers stand through the service as a sign of respect), tall and skinny candles (representing prayers), and a screen of icons, called an iconostasis, in the middle of the sanctuary to separate the material world from the holy world (where the Bible is kept). For more about Orthodox worship, see the sidebar on page 44.

Before continuing on, enjoy this square's lazy ambience. The big building fronting the square is a music school, and the students practicing here fill this already pleasant public space with an appealing soundtrack.

• *If you go down the street to your left as you face St. Nicholas, you'll wind up back at the Square of Arms. But first try getting lost, then found again, in Kotor's delightful maze of streets.*

The town's final attraction is above your head. To go there directly, face St. Nicholas' Church, turn right, and walk straight for two blocks until you reach St. Mary's Church (named for one of four Catholic saints who came from the Bay of Kotor—which some faithful locals call the "Bay of Saints"). If you skirt the church along its right side—down the narrow lane with two arches—you'll find the entrance to the town walls.

▲▲Town Walls (Gradske Zidine)

Kotor's fortifications begin as stout ramparts along the waterfront, then climb up the sheer cliff face behind town in a dizzying zigzag line. If there's a more elaborate city wall in Europe, I haven't seen it. A proud Kotorian bragged to me, "These fortifications cost more to build than any palace in Europe."

Imagine what it took to create this "Great Wall of Kotor." The wall is nearly three miles long and sits on some extremely inaccessible terrain. It was built in fits and starts over a millennium (9th-19th centuries, though most of it was completed during the Venetian occupation in the 17th and 18th centuries). Its thickness varies from 6

to 50 feet, and the tallest parts are 65 feet high. Sections higher on the hill—with thinner walls, built before the age of gunpowder—are the oldest, while the thick walls along the water are most recent. It was all worth it: The fortified town survived many attacks, including a two-month Ottoman siege in 1657.

If you're in great shape, consider scrambling along the walls and turrets above the Old Town.

Cost and Hours: Entry to the walls is €8 May-Oct daily 8:00-20:00; otherwise they're free.

Hiking the Walls: If you go all the way up to the top fortress and back again, it'll take around an hour and a half round-trip (depending on how fast you go). This involves climbing 1,355 steps (an elevation gain of more than 700 feet)—don't overestimate your endurance or underestimate the heat. ("Am-I-*that*-out-of-shape?" tourists routinely find themselves winded and stranded high above town.) Bring plenty of water, along with a hat and sunscreen, and wear sturdy shoes. Most of the way, there's both a ramp and uneven stairs, but the route is in poor repair, with a lot of rough, rocky patches.

It's best to tackle the walls clockwise. (Even if you're not doing the hike, you can visually trace this route.) Find the entrance at the back-left corner of town (near St. Mary's Church, through the alley with the two arches over it). Pay the entry fee and begin hiking up. On the way up, notice the sign explaining that the fortress reconstruction was funded by the United States (Nov 2004)—if you're a US taxpayer, consider this hike your tax dollars at work.

First climb as high as the **Church of Our Lady of Health** (Crkva Gospe od Zdravlj). This is the halfway mark—about 20 minutes from the base at a good pace. While some believe this church has miraculous healing powers, everyone agrees it offers some of the best views down over Kotor.

From this church, you can either cut back down toward the Old Town, or—if you're not exhausted yet—keep hiking up to the tippy-top **Fortress of St. John** (figure another 30 minutes from the church, if you're in decent shape). Built on the remains of fortifications from the Illyrians (you can scan the third-century B.C. remains just beyond the fort), this was the headquarters for the entire wall network below it. There's not much to see here, but it is fun to play "king of the castle" exploring the ruined shell—and the views, with 360 degrees of Montenegrin cliffs, are spectacular.

Then head back down, enjoying your reward: a downhill walk with head-on views of the Bay of Kotor. On the way down, watch your step on the slippery-even-when-dry marble stairs, highly polished by the feet of centuries of visitors. At the round terrace below the church, you can head to the right (back the way you came); or, for a different path, head left following *powder magazine* signs, then down (right) at the fork. The ticket-seller warned me that he's often seen people wipe out on the very last step on their way down—so exhausted after the demanding hike that they let their guard down.

Sleeping in Kotor

Kotor is an enjoyable place to spend the night. (Given its popularity as a cruise port, and among side-trippers from Dubrovnik, only a tiny fraction of visitors bother to sleep here.) However, the town has two big disadvantages: inexplicably high prices (you'll sleep more affordably in Dubrovnik) and lots of nighttime noise from boisterous bars. Assume it'll be loud anywhere, and pack earplugs.

$$$ Hotel Villa Duomo is a stylish refuge just down the street from the cathedral. The 13 stony-chic rooms share an interior terrace where breakfast is served in good weather (Stari Grad 358, tel. 032/323-111, www.villaduomo.com, villaduomo@yahoo.com).

$$$ Hotel Vardar has 24 rooms with mod bathrooms smack-dab in the middle of the Old Town. This classic old copper-roofed hotel has been renovated from top to bottom, leaving it tastefully chic. While convenient, the dead-central location can come with some noise, especially on weekends—request a quieter room (elevator, Stari Grad 476, tel. 032/325-084, www.hotelvardar.com, info@hotelvardar.com).

$$ Hotel Marija, an Old World throwback on an Old Town

square, offers 17 rooms and wood-paneled halls. Request a quieter room in the back (on Trg od Kina, Stari Grad 449, tel. 032/325-062, hotel.marija.kotor@t-com.me).

$ D&Sons Apartments has six good, modern apartments along an atmospheric, café-lined lane at the back edge of the Old Town (no breakfast but kitchenettes, Stari Grad 490, mobile 069-050-094, www.dandsons.com, dandsons@t-com.me, Dražan).

¢ Old Town Hostel is a budget option in the Old Town, filling a stony, labyrinthine 13th-century building with 10 rooms, ranging from 10-bed dorms to overpriced private rooms. Youthful conviviality fills the inviting lounge (no breakfast but kitchen in each room, Stari Grad 284, tel. 032/325-317, mobile 067-737-825, www.hostel-kotor.me, info@hostel-kotor.me).

Eating in Kotor

In coastal, Italian-influenced Kotor, the cuisine is very similar to Croatia's: seafood, pasta, and pizza. There are a few local specialties to look for, and at the top of the list is *Njeguški pršut*, the delicious smoked ham from the village of Njeguši high in the mountains above town (described later, under "The Montenegrin Interior"). While *pršut* (prosciutto) is beloved throughout the Balkans, *Njeguški pršut*'s rich, salty, smoky flavor is perhaps the best. It goes well with the local cow's cheese—smoked, of course.

Montenegro produces some surprisingly good (and expensive) wines. The biggest producer in the country—and one of the biggest in the Balkans—is Plantaže Podgorica, which corks up some 20 million bottles each year. While that kind of volume often doesn't come with quality, Plantaže's vintages are quite good and worth trying (if not impossible to avoid). The most popular red-wine grape is the dry, medium-bodied *vranac* (VRAH-nahts), which is distantly related to Italian *primitivo,* Californian zinfandel, and Croatian *plavac mali.* For white, you'll see the dry, fruity *krstač* (kur-STACH), similar to riesling.

As far as choosing restaurants in Kotor, there's not much to recommend. Truly great cuisine is rare here—I'd just settle for something scenic and functional. For a better-quality, memorable meal in a romantic setting, drivers can consider heading to Konoba Ćatovića Mlini or Restoran Stari Mlini (described later).

Simple Meals near the Cathedral: $$ City Restaurant, with breezy outdoor tables next to the Cathedral of St. Tryphon, offers a fine, shady perch. Its well-varnished picnic tables are set within the little forest in the Old Town, and more tables fill a small square out front (daily 8:00 until late; mobile 069-049-653).

Local Fish: $$$ Cesarica offers unpretentious seafood in a casual, stony interior buried deep in the Old Town. They enjoy bragging that the owner, Petar, was a fisherman, so he has a line on the freshest ingredients (daily 9:00-23:00, Stari Grad 375, mobile 069-049-733).

Market: Just outside the Old Town wall, facing the harbor, is a lively open market that hops each morning (typically 9:00-14:00, busiest on Sat). This is a great place to gather ingredients for a picnic, including the delicious local smoked ham, *Njeguški pršut*.

Wine Bar: $$$$ The Old Winery (Stara Vinarija) fills an inviting stony-chic space on a tight Old Town lane with convivial indoor and outdoor seating. It's a chance to enjoy a limited but appealing range of dishes that work well with wines from throughout the former Yugoslavia—with an emphasis on Montenegrin vintages. Hang out in the wine bar itself (about 20 wines available by the glass; frequent live music—piano in the morning, blues after 21:00). Or stop in their wine shop—called Mon Ami—next door. Both are open long hours daily (Stari Grad 483, mobile 068-517-417, Goran). You can sample three wines in the shop for cheap, or spring for a more elaborate five-wine tasting in the bar (call or drop by in advance to reserve).

NEAR KOTOR

These very scenic options are situated on or near the bayside road, handy for dinner on your way back to Croatia. The first two restaurants sit in oasis-like settings near running water, which helps keep them cool during the hot summer months. Another dinner option on the way home to Dubrovnik—just over the Croatian border— are similar restaurants in Konavoski Dvori (see page 81).

In Ljuta

$$$$ Restoran Stari Mlini has a cozy interior and wonderful outdoor seating scattered around a spring-fed stream near an old, namesake water mill. Surrounded by trickling water, you'll dine on local cuisine, with an emphasis on seafood. If you prefer freshwater fish, you can choose your own trout from the pond (daily 12:00-24:00, tel. 032/333-555).

Near the Verige Strait, in Morinj

$$$$ Konoba Ćatovića Mlini is a memorable restaurant worth going out of your way to reach. Hiding in a sparse forest off the main fjordside road, this oasis is situated amidst a series of ponds, streams, waterfalls, and bubbling springs. The

traditionally clad waiters are stiffly formal, mindful of this place's good reputation. Choose between several different stony seating options, indoors and out. Family-run for 200 years, this place is a local institution, yet it feels like a well-kept secret. Reservations are essential in summer (extensive wine list, daily 11:00-23:00, tel. 032/373-030, www.catovicamlini.me). At the town of Morinj, watch for burgundy *Konoba Ćatovića Mlini* signs leading away from the water.

$$ Tramontana is a more affordable, still very scenic option overlooking a beach with grand fjord views, right along the main waterfront road on the way out of Morinj (daily 8:00-24:00, mobile 068-737-737).

Kotor Connections

From Kotor by Bus to: Perast (hourly, usually at :15 past the hour, every 2 hours on Sun, departs from small bus stop near Old Town rather than bus station), **Herceg Novi** (2/hour, 1 hour), **Budva** (1-4/hour, 40 minutes), **Cetinje** (2/hour, 1 hour), **Dubrovnik** (7/day in summer, less off-season, 2.5 hours—or can take much longer due to border delays), **Mostar** (2/day via Trebinje—likely at 11:00 and 22:00, 9 hours; also 1/day via Dubrovnik—likely at 14:40, 5.5 hours; all operated by Globtour), **Zagreb** (2/day, including overnight option, 13-16 hours). Bus info: Tel. 032/325-809, www. autobuskastanicakotor.me.

The Montenegrin Interior

Although Montenegro is trying to cultivate a glitzy beach-break cachet, for most of its history it has been thought of as a rugged mountain kingdom. While the coast—the focus of most of this chapter—was traditionally Venetian or Austrian, the true heart of Montenegro beat behind the sheer wall of mountains rising up from that seafront. And romantics, caught up in misty Balkan fantasies, still think of this inland area as the "real" Montenegro.

While the Bay of Kotor is the most accessible and appealing part of the country, those with more time might enjoy a detour up into the mountains. For a quick look at this area, the easiest loop takes you to the historic capital of Cetinje—a dull little town in its own right, but a fine excuse for a mountain joyride. You could do this whole loop in about two and a half hours without stopping (about an hour from Kotor to Cetinje, then another hour to Budva, then a half-hour back to Kotor)—but if you want to stretch your legs in Njeguši or Cetinje, allow more time.

Self-Guided Driving Tour

The Road into the Mountains

The road to Cetinje twists you up the mountain face that stretches high above Kotor—it's an incredibly scenic, white-knuckle drive. (Particularly since it can be clogged with cruise excursion buses, timid drivers may want to skip it.)

From Kotor, leave town toward Budva (bearing left at the roundabout). At the edge of Kotor, after the cemetery but before the big tunnel, take a right (marked for *Cetinje*) and begin your ascent. Cresting the first hill, go left to get to Cetinje (also marked for *Njeguši*). You'll wind up and up (past a small Roma encampment) on 25 numbered switchbacks. The road is a souvenir from the Habsburg era (1884). While Venetian rule brought sea trade, Austrian rule brought fortresses and infrastructure. After switchback #13, you'll pass an old customs house marking the former border between the Austro-Hungarian Empire and the Kingdom of Montenegro—a reminder that the coastline was not historically an integral part of Montenegrin cultural identity. As you near the top, look across the canyon to the left to spot the impossibly rough little donkey path that once was Cetinje's connection with the coast... like a tenuous umbilical cord tethering the mountainous interior to the outside world.

As you crest the hill, the vegetation changes—you're high above the Adriatic, with commanding views of Kotor and its bay (and great photo-op pullouts; the best is just after switchback #25). Continuing inland, you find yourself in another world: poor, insular, and more Eastern (you'll see more Cyrillic lettering). Country farmhouses sell smoked ham, mountain cheese, and *medovina* (honey brandy). Before long, you reach a broad plain and the hamlet of...

Njeguši

The humble-seeming village of Njeguši (NYEH-goo-shee) is actually well-known among Montenegrins, with two very important claims to fame. This was the hometown of the House of Petrović-Njegoš, the dynasty that ruled Montenegro for much of its history (1696-1918). The family's favorite son was Petar II Petrović-Njegoš (1813-1851). Aside from ruling the country, Petar II is remembered most fondly as a great poet and playwright—sort of the Montenegrin Shakespeare.

Njeguši is also famous for producing its own special type of air-dried ham, called *Njeguški pršut*. Locals explain that, because this meadow overlooks the sea on one side, and the mountains on the other, the wind changes direction 10 times each day, alternating between dry mountain breeze and salty sea air—perfect for seasoning and drying ham hocks. For good measure, the *pršut* is also smoked with beech wood. The blocky, white buildings lining the road that look like giant Monopoly houses are actually smoke-houses, jammed with five layers of hanging ham hocks—thousands of euros' worth—silently aging. (More industry than you realize hides out in sleepy villages.) A couple of traditional restaurants at the heart of the village are happy to serve passing tourists a lunch of this local specialty.

From Njeguši to Cetinje

Continuing through Njeguši toward Cetinje, you'll twist up into more mountains—soon arriving in an even more rugged and in-hospitable landscape than you passed on the road that brought you here from the coast. Eyeing this desolate scenery, you can un-derstand why the visiting Lord Byron said of this place, "Am I in paradise or on the moon?" Along the mountain road that drops you down into Cetinje, each rock has the phone number of a vulture-esque road repair service *(auto slep)* spray-painted onto it. Low-pro-file plaques mark the site of Tito-era ambush assassinations.

Keep an eye out (on the horizon to the right) for the pointy peak of the mountain called **Lovćen,** which is capped by an elab-orate mausoleum, designed by the great Croatian sculptor Ivan Meštrović, and devoted to King Petar II Petrović-Njegoš. With more time, you could actually drive up to the top of this mountain for sweeping views across Montenegro.

Soon you reach the outskirts of...

Cetinje

Cetinje (TSEH-teen-yeh)—the historic capital of Montenegro—is a fine but fallen-on-hard-times little burg that sits cradled in a desolate valley surrounded by mighty peaks. Observing Cetinje from afar, it seems made to order as the historic capital of a re-mote and rustic people. It was the home of the Montenegrin king since the 15th century, but has always been pretty humble. In fact, it's said that when the Ottomans conquered it and moved in ready to rampage, they realized there wasn't much to pillage and plun-der—so they just destroyed the town and moved on. The town was destroyed several other times, as well—and each time, the local people rebuilt it.

This "Old Royal Capital," once the leading city in the realm, is today recovering from its status as a victim of Tito's quirky eco-nomic program for Yugoslavia. It used to provide shoes and re-frigerators for the country, but when Yugoslavia disintegrated, so did the viability of Cetinje's economy. As you explore the two-story town today, it seems there's little more than a scruffy dollop of tourism to keep its 17,000 people housed and fed. Many of its younger generation have left for employment along the coast in the tourism industry.

Park in the town center and stroll the main street (Njegoševa) past kids on bikes, old-timers with hard memories, and young adults with metabolisms as low as the town's. At the end of this drag is the main square (Balšića Pazar), surrounded by low-key sights with sporadic opening hours: the **Ethnographic Museum** (traditional costumes and folk life), **Historical Museum** (tracing the story of Montenegro), **Njegoš Museum** (dedicated to the beloved poet-king Petar II Petrović-Njegoš), and **National Museum,** which honors King Nikola I, who ruled from 1860 until 1918. While his residence is as poor and humble a royal palace as you'll see in Europe, Nikola I thought big. He married off five of his daughters into the various royal families of Europe.

A short walk from the palace is the birthplace of the town, **Cetinje Monastery.** It's dedicated to St. Peter of Cetinje, a leg-

endary local priest who carried a cross in one hand and a sword in the other, established the first set of laws among Montenegrins, and inspired his people to defend Christian Montenegro against the Muslim Ottomans. The monastery also holds the supposed right hand of St. John the Baptist. You are free to wander respectfully through the courtyard and church of this spiritual capital of Serbian Orthodox Montenegro.

From Cetinje Back to the Coast

To avoid backtracking down the same twisty road you came up, consider heading more directly back toward the coast from Cetinje. Just follow signs for *Budva*. A few miles outside of Cetinje along this road, look for the good **$$ Restoran Konak,** which serves up tasty traditional dishes with indoor and outdoor seating (open long hours daily, tel. 041/761-011).

Continuing along this road, you'll pop out high above the **Budva Riviera.** Looking out to sea, you'll spot the distinctive peninsula of Sveti Stefan off to the left, and the town of Budva to the right. If you have even more time, linger along the coast to visit these sights (described next). Otherwise, head right to return to Kotor or Dubrovnik.

MONTENEGRO

The Budva Riviera

Montenegrins boast, "Croatia's got islands, but we've got beaches!" Long swaths of coarse-sand and fine-pebble beaches surround the resort town of Budva, just south of Kotor. This 15-mile stretch of coast, called the "Budva Riviera," is unappealingly built up with a mix of cheap and luxury resort hotels—making it pale in comparison to the jagged saltiness of the Bay of Kotor or the romantic tidiness of Dalmatia. This region is a mecca for super-wealthy Russians, staking their claim to this patch of Adriatic seafront. But the area isn't without its charms. Aside from the pleasant Old Town of the region's unofficial capital, Budva, you'll discover a near-mythical haunt of the rich and famous: the highly exclusive resort peninsula of Sveti Stefan (not possible to visit, but alluring from afar). For me, more time in Kotor or an earlier return to Dubrovnik would be more satisfying than the trek to the Budva Riviera. But beach lovers who have plenty of time and a spirit of adventure will find this area merits a look.

GETTING TO THE BUDVA RIVIERA

Budva is about a 30-minute drive south of **Kotor.** The easiest approach is to continue past Kotor along the fjord, left at the roundabout, then through the tunnel (following *Budva* signs; exiting the tunnel, notice the sign in Cyrillic letters for Russki Radio 107.3—catering to the Russian jet-setters). First, you'll reach the town of **Budva** (turn right at traffic light, following brown *Stari Grad* signs to the Old Town; parking is well-marked in modern complex next to Old Town). Continuing around the bay, you'll pass the busy, modern resort cluster of Bečići before reaching **Sveti Stefan.**

Sights on the Budva Riviera

Between the strings of resort hotels are two towns that deserve a quick visit.

Budva

The Budva Riviera's best Old Town has charming Old World lanes crammed with souvenir shops and holiday-making Serbs and Russians. While less appealing than Kotor, Budva at least offers a taste of romance between the resort sprawl.

Budva began as an "emporium" (market and trading center) for Greek seamen, and extremely valuable jewelry uncovered here indicates that some pretty important people spent time here. Today, Budva's layout is simple and intuitive—a peninsula (flanked by beaches) with a big Venetian-style bell tower.

From the parking lot, head inside the Old Town walls and wander up the main drag, Njegoševa. Out at the tip of town, you'll pop out into a small café-lined square with a **Catholic church** (on the left, with an unusually modern 1970s mosaic behind the altar depicting St. John preaching on the Montenegrin coast) facing the Orthodox **Holy Trinity Church,** with gorgeous and colorful Orthodox decorations inside. Beyond that is a huge **citadel** that's imposing on the outside but dull on the inside; it's not worth paying to tour its museum of model ships, antiquarium (old library), restaurant, and less-than-thrilling sea views.

Sveti Stefan

Like a mirage hovering just offshore, the famously exclusive luxury hotel that makes up the resort peninsula of Sveti Stefan beckons curious travelers to come, see, snap a photo...and then wish they'd spent more time elsewhere. While scenic, there's not much to actually experience at Sveti Stefan (unless you've got more than a thousand bucks to rent a room); while it's a great photo op, it disappoints many who make the trip.

Once an actual, living town (connected to the mainland only by a narrow, natural causeway), Sveti Stefan was virtually abandoned after World War II. The Yugoslav government developed it into a giant resort hotel in the 1950s. As old homes were converted to hotel rooms, the novelty of the place—and its sterling location, surrounded by pebbly beaches and lush scenery—began to attract some seriously wealthy guests.

During this resort's heyday in the 1960s and 1970s, it ranked alongside Cannes and St-Tropez as *the* place to see and be seen on Europe's beaches. You could rent a room, a house, an entire block of houses, or even the entire peninsula. Anonymity was vigilantly protected, as the nicest "rooms" had their own private pools (away from public scrutiny), lockable gates, and security guards. Lured by Sveti Stefan's promise of privacy, celebrities, rock stars, royalty, and dignitaries famously engaged in bidding wars to decide who'd be granted access to the best suites: Whoever put the most money in a sealed envelope and slipped it to the manager, won. (According to local legend, Sly Stallone's money talked.) Guests were pam-

MONTENEGRO

pered—indulged no matter how outrageous their requests. Sophia Loren, Kirk Douglas, Doris Day, and Claudia Schiffer are just a few of the big names who basked on Sveti Stefan's beaches.

By the late 2000s, Sveti Stefan had experienced a dramatic decline. The Yugoslav Wars scared visitors away, its cachet faded, and the resort grew a bit rough around the edges. Then the Indian company Aman Resorts swept in with ambitious plans to restore the island to its former status as one of the world's most exclusive, crème-de-la-crème resorts (www.aman.com). These days, no-neck thugs guard the causeway, letting only guests (no exceptions) cross over into the fantasy world of Sveti Stefan. If you're desperate to check it out, you can reserve a table at the expensive restaurant. If you want to relax on the beaches flanking the causeway, most areas charge €30-50 per person for the day, but there are a few free areas—ask the guard for pointers.

Even if you can't enter the peninsula, let your imagination run as you gaze upon it. Strolling through the dead town, peeking through gates, visitors hope to spot a withered old celebrity who forgot to go home. "Rooms" come with varying degrees of privacy (each more expensive than the last): no fence, small fence, big fence. At the far end is the biggest and most famous "suite," where guests have an entire corner of the peninsula to themselves. At the top of the peninsula is a big Russian Orthodox church and a smaller Serbian Orthodox church—though both are little more than hotel decorations today.

Across the water from Sveti Stefan, on its own little cove, is one of Tito's former vacation villas (Villa Miločer, also part of the Aman resort). From here, you can enjoy the promenade that runs from the beach in front of the villa and to the next cove; eventually, this path will let you stroll along the water all the way to Budva.

Getting to Sveti Stefan: Sveti Stefan is just three miles beyond Budva. Coming around the bay from Budva (following signs toward *Bar*), you'll pass above the peninsula on the main road, watching for the well-marked pullout on the right that offers classic views. After snapping your photos, if you want to get closer, continue down and turn off to the right, following signs to *Hotel Sveti Stefan;* you can park in the pay lot and walk along the beach as far as the causeway.

From Sveti Stefan to Dubrovnik: Figure 1.5 hours to the Croatian border (if you go via Tivat—rather than Kotor—and use the shortcut ferry across the Bay of Kotor, described on page 119), then another 45 minutes to Dubrovnik.

BOSNIA-HERZEGOVINA

Bosna i Hercegovina

BOSNIA-HERZEGOVINA

The 1990s weren't kind to Bosnia-Herzegovina: War. Destruction. Genocide. But apart from the tragic way it separated from Yugoslavia, the country has long been—and remains—a remarkable place, with ruggedly beautiful terrain, a unique mix of cultures and faiths, kind and welcoming people who pride themselves on their hospitality, and some of the most captivating sightseeing in southeastern Europe.

Little Bosnia-Herzegovina is a country with three faiths, three languages, and two alphabets. While the rest of Yugoslavia has splintered into countries dominated by one ethnicity, Bosnia remains an uneasy mix of scattered communities, with large contingents of all three major Yugoslav groups: Muslim Bosniaks, Eastern Orthodox Serbs, and Catholic Croats. These same three factions fought each other in that brutal war several decades ago, and today they're still working on reconciliation.

A visit here offers a fascinating opportunity to sample the cultures of these three major faiths within a relatively small area. In the same day, you can inhale incense in a mystical-feeling Serbian Orthodox church, hear the subtle clicking of rosary beads in a Roman Catholic church, and listen to the Muslim call to prayer echo across a skyline pricked by minarets. Few places in Europe—or the world—cram so much diversity into such a small area.

About half of the people in Bosnia are "Bosniaks"—that is, Muslims. Travel in Bosnia offers an illuminating and unique glimpse into a culture that's both devoutly Muslim and fully European. Here, just a short drive from the touristy Dalmatian Coast, you can step into a mosque and learn about Islam directly from a Muslim. The country also holds one of the most important pilgrimage sites of the Roman Catholic world: Međugorje, where six residents have reported seeing visions of the Virgin Mary.

Bosnian coffee *(bosanska kafa)* is not just a drink, but a complex ritual that captures this culture's deliberate, stop-and-smell-the-tulips approach to life. Similar to what you might call "Turkish coffee," this unfiltered brew is prepared—and enjoyed—according to a very specific routine: The fine grounds are stirred with water in

Bosnia-Herzegovina

Bosnia-Herzegovina Political Regions

☐ Republika Srpska

☐ Muslim-Croat Federation

a small copper-plated kettle with a long, straight handle (called a *džezva*). When it's ready to drink, it's done slo-o-o-owly: Carefully decant the coffee—easy now, don't pour off too many grounds—into a small ceramic cup. If you take sugar, put the sugar cube in the cup first, then pour the coffee over it. Sip your coffee gradually, and swirl the cup periodically to agitate and recaffeinate your brew. (If it's prepared—and drunk—properly, you won't even wind up with mud at the bottom of the cup.) Nibble on the Turkish delight candy *(rahatlokum)* that usually accompanies Bosnian coffee, and take time to chat with your travel partner or a new Bosnian friend. The point is not to slam down caffeine, but to have an excuse to slow your pulse and focus on where you are and who you're with.

Bosnian coffee is just one of the many facets of local culture that were adopted from the Ottomans (from today's Turkey) who ruled here for centuries. Thanks largely to this influence, Bosnian culture is permeated with a deep and abiding soulfulness that's rare in Europe. The Bosnian language features an entire lexicon of words that have no clear translation in other tongues or cultures.

Sarajevans embrace the concept of *raja*, meaning an unpretentious humility that stems from being one with a community or a circle of friends. *Merak* is enjoyment, particularly a relaxed atmosphere that arises when you're among friends—perhaps while listening to *sevdah* music (explained below) and sipping Bosnian coffee. Enjoying the company of friends while going out for snacks is called *mezetluk* (related to the Greek *mezedes*, or tapas-like small plates). And the insult *papak* (literally "hoof") means primitive, naive, tacky, or generally "outsider"—such as wearing white socks with dark shoes (a stereotypical Bosnian faux pas).

My favorite Bosnian word is *ćejf* (pronounced "chayf"), which means a sense of well-being while engaged in a highly idiosyncratic routine. These rituals—from the way someone spins their worry beads, to their own unique procedure for preparing and drinking coffee or smoking a water pipe, to a dervish whirling in a worshipful trance—might be considered "OCD" (or simply "annoying") by many Americans...but Bosnians understand that it's simply *ćejf*. As long as your *ćejf* is not hurting anyone, it's tolerated—because everyone has one.

Sevdah—sometimes called "the Bosnian blues"—is a traditional folk music that mingles powerful emotions: sad and happy, convivial and nostalgic. Bosnians explain how the passionate, mournful strains of *sevdah* (which sounds distinctly eastern) pair perfectly with falling in love, drinking with friends, or contemplating loss. *Sevdah* is also the word for a poignant, melancholic mood—sort of the counterpoint to *merak*. Balancing these moods, Bosniaks explain, is key to emotional satisfaction.

To strike up a conversation, ask your new Bosnian friend to tell you more about what any of these terms means. All of them are examples of how Bosnians celebrate the "little things" that make life worth living...things that mainstream American and European cultures, all too often, see as barriers to progress.

In keeping with their generally relaxed culture, Bosnians are known for their gregarious sense of hospitality and their sharp sense of humor. Even during the darkest days of the war, they found ways to joke about the horrors unfolding around them. And today, they're quick to chuckle at their complicated political system and shambolic economy. Pointing to an ATM, your new Bosnian friend may say, "That's what we call our 'wailing wall.'" And they like to quip about their unfortunate circumstances in life: "Just our luck. Bosnia has so many Muslims—but no oil."

This unique Muslim culture seems fitting in this porous and mountainous land, where streams and rivers trickle endlessly. After all, the very name "Bosnia" comes from a term that means "running water" or "saturated"—and Muslim culture prizes constantly flowing water. While Christians bless still water and call it holy, for Muslims, the power of nature is in its movement; they prefer water to be continually flowing, cleansing, replenishing, circulating. Just as a dervish whirls to connect with the spirituality of the earth and the heavens, so, too, should water be in motion. When the Ottomans arrived here from their Turkish homeland, they must have felt right at home.

Bosnia rearranges your mental furniture more than any other country in this book. It offers an enticing glimpse at a completely different, very eastern worldview. And it comes with some in-your-face lessons about recent history.

While repairs are ongoing, you'll still be confronted by vivid and thought-provoking scars of the Yugoslav Wars, especially outside of the tourist zones. Poignant roadside memorials to fallen soldiers, burned-out husks of buildings, unmistakable starburst patterns in the pavement, and bullet holes in walls are a constant reminder that the country is still recovering—physically and psychologically. Driving through the countryside, you'll pass between Muslim, Croat, and Serb towns—each one decorated with its own provocative sectarian symbols. Bosnia teaches an essential lesson about how real—and destructive—war and interethnic strife truly are.

Of all the former Yugoslav states, Bosnia is where you'll sense the most nostalgia for communist-era leader Marshal Tito (at least, in the Bosniak-dominated parts of Bosnia, like Mostar and Sarajevo). This is likely because Bosniaks suffered the most from the breakup of Yugoslavia. It was only under Tito—who made it clear that ethnic division mattered far less than Yugoslav unity—that Bosniaks felt protected and respected.

And there's another throwback to the past here: In Bosnia, you'll be exposed to more cigarette smoke than in most of Europe. Hotels and restaurants permit smoking to an unusual degree.

In this book, I focus on a few user-friendly Bosnian destinations within easy reach of the Dalmatian Coast: the Turkish-flavored city of Mostar (with its restored Old Bridge—one of Europe's most inspiring sights), some nearby attractions offering a more complete view of Herzegovina (Blagaj, Počitelj, and Stolac), the Catholic shrine at Međugorje, and—just over the Croatian border—an excellent Roman museum near Metković. A longer trip

Bosnia-Herzegovina Almanac

Official Name: Bosna i Hercegovina (abbreviated "BiH")—that's Bosnia and Herzegovina, the country's two regions. For simplicity, I generally call the whole country "Bosnia" in this book.

Snapshot History: Bosnia-Herzegovina's early history is similar to the rest of the region: Illyrians, Romans, and Slavs (oh, my!). In the late 15th century, Turkish rulers from the Ottoman Empire began a 400-year domination of the country. Many of the Ottomans' subjects converted to Islam, and their descendants remain Muslims today. Bosnia-Herzegovina became part of the Austro-Hungarian Empire in 1878, then Yugoslavia after World War I, until it declared independence in the spring of 1992. The bloody war that ensued came to an end in 1995. (For details, see the Understanding Yugoslavia chapter.)

Population: About 3.9 million. (There were about 100,000 identified casualties of the Yugoslav Wars in the 1990s, but many estimates of total casualties are double that number.) Someone who lives in Bosnia-Herzegovina, regardless of ethnicity, is called a "Bosnian." A southern Slav who practices Islam is called a "Bosniak." Today, about half of all Bosnians are Bosniaks (Muslims), about a third are Orthodox Serbs, and nearly 15 percent are Catholic Croats.

Area: 19,741 square miles (about the size of West Virginia). In both size and population, Bosnia is comparable to Croatia.

Geography: Bosnia and Herzegovina are two distinct regions that share the same mountainous country. Bosnia constitutes the majority of the country (in the north, with a continental climate), while Herzegovina is the southern tip (about a fifth of the total area, with a hotter Mediterranean climate). The nation's capital, Sarajevo, has an estimated 310,000 people; Mostar is Herzegovina's biggest

from Dalmatia—and well worth the trek—is the Bosnian capital of Sarajevo, with a spectacular mountain-valley setting, a multilayered history, powerful wartime stories, and a resilient populace of proud Sarajevans eager to show you their city.

Bosnia is highly recommended as a detour—both geographical and cultural—from the Croatian and Slovenian mainstream. Inquisitive visitors come away from a visit to Bosnia with a more nuanced understanding of the former Yugoslavia. And Bosnia offers lower prices and a warmer welcome than you'll find on the Croatian coast. Overcome your jitters and dive in.

BOSNIAN HISTORY

With its mountainous landscape, remote from the more mainline areas of the western Balkans, Bosnia's evolution has followed

city (with approximately 130,000 people) and unofficial capital.

Red Tape: To enter Bosnia-Herzegovina, Americans and Canadians need only a passport.

Economy: The country's economy has struggled since the war—the per-capita GDP is just over $10,000, and the official unemployment rate is around 25 percent.

Currency: The official currency is the Convertible Mark (Konvertibilna Marka, abbreviated KM locally, BAM internationally). The official exchange rate is $1 = about 1.50 KM. But merchants are usually willing to take euros, and (in Mostar) they'll often accept Croatian kunas, roughly converting prices with a simple formula: 2 KM = €1 = 7 kn (= about $1.20).

Telephones: Bosnia-Herzegovina's country code is 387. If calling from another country, first dial the international access code (00 in Europe, 011 in the US), then 387, then the area code (minus the initial zero), then the number.

Flag: The flag of Bosnia-Herzegovina is a blue field with a yellow triangle along the top edge. The three points of the triangle represent Bosnia-Herzegovina's three peoples (Bosniaks, Croats, Serbs), and the triangle itself resembles the physical shape of the country. A row of white stars underscores the longest side of the triangle. These stars—and the yellow-and-blue color scheme—echo the flag of the European Union (a nod to the EU's efforts to bring peace to the region). While this compromise flag sounds like a nice idea, almost no Bosnian embraces it; each group has its own unofficial but highly prized symbols and flags (such as the fleur-de-lis for the Bosniaks, the red-and-white checkerboard shield for the Croats, and the cross with the four C's for the Serbs)—many of which offend the other groups.

a unique course. Even in the present day, the people of Bosnia struggle with being outsiders—afloat on an oddball cultural island flanked by the Roman Catholic West (Croatia) and the Orthodox East (Serbia), borrowing elements from both but not fully belonging to either.

After periods of rule by the Illyrians and the Romans, Bosnia fostered its own thriving Slavic civilization during the Middle Ages. The local Bogomils were a homegrown branch of Christianity that was neither Catholic nor Orthodox—and was viewed with suspicion by both faiths. Literally "dear to God," the Bogomil faith was simple, ascetic, and somewhat mystic, combining elements of Slavic, Illyrian, and Celtic traditions. The Bogomils—who comprised a majority of the population of medieval Bosnia—had a thriving civilization. Vivid artifacts of the Bogomil kingdom still survive, such as their engraved burial grave markers, called *stećaks* (some of the best-preserved are in Stolac, near Mostar—see page 191).

When the Ottomans (from today's Turkey) took over this land in the 15th century, they tolerated different faiths, but offered generous economic and political incentives to those who converted to Islam. In negotiating their religious freedoms with the sultans, Bosnia's Roman Catholics (who identified as Croats) and Eastern Orthodox (who identified as Serbs) both had the support of larger church hierarchies outside of Bosnia. But the Bogomils had no bargaining power, and were more likely to swap one monotheistic faith for another—creating the Muslim South Slav ethnicity that would come to be known as "Bosniak."

Under the Ottomans, Bosnia flourished. The Ottoman sultans invested in infrastructure (primarily bridges—including Mostar's Old Bridge—and fountains) and architecture, including many mosques, hammams (baths), caravanserais (inns), madrassas (theological schools), and so on. Bosnian Muslims rose through the ranks of the empire, becoming military generals, religious leaders, beloved poets, and even grand viziers (advisers to the sultans).

After four centuries of rule, the Ottoman Empire entered a steep decline. The Bosniak military hero Husein Gradaščević—nicknamed "The Dragon of Bosnia" (Zmaj od Bosne)—led an armed uprising in the 1830s. Though he died in battle, his movement eventually brought about the end of the archaic Ottoman system of rule in Bosnia, leading to a greater degree of autonomy.

But Bosnia was bound for even bigger changes. Unable to manage their vast holdings, in 1878 the Ottomans passed control of Bosnia-Herzegovina to their Habsburg rival, the Austro-Hungarian Empire (which already controlled neighboring Croatia and Slovenia). The Habsburgs quickly moved to modernize Bosnia, erecting buildings and investing in infrastructure. Sarajevo, Mostar, and many other Bosnian cities still show the impressive results of these efforts, which pulled Bosnia from their antiquated Ottoman ways into the modern world. Habsburg rule piped in mainstream European culture for the first time. Now Bosnian urbanites and aristocrats exchanged their ornate Turkish gowns for snazzy Austrian business suits...which they wore with their old fezzes and turbans.

Of course, not everybody bought what the Habsburgs were selling. Fierce underground resistance movements—such as the Black Hand—were determined to bring about self-rule for the South Slavs. Just 40 years after the Habsburgs took over, their empire began to topple—losing a Great War that began when the Habsburg heir, Archduke Franz Ferdinand, was assassinated in Sarajevo.

Following World War I, Bosnia was swept up in the movement to create a union of the South Slavs. The original incarnation of Yugoslavia, called "the Kingdom of the Serbs, Croats, and Slovenes," ignored the Bosniaks both in name and in political influence—they were merely along for the ride.

During World War II, Bosnia was part of the so-called "Independent State of Croatia" (run by the Nazis' puppet Ustaše government). Hitler's right-hand man, Heinrich Himmler, came to Bosnia to assess where the Bosniaks might fit into the Führer's ethnic vision. He determined that they were "Croats with Muslim culture"—that is, good ol' Aryans, who would be conscripted to fight. Himmler and the Ustaše leader, Ante Pavelić (a Bosnian-born Croat), squabbled over whether the Bosniaks would fight for the SS or the Ustaše. Ultimately they created an SS Hanjar/ Handschar unit (named for a Turkish knife), issuing the conscripts a Germanic-style uniform with a ceremonial fez. The unit fought fiercely against Tito's Partisan Army, and participated in the Ustaše's genocidal efforts against Serbs, Jews, and other "undesirables." But as the war wore on, more and more of these troops became disillusioned with the Nazi cause, and deserted in large numbers.

Some of the most dramatic WWII battles between the Yugoslav Partisans and the Nazis took place here in Bosnia. One of the most famous was the Battle of the Neretva, in which Tito ingeniously saved more than 4,000 of his wounded troops—effectively turning the tide of the war.

The postwar communist country of Yugoslavia was born in the Bosnian town of Jajce on November 29, 1943, when Partisan generals met to outline the future of a hoped-for post-Nazi state. But in the new incarnation of Yugoslavia, many Bosniaks still felt like second-class citizens. Local Muslims recall that Yugoslav government-issued textbooks reinforced negative stereotypes. For example, they might say, "Sasha [a typically Serb name] is working," but "Mujo [a typically Muslim name] is a bad boy."

Even after the outbreak of violence between breakaway republics Slovenia and Croatia and Serb-dominated Yugoslavia in 1991, things stayed strangely calm in Bosnia. But when the Bosnian conflict finally erupted in 1992, it was war of the most brutal kind. A three-way war exploded between Bosnian Croats (supported by Croatia proper), Bosnian Serbs (supported by Serbia proper), and Bosniaks (who, caught in the crossfire, realized they had no real European allies). The early to mid-1990s saw the worst human, architectural, and cultural devastation in Bosnian history. Sarajevo, Srebrenica, and Mostar became synonymous with sectarian strife, horrific sieges, and shocking genocide. (For more details on the war, the Understanding Yugoslavia chapter.)

The Dayton Peace Accords that ended the conflict here in 1995 gerrymandered the nation into three separate regions: the Federation of Bosnia and Herzegovina (FBiH, shared by Bosniaks and Croats, roughly in the western and central parts of the country), the Republika Srpska (RS, dominated by Serbs, generally to the north and east), and the Brčko District (BD, a tiny corner of the country, with a mix of the ethnicities). For the most part, each of the three native ethnic groups stay in "their" part of this divided country, but tourists can move freely among them.

On your visit, tune into the many ways that the Bosniaks, Croats, and Serbs of Bosnia are working to coexist. To satisfy the country's various factions, the currency uses both the Roman and the Cyrillic alphabets, and bills have different figureheads and symbols (some bills feature Bosniaks, others Serbs). Until recently, the alphabet used on road signs changed with the territory: Roman alphabet in Muslim and Croat areas, Cyrillic alphabet in Serb lands. Now all road signs throughout Bosnia-Herzegovina are required to appear in both alphabets—though that doesn't prevent vandals from spray-painting over the alphabet they don't like. License plates also used different alphabets, but this led to vandalism. Today's license plates use only letters that are common to both alphabets.

Towns with mixed populations are either effectively divided in half, or have buildings clearly marked with symbols indicating the ethnicity of the occupant. Small-town schoolhouses often operate "two schools under one roof," with separate entrances and staggered shifts for the Bosniak and Croat kids...who, virtually from birth, are constantly reminded they are very different from each other. In some towns, a beautifully restored Orthodox church may sit across from the battered footprint of a long-gone mosque, or vice versa.

Bosnia has a central government, but each population group also has its own autonomous government and sub-agencies, resulting in four essentially redundant bureaucracies. The country is also divided into 10 state-like cantons, each of which also has some governmental authority. Imagine the inefficiency. On top of all this, Bosnia is still navigating the complex transition from communism to capitalism, and rebuilding from a devastating war. It's a miracle that things here work at all.

Fundamentalist Islam in Bosnia?

Islam is a hot topic in today's Europe, where some citizens scapegoat Muslim immigrants. And even though Bosnia's Muslims are indigenous, they're not immune to criticism—especially from their Serb and Croat rivals. While Bosniaks have a long history as a peace-loving people, critics allege that elements of the population are experimenting with some alarming fundamentalist Islamic ideologies.

These allegations do have some basis in fact. During the war and genocide of the 1990s, many Bosniaks felt abandoned by Europe and the US, who were too timid to step in and "take sides" to end the violence. In his people's darkest hour, desperate Bosnian President Alija Izetbegović recruited assistance from the only group willing to offer help: Muslim fundamentalists from the Middle East and North Africa. Several hundred mujahideen (Islamic jihadists) came to Bosnia to train Bosniak soldiers—and participated in bloody massacres of Serbs and Croats. They brought with them the dangerous ideas of Wahhabism, an ultraconservative movement bent on "purifying" Islam, often through violent means. According to reports, Izetbegović was even in contact with Osama bin Laden. In some cases, the mujahideen offered donations to widows of *šehids* (Bosniak martyrs).

Today, while waning, these groups' influence persists. At the legitimate end of the spectrum, Muslim countries have helped to fund the postwar reconstruction of Bosnia—especially the rebuilding of mosques and madrassas. Just as the end of atheistic, communist Yugoslav rule kick-started a passion for Catholicism in Croatia and the Orthodox faith in Serbia, many Muslims in Bosnia are today actively pursuing their faith. You may even see women wearing traditional Muslim headscarves—a rare sight before the war, when most Bosniaks dressed just like their Serb and Croat neighbors. (But note that many veiled women are likely Muslim tourists from elsewhere.)

And what about those mujahideen fighters? Most left the country after the war, as dictated by the Dayton Peace Accords. But small pockets of Wahhabists still live in remote areas high in the mountains. The vast majority of practicing Muslims in Bosnia explicitly denounce the Wahhabists—just as any peaceful, moderate country looks with concern upon its lunatic fringe.

Nearly 25 years later, the delicate compromises that were necessary to end a horrifying war have become almost too complicated to maintain. For Bosnia-Herzegovina to fully recover, all three groups must learn to truly set aside their differences and work together. Pessimists (who are abundant in this region) don't like Bosnia's chances, and Bosnian Serbs still talk loudly about secession (Republika Srpska's president, Milorad Dodik, is an outspoken separatist). But others see signs of hope, such as the young people from the three faiths now beginning to cautiously intermingle, as their ancestors did for centuries. Will Bosniak, Serb, and Croat youth manage to transcend the fear and anger that tainted their parents' and grandparents' country in the 20th century? That history is yet to be written.

BOSNIAN FOOD

Bosnia-Herzegovina dines on grilled meat, stewed vegetables, soft cheeses, and other foods you may think of as "Turkish" or "Greek." On menus, look for the word *domaća*—"homemade." Another key term is *pod saća,* which means "under the bell" (similar to *peka* in Croatia); this means that it has been slow cooked under a copper lid covered with hot coals. For a rundown of the most common items you'll eat in Bosnia—and throughout the Balkans—see the "Balkan Flavors" sidebar.

Dolma is a bell pepper stuffed with minced meat, vegetables, and rice. A *sarma* or *sarmica* is similar, but stuffed in cabbage leaves rather than in a pepper, while *japrak* is stuffed grape leaves. *Begova ćorba* ("nobleman's stew") is a meaty vegetable soup. *Grah* is bean soup. And one Bosnian institution—which you'll see at roadside truck stops across the country—is the whole lamb grilled on a spit.

While Balkan cuisine favors meat, a nice veggie complement is *đuveđ* (JOO-vedge)—a spicy mix of stewed vegetables, flavored with tomatoes and peppers. And the best salad option is *šopska salata*—a Greek-style salad of tomatoes, cucumbers, onions, and peppers, smothered in grated feta-like *sirene* cheese. *Srpska salata* ("Serb salad") is often the same thing, but may have extra cheese.

Bosnian desserts—typically sweetened with honey rather than sugar—are another local treat. Drop by a sweets shop and peruse your options. *Baklava,* a phyllo-dough pastry with nuts and honey, is a familiar choice. *Kadaif* is similar, but made with shredded sheets of dough. *Tulumba* is a pastry cylinder drenched in honey, and *tufahija* is an apple stuffed with walnuts, soaked in honey, and topped with whipped cream. *Smokvaća* is a dense, very sweet fig pie. You'll also see blocks of nougat-like *halva,* made from sesame paste. And every cup of Bosnian coffee comes with a Turkish delight candy.

Bosnia produces some wine, but it's mostly consumed domestically. Sarajevso Pivo, brewed in the capital, is the favored brand of beer. In Bosnia, "coffee" is *kafa* (not *kava,* as in Croatia and Slovenia). While you can easily get espresso-style coffee, *bosanska kafa* (unfiltered "Bosnian coffee") is more local—and more fun to drink. (For tips on this ritual, see earlier.)

Balkan Flavors

All of the countries of the Balkan Peninsula—from Slovenia to Greece—have several foods in common: The Ottomans who

controlled much of this territory for centuries imported some goodies that remained standard fare here long after they left town. Whether you're in Bosnia-Herzegovina, Slovenia, Croatia, Montenegro, or Serbia, it's worth seeking out some of these local tastes.

A popular, cheap fast food you'll see everywhere is *burek* (BOO-rehk)—phyllo dough filled with meat, cheese, spinach, or apples. *Burek* rivals pizza-by-the-slice as the most popular takeaway snack food in southeastern Europe. The best *burek* is *pod sača*—cooked under a baking lid.

Grilled meats are a staple of Balkan cuisine. You'll most often see *ćevapčići* (cheh-VAHP-chee-chee), or simply *ćevapi* (cheh-VAH-pee)—minced meat (typically a mix of lamb and beef) formed into a sausage-link shape, then grilled. There are variations: Sarajevo-style *(sarajevski ćevapi)* is typically eaten with grilled onions and stuffed into a pita-like flatbread called *somun;* Banja Luka-style *(banjalučki ćevapi)* is one long, continuous *ćevap* with hot peppers on the side.

Ražnjići (RAZH-nyee-chee) is small pieces of steak on a skewer, like a shish kebab. *Pljeskavica* (plehs-kah-VEET-suh) is similar to *ćevapčići,* except the meat is in the form of a hamburger-like patty. *Pileći* is chicken, and *piščančje* is grilled chicken breast. *Sudžukice* are sausages, and *ćufte* are meatballs.

You just can't eat any of this stuff without the ever-present condiment *ajvar* (EYE-var). Made from red bell pepper and eggplant, *ajvar* is like ketchup with a kick. Many Americans pack a jar of this distinctive sauce to remember the flavors of the Balkans when they get back home. (You may even be able to find it at specialty grocery stores in the US—look for "eggplant/red pepper spread.")

Particularly in Bosnia, another side dish you'll see is the soft, spreadable—and tasty—cheese called *kajmak. Lepinje* is a pita-like grilled bread, which is often wrapped around *ćevapčići* or *pljeskavica* to make a sandwich. *Uštipci* is a fry bread that's especially popular throughout Bosnia-Herzegovina.

Ajvar, kajmak, lepinje, and diced raw onions are the perfect complement to a "mixed grill" of various meats on a big platter—the quintessence of Balkan cuisine on one plate.

BOSNIAN LANGUAGE

Technically, Bosnia-Herzegovina has three languages—Bosnian, Serbian, and Croatian. But all three are mutually intelligible variants of what was until recently considered a single language: Serbo-Croatian. The Croatian survival phrases on page 211 will work just fine throughout Bosnia-Herzegovina. Bosniaks and Croats use basically the same Roman alphabet we do, while Serbs use the Cyrillic alphabet. You'll see both alphabets on currency, official documents, and road signs, but the Roman alphabet predominates in virtually every destination covered in this book. Most people also speak English.

MOSTAR & NEARBY

Mostar • Blagaj • Počitelj • Metković • Stolac • Međugorje

Mostar (MOH-star) encapsulates the best and the worst of the former Yugoslavia. During the Tito years, its residents—Catholic Croats, Orthodox Serbs, and Muslim Bosniaks—enjoyed an idyllic mingling of cultures, all living together in harmony. Their differences were spanned by an Old Bridge that epitomized an optimistic vision of a Yugoslavia in which ethnic differences were accepted and celebrated. But then, as the country unraveled in the early 1990s, Mostar was gripped by a gory three-way war among those same peoples...and that famous bridge crumbled into the Neretva River.

Mostar is still rebuilding, and the bullet holes and destroyed buildings are ugly reminders that the last time you saw this place,

it was probably on the nightly news. Western visitors may also be struck by the immediacy of the Muslim culture that permeates Mostar, where minarets share the horizon with church steeples. During the Ottomans' 400-year control of this region, many Slavic subjects converted to Islam (see sidebar on page 149). And, although they retreated in the late 19th century, the Ottomans left behind a rich architectural, cultural, and religious legacy that has forever shaped Mostar. Five times each day, loud-speakers on minarets crackle to life, and the call to prayer warbles through the streets. In many parts of the city, you'd swear you were in Turkey.

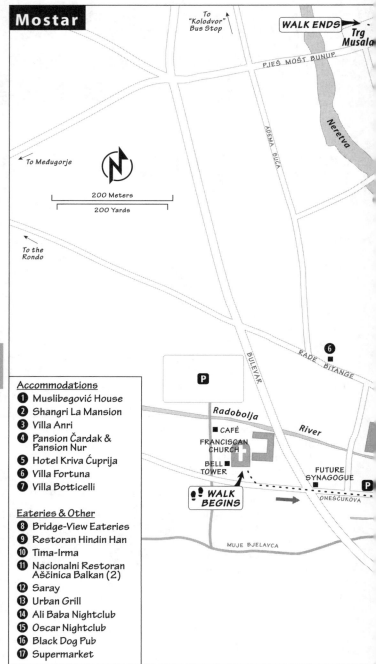

Mostar

To "Kolodvor" Bus Stop

WALK ENDS → Trg Musala

PJEŠ MOST BUNUP

ADEMA BUĆA

Neretva

To Medugorje

200 Meters
200 Yards

To the Rondo

RADE BITANGE

6

BULEVAR

P

Radobolja

River

CAFÉ

FRANCISCAN CHURCH

BELL TOWER

FUTURE SYNAGOGUE

P

ONEŠĆUKOVA

WALK BEGINS

MUJE BJELAVCA

Accommodations
1 Muslibegović House
2 Shangri La Mansion
3 Villa Anri
4 Pansion Čardak & Pansion Nur
5 Hotel Kriva Ćuprija
6 Villa Fortuna
7 Villa Botticelli

Eateries & Other
8 Bridge-View Eateries
9 Restoran Hindin Han
10 Tima-Irma
11 Nacionalni Restoran Aščinica Balkan (2)
12 Saray
13 Urban Grill
14 Ali Baba Nightclub
15 Oscar Nightclub
16 Black Dog Pub
17 Supermarket

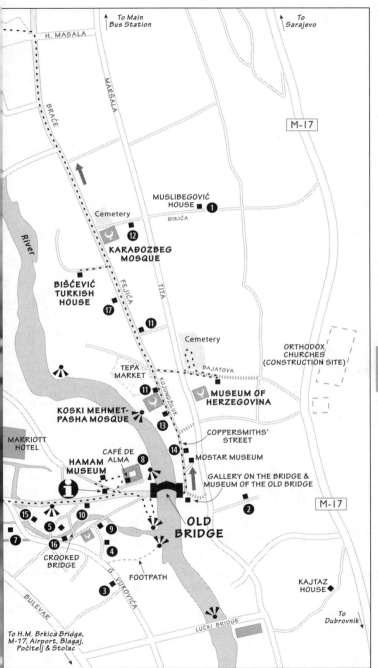

Despite the scars of war, Mostar's setting is stunning: straddling the banks of the gorgeous Neretva River, with tributaries and waterfalls carving their way through the rocky landscape. The sightseeing—mosques, old Turkish-style houses, and that spine-tingling Old Bridge—is more engaging than much of what you'll find in Croatia or Slovenia. And it's cheap: Hotels, food, and museums cost less than half of what you'll pay in Dubrovnik or Ljubljana.

In this chapter, I've also included some worthwhile attractions near Mostar: the river spring and whirling dervish house at Blagaj, the striking fortified hill town of Počitelj, and workaday Stolac, which sits upon some very impressive history. The top Croat sight in Bosnia-Herzegovina is Međugorje, where Catholic pilgrims flock from around the world to hear tales of a Virgin Mary apparition. And just over the Croatian border, near Metković, is a fine Roman museum. All of these places are within a half-hour's drive of Mostar; take your pick for the drive between Mostar and coastal destinations.

While a visit to Mostar was depressing not that long ago, the city gets more uplifting all the time: Mostarians are rebuilding at an impressive pace, tentatively reintegrating, and working hard to make Mostar tourist-friendly. Mostar is well on its way to reclaiming its status as one of the premier destinations in the former Yugoslavia.

PLANNING YOUR TIME

Bosnia-Herzegovina is a major cultural detour on your Dalmatian vacation—but it's easy to reach, just a three-hour drive or four-hour bus ride from Dubrovnik or Split. To fit a Mostar overnight into your itinerary, consider a round-trip plan that takes you south along the coast, then back north via Bosnia-Herzegovina (for example, Split-Hvar-Korčula-Dubrovnik-Mostar-back to Split).

Mostar's Old Town is packed with day-trippers at midday, but empty in the morning and evening. You can get a good feel for Mostar in just a few hours, but a full day—and, ideally, an overnight—gives you time to linger and ponder. My self-guided walk provides a framework for a visit of any duration. With extra time, venture to the western (Croat) part of the city, which most tourists miss.

If you're day-tripping from Dubrovnik (a common plan), you have several choices. The easiest option is to hire a driver, or take a package excursion with a company based in Dubrovnik. If you have your own car, Mostar is a fairly easy side-trip (with the option of going down and back by different routes, outlined in this chapter)—or it works great on the way to Sarajevo, or even for those heading overland to Split. In summer, it's typically possible to do a same-day round-trip using public buses (though it's a long day)—

but, because the specific bus connections change from year to year, carefully check your options.

GETTING AROUND HERZEGOVINA

By Car: Coming with your own car gives you maximum flexibility, and a number of interesting routes connect Mostar to the coast (but be aware that GPS is often wrong in Mostar; for detailed route information, see "Route Tips for Drivers," later). If you do plan to drive here, let your car-rental company know in advance, to ensure you have the appropriate paperwork for crossing the border. If you're not up for driving yourself, consider splurging on a **driver** to bring you here (for drivers based in Dubrovnik, see the Dubrovnik chapter; for a Mostar-based driver, see "Helpful Hints," later). Drivers may suggest several detours en route. Do your homework to know which ones interest you (for example, Međugorje isn't worth the extra time for most visitors), and don't hesitate to say that you want to just max out on time in Mostar itself.

By Bus: Public buses connect Mostar with destinations on the Dalmatian Coast (particularly Split and Dubrovnik), but doing Mostar as a one-day side-trip from Dubrovnik only works in peak season (June-Aug) due to limited buses; otherwise you'll need to pay for an excursion, drive yourself, or spend the night. For bus details, see "Mostar Connections," later.

By Package Tour: Taking a package excursion from a Dalmatian resort town sounds like an efficient way to visit Mostar or Međugorje. But it has its cons: Count on lots of hours on a crowded bus, listening to a lackluster, multilingual tour guide reading from a script, and precious little time in the destinations themselves. I'd pick an itinerary focusing on Mostar itself, and avoid tours that include a pointless boat trip on the Neretva River or time in Međugorje. Those that add a quick visit to the worthwhile town of Počitelj are a better deal. Ask for details at any travel agency in Dalmatia.

Orientation to Mostar

Mostar (pop. 130,000) fills a basin surrounded by arid mountains and split down the middle by the emerald-green Neretva River. Bosniaks live mostly on the east side of the river (plus a strip on the west bank) and Croats in the modern sprawl to the west—though the populations are beginning to mix again. Virtually all of the sights are in the Bosniak zone, but visitors move freely throughout the city, and don't even notice the division. The cobbled, Turkish-feeling Old Town (called the "Stari Grad" or "Stara Čaršija") surrounds the town's centerpiece, the Old Bridge.

The skyline is pierced by the minarets of various mosques, but none is as big as the two major Catholic (Croat) symbols in town, both erected after the Yugoslav Wars: the giant white cross on the hilltop (marking the place from where Croat forces shelled the Bosniak side of the river, including the Old Bridge); and the enormous (almost 100-foot-tall) bell tower of the Franciscan Church of Sts. Peter and Paul. A monumental Orthodox cathedral on the hillside across the river, destroyed during the war, is now being rebuilt.

A note about safety: You'll see bombed-out buildings everywhere, even in the core of the city. A few are marked with *Warning! Dangerous Ruin* signs; for safety's sake, never wander into any building that appears damaged or deserted. Also, pickpockets operate in the tourist zone; watch your valuables, especially on the Old Bridge.

TOURIST INFORMATION

The virtually worthless TI shares a building with a tour office, but it does give out a free town map and a few other brochures on Mostar and Herzegovina (sporadic hours, a block from the Old Bridge at Rade Bitange 5, tel. 036/580-275, www.turizam.mostar.ba).

ARRIVAL IN MOSTAR

By Bus or Train: The **main bus station** sits next to the giant but mostly deserted **train station,** north of the Old Town on the east side of the river. At the bus station, you'll find ticket windows and a left-luggage counter in the Autoprevoz lobby facing the bus stalls. You can check schedules and buy tickets in this office for most buses *except* the many connections operated by Globtour, whose office is nearby (exit Autoprevoz, turn left, and walk to the end of the bus-station area; look for *Mediteran Tours* sign). Because these two companies don't cooperate well, you may have to check with both to get the complete schedule; most departures with either company are also listed at www.getbybus.com. To find your way to the town center, walk through the bus stalls and parking lot and turn left at the big road, which leads you to the Old Town area in about 15 minutes. A taxi into town costs about 5-10 KM.

It's possible (though unlikely) that you'll arrive at Mostar's secondary bus station, called **"Kolodvor,"** on the west/Croat side of town. From here, it's a dreary 20-minute walk into town: Turn right out of the bus station area, turn left down the busy Dubrovačka street, and head straight to the river (which you can follow south into the Old Town). Globtour buses that stop at Kolodvor will likely continue to the main bus station; those run by other companies probably won't (in either case, ask).

For details on both stations, see "Mostar Connections," later.

By Car: There are two good options for **parking** close to the Old Town, as you approach on the main drag called the Bulevar. For both options, be ready to turn just before the giant church tower. The cheaper, slightly farther option is the "Campanile" parking lot: Turn left on Franjevačka just before the church, then turn right immediately after the bell tower. This takes you to a cheap parking lot (2 KM all day), with pay WCs and café. The nearby church is also the starting point for my self-guided walk.

For a speedy, targeted visit, you can pay more for a parking lot closer to the Old Bridge: Approaching on the Bulevar, just before the church, turn right on Onešćukova and go two short blocks to where it dead-ends at the Old Town cobbles; on the left is a fancy pay lot (4 KM/hour, 20 KM/24 hours).

For tips on driving to Mostar from the Dalmatian Coast, see "Route Tips for Drivers," later.

HELPFUL HINTS

Local Cash: Need Convertible Marks? The most convenient ATM in town is to the left of Fortuna Tours' door, right at the top of Coppersmiths' Street (but on a short visit, you can generally skip a trip to the ATM, as many vendors here also accept Croatian kunas and euros).

Travel Agency: The handy **Fortuna Tours** travel agency, right in the heart of the Old Town (at the top of Coppersmiths' Street), sells all the tourist stuff, can book a local guide or arrange a transfer, and answers basic questions (long hours daily, Kujundžiluk 2, tel. 036/551-887, main office tel. 036/552-197, www.fortuna.ba, headoffice@fortuna.ba).

Local Guides: Hiring a guide is an excellent investment to help you understand Mostar. I've enjoyed working with **Alma Elezović,** a warm-hearted Bosniak who loves sharing her city and her wartime stories with visitors (€20/person, up to €70/group for 2-3-hour tour, mobile 063-282-142, http://almasguidedtours.blogspot.com, aelezovic@gmail.com). If Alma is busy, she may send you with her son **Jaz** (pronounced "yahz"), who speaks perfect English and offers a younger generation's perspective. Other companies around town can arrange for a local guide at extremely reasonable prices (2-hour tour-€30/2 people, €40/4 people, includes entry to mosque and/or Turkish house); try **Fortuna Tours,** listed above.

Local Driver: Ermin Elezović, husband of local guide Alma (see above), is a gregarious, English-speaking driver who enjoys taking visitors on day trips from Mostar. You can also hire him for a transfer between Mostar and destinations anywhere in Croatia (prices for 2 people: €100 for one-way transfer to Sarajevo, €120 one-way to Split or Dubrovnik with a few brief sightseeing stops on the way, €150 one-way to Split airport or the Korčula ferry; also available for longer trips for around €1/

MOSTAR & NEARBY

kilometer—contact Ermin and Alma for help planning a mul-
tiday itinerary; mobile 061-908-597, elezovicermin@gmail.
com).

Sights in Mostar

CENTRAL MOSTAR

Mostar's major sights line up along a handy L-shaped axis. I've
laced them together as an enjoyable orientation walk: From the
Franciscan Church, you'll walk straight until you cross the Old
Bridge. Then you'll turn left and walk basically straight (with a
couple small detours) to the big square at the far end of town. This
walk is designed to help you see both the main tourist zones, and
the parts of workaday Mostar that many visitors miss.

• *Begin at the...*

▲Franciscan Church of Sts. Peter and Paul

In a town of competing religious architectural exclamation points,
this spire is the tallest. The church, which adjoins a working Fran-

ciscan monastery, was built in 1997, after the
fighting subsided (the same year as the big
cross on the hill). The tower, which looks like
a minaret on steroids, is modeled after typical Croatian/Venetian, campanile-style bell
towers. Step inside to see the cavernous interior, still not fully decorated. (Sunday Mass
here is an inspiration.) Downstairs—but often
closed to the public—is another sanctuary,
with naked concrete walls that make it feel
like a bomb shelter, as well as a small museum
documenting the history of Franciscans in
Mostar. Seeing photos of older versions of this
church—one destroyed by WWII fighting in
1945 (when many friars were killed by communists), and the other
destroyed by the Yugoslav Wars in 1992—is a reminder that Mostarians of all stripes have suffered loss over time.

It's possible to ascend the church's 350-foot-tall **bell tower**—
called the "Mostar Peace Bell Tower." You'll ride the elevator up
about 250 feet, then hike up 148 steps around the bells (some of
which were salvaged from the original church) to reach fine views
over the city. They plan to gradually add peace-related exhibits to
the staircase (6 KM, Mon-Sat 9:00-17:00, Sun from 12:00).

• *The church fronts the busy boulevard called the...*

▲Bulevar

"The Boulevard" was once the modern main drag of Mostar. In the early 1990s, this city of Bosniaks, Croats, and Serbs began to fracture under the pressure of politicians' propaganda. In October of 1991, Bosnia-Herzegovina—following Croatia's and Slovenia's example, but without the blessing of its large Serb minority—began a process of splitting from Yugoslavia. Soon after, the Serb-dominated Yugoslav People's Army invaded. Mostar's Bosniaks and Croats joined forces to battle the Serbs and succeeded in claiming the city as their own, forcing out the Serb residents.

But even as they fended off the final, distant bombardments of Serb forces, Mostar's Bosniaks (Muslims) and Croats (Catholics) turned their guns against each other. This street became the front line—and virtually all its buildings were destroyed. The area to the east of here (toward the river) was held by Bosniaks, while the western part of town was Croat territory.

While many of the buildings along here have been rebuilt, some damage is still evident. Stroll a bit, imagining the hell of a split community at war. Neighbors, friends, and even families fought among themselves. Mortar craters in the asphalt leave poignant scars. During those dark war years, the Croats on the hill above laid siege to the Bosniaks on the other side, cutting off electricity, blocking roads, and blaring Croatian rabble-rousing pop music and propaganda speeches from loudspeakers. Through '93 and '94, when the Bosniaks dared to go out, they sprinted past exposed places, for fear of being picked off by a sniper. Local Bosniaks explain, "Night was time to live"—cloaking themselves in black clothes, under cover of darkness. When people were killed along this street, their corpses were sometimes left here for months, because it wasn't safe to retrieve the bodies. Tens of thousands fled, many taking refuge elsewhere in Europe, in the US, and in Canada.

The stories are shocking, and it's difficult to see the war impartially. But looking back on this complicated war, I try not to broadly cast one side as the "aggressors" and another as the "victims." Bosniaks were victimized in Mostar, just as Croats were victimized during the siege of Dubrovnik (explained on page 24). And, as the remains of a destroyed Orthodox cathedral on the hillside above Mostar attest, Serbs also took their turn as victims. Every conflict has many sides, and it's the civilians who often pay the highest toll—no matter their affiliation.

Head down Oneščukova street, across the Bulevar from the church. A few steps down on the left, the vacant lot with the menorah-ornamented metal fence will someday be the **Mostar Synagogue.** While the town's Jewish population has dwindled to a handful of families since World War II, many Jews courageously served as aid workers and intermediaries when Croats and Bosniaks were killing each other. In recognition of their loving help, the community of Mostar gave them this land for a new synagogue.
• *Continue past the synagogue site, walking two short blocks along a row of modern storefronts. Soon, you'll enter the Old Town and follow the canyon of the...*

Radobolja River Valley

Cross the small river called Radobolja, which winds over waterfalls and several mills on its way to join the Neretva, and enter the

city's cobbled historic core (keeping the river on your right). As you step upon the smooth, ankle-twisting river stones, you suddenly become immersed in the Turkish heritage of Mostar. Around you are several fine examples of Mostar's traditional heavy limestone-shingled roofs. From the arrival of the Ottomans all the way through the end of World War II, Mostar had fewer than 15,000 residents—this compact central zone was pretty much all there was to the city. It wasn't until the Tito years that it became industrialized and grew like crazy. As you explore, survey the atmospheric eateries clinging to the walls of the canyon—and choose one for a meal or drink later in the day (I've noted a couple under "Eating in Mostar," later).

Walk straight ahead until you reach a break in the buildings on your right. Belly up to the wall (you may have to squeeze between souvenir stands). The mosque you see across the river is one of 10 in town. Before the Yugoslav Wars there were 36, and before World War II there were even more (many of those damaged or destroyed in World War II were never repaired or replaced, since Tito's communist Yugoslavia discouraged religion). But the recent war inspired Muslims to finally rebuild. Each of the town's reconstructed mosques was financed by a Muslim nation or organization (this one was a gift from an international association for the protection of Islamic heritage). Some critics (read: Croats) allege that these foreign Muslim influences—which generally interpret their faith more strictly than the typically progressive and laid-back Bosniaks—are threatening to flood the country with a rising tide of Islamic fundamentalism. For more on this debate, see page 149.

• *Look upriver. Spanning the river below the mosque (partly obscured by trees) is the...*

▲Crooked Bridge (Kriva Ćuprija)

This miniature Old Bridge was built nearly a decade before its more famous sibling, supposedly to practice for the real deal. Damaged—but not destroyed—during the war, the original bridge was swept away several years later by floods. The bridge you see today is a reconstruction.

• *Continue on the same street deeper into the city center. After a few steps, take a detour to the left, to the area I like to call...*

"Hammam Square"

Heading up this relatively calm eddy off the rushing river of the main tourist strip, you'll emerge into a small square. The glimmering domes mark the hammam, or Turkish bathhouse, which has been turned into an excellent ▲**Hammam Museum** (4 KM, daily May-Sept 9:00-19:00, Oct-April until 17:00). Destroyed in World War II, this was only rebuilt a few years ago by a Turkish organization (as if restaking their original Ottoman claim here). You can step inside under the beautiful soaring dome and read helpful English explanations of Turkish bathing culture. You'll also see several artifacts that were used in baths like this one: soaps, tea sets, artfully crafted copper soap boxes, towels, and so on.

As you face the hammam, notice the long building to your right. If you go in the door near the left end of this building, then cross straight through the courtyard, you'll pop out at a **terrace** where various restaurants offer mediocre food with stunning views of the Old Bridge—a great spot for a floodlit dinner.

Near the right end of that same long building is one of Mostar's best-kept secrets. At **Café de Alma,** soulful Jaz ("yahz") loves to explain the rich heritage and traditions around Bosnian coffee (which you may think of as "Turkish coffee"). For 2 KM, he'll show you his coffee roaster (the only one in Mostar), then grind and pour you a cup of Bosnian coffee. The coffee is good, but learning about this important facet of Bosnian culture is even better. He also has teas and handmade syrups for refreshing drinks, and sells bags of his coffee (either beans or ground) and Bosnian coffee gear (daily 9:00-18:00 but may be closed sporadically).

• *Head back to the main drag and continue toward the bridge, passing several more market stalls. Because the bridge itself can be crowded with tourists (and pickpockets), I'd hike down to the **riverbank** below to read the following description while enjoying a dramatic view of the stunning structure. To get there, hook right at the Šadrvan restaurant, then watch for the steps down to the river on your left.*

▲▲▲Old Bridge (Stari Most)

One of the most evocative sights in the former Yugoslavia, this iconic bridge confidently spanned the Neretva River for more than four centuries. Mostarians of all faiths love the bridge and speak of "him" as an old friend. Traditionally considered the point where East meets West, the Old Bridge is as symbolic as it is beautiful. Dramatically arched and flanked by two boxy towers, the bridge is stirring—even if you don't know its history.

Before the Old Bridge, the Neretva was spanned only by a rickety suspension bridge, guarded by *mostari* ("watchers of the bridge"), who gave the city its name. Commissioned in 1557 by the Ottoman Sultan Süleyman the Magnificent, and completed just nine years later, the Old Bridge was a technological marvel for its time..."the longest single-span stone arch on the planet." (In other words, it's the granddaddy of the Rialto Bridge in Venice.) Because of its graceful keystone design—and the fact that there are empty spaces inside the structure—it's much lighter than it appears. And yet, nearly 400 years after it was built, the bridge was still sturdy enough to support the weight of the Nazi tanks that rolled in to occupy Mostar. Over the centuries, it became the symbol of the town and region—a metaphor in stone for the way the diverse faiths and cultures here were able to bridge the gaps that divided them.

All of that drastically changed in the early 1990s. Beginning in May of 1993, as the city became engulfed in war, the Old Bridge frequently got caught in the crossfire. Old tires were slung over its sides to absorb some of the impact from nearby artillery and shrapnel. In November of 1993, Croats began shelling the bridge from the top of the mountain (where the cross is now). The bridge took several direct hits on November 8; on November 9, another shell caused the venerable Old Bridge to lurch, then tumble in pieces into the river. The mortar inside, which contained pink bauxite, turned the water red as it fell in. Locals said that their old friend was bleeding.

The decision to destroy the bridge was partly strategic—to cut off a Bosniak-controlled strip on the west bank from Bosniak forces on the east. (News footage from the time shows Bosniak soldiers scurrying back and forth over the bridge.) But there can be no doubt that, like the Yugoslav Army's siege of Dubrovnik, the attack was also partly symbolic: the destruction of a bridge representing the city's Muslim legacy.

After the war, city leaders decided to rebuild the Old Bridge. Chunks of the original bridge were dredged up from the river. But the limestone had been compromised by soaking in the water for so long, so it couldn't be used (you can still see a few chunks of the old Old Bridge on the riverbank below). Having pledged to rebuild the bridge authentically, restorers cut new stone from the original quarry, and each block was hand-carved. Then they assembled the stones with the same technology used by the Ottomans 450 years ago: Workers erected wooden scaffolding and fastened the blocks together with iron hooks cast

in lead. The project was overseen by UNESCO and cost over $13 million, funded largely by international donors.

It took longer to rebuild the bridge in the 21st century than it did to build it in the 16th century. But on July 23, 2004, the new Old Bridge was inaugurated with much fanfare and was immediately embraced by both the city and the world as a sign of reconciliation.

Since its restoration, another piece of bridge history has fully returned, as young men once again jump from the bridge 75 feet down into the Neretva (which remains icy cold even in summer). Done both for the sake of tradition and to impress girls, this custom carried on even during the time when the destroyed bridge was temporarily replaced by a wooden one. Now the tower on the west side of the bridge houses the office of the local "Divers Club," a loosely run organization that continues this long-standing ritual. On hot summer days, you'll see divers making a ruckus and collecting donations at the top of the bridge. They tease and tease, standing up on the railing and pretending they're about to jump...then getting down and asking for more money. (If he's wearing trunks rather than Speedos, he's not a diver—just a teaser.) Once they collect about €30, one of them will take the plunge. Recently, this custom has gotten even more attention: Each autumn the bridge becomes the venue for a Red Bull-sponsored cliff diving contest.

• *Now begin to walk across the Old Bridge. Watch your footing—the big, chunky steps, spaced at awkward intervals, seem designed to trip up distracted tourists.*

Inside the Halebija Tower at the near end of the bridge, up the stairs (above the Divers Club), the **War Photo Exhibition** displays 50 somber, poignant wartime images taken by photojournalist Wade Goddard. While small, the collection of black-and-white images puts a human face on the suffering by focusing not on the conflict itself, but on the everyday people whose lives were ripped apart by the war (6 KM, daily July-Sept 9:00-21:00, March-June and Oct-Nov 11:00-18:00, closed Dec-Feb).

From the top of the bridge, see how many of the town's 10 mosques you can spot (I counted seven minarets).

• *Once across the bridge, three exhibits are on your right; unless you have a special interest, I'd skip these and save your time for the more worthwhile sights described later.*

Exhibits near the Old Bridge

The **Gallery on the Bridge** is a bookstore operated by the local Islamic cultural center, filling a former mosque for soldiers who guarded the bridge. Explore the good, free photo exhibition of powerful images of war-torn Mostar. The shop sells an impressively wide range of books about the former Yugoslavia and its troubled breakup. You can pay 4 KM to watch a seven-minute montage of videos and photos of the bridge—before, during, and after the war (entry free, daily 8:00-23:00).

Just beyond the bookstore, tucked into the corner on the right, look for the stairs leading up to the **Museum of the Old Bridge** (Muzej Stari Most). Located within one of the Old Bridge's towers, this museum features a 45-minute film and photos about the reconstruction of the bridge, archaeological findings, and a few other paltry exhibits about the history of the town and bridge, all in English. The museum offers more detail than most casual visitors need (10 KM, daily 10:00-18:00, closed Nov-March, lots of stairs, Bajatova 4, tel. 036/551-6021).

Finally, as you round the bend and proceed along Coppersmiths' Street (described next), you could head up the wide staircase on your right, then hook to the left on the main road to find the **Mostar Museum** (Muzej Mostar, or MuM for short). This offers a look at traditional lifestyles in Mostar and Herzegovina, with a scant few artifacts well-described by the included audioguide (5 KM, daily 10:00-16:00, Nov-April until 14:00, www.muzejhercegovine.com).

• *After the Old Bridge, the street swings left and leads you along...*

▲▲Coppersmiths' Street (Kujundžiluk)

This lively strip, with the flavor of a Turkish bazaar, offers some of the most colorful shopping this side of Istanbul. You'll see Mostar's characteristic bridge depicted in every possible way, along with blue-and-white "evil eyes" (believed in the Turkish culture to keep bad spirits at bay), old Yugoslav Army kitsch (including spent bullet and shell casings engraved with images of Mostar), and hammered-

copper decorations—continuing the long tradition that gave the street its name. Partway up, the homes with the colorfully painted facades double as galleries for local artists. The artists live and work upstairs, then sell their work right on this street. Pop into the *atelier d'art* "Đul Emina" on the right (under wooden beams) to meet Sead Vladović and enjoy his impressive iconographic work. This is the most touristy street in all of Bosnia-Herzegovina, so don't expect any bargains. Still, it's fun. As you stroll, check out the fine views of the Old Bridge.

• *Continue uphill. After the street levels out, about halfway along the street on the left-hand side, look for the entrance to the...*

▲Koski Mehmet-Pasha Mosque (Koski Mehmet-Paša Džamija)

Step into this courtyard for a look at one of Mostar's many mosques. Dating from the early 17th century, this mosque is notable for its cliff-hanging riverside location, and because it's particularly accessible for tourists.

Cost and Hours: 6 KM to enter mosque, 12 KM includes minaret climb, daily in summer 8:00-21:00, progressively shorter hours off-season. If it seems crowded with tour groups, you can enter a very similar mosque later on this walk instead (which has most of the same features).

Visiting the Mosque: The **fountain** *(šadrvan)* in the courtyard allows worshippers to wash before entering the mosque, as directed by Islamic law. This practice, called ablution, is both a literal and a spiritual cleansing in preparation for being in the presence of Allah. It's also refreshing in this hot climate, and the sound of running water helps worshippers concentrate.

The **minaret**—the slender needle jutting up next to the dome—is the Islamic equivalent of the Christian bell tower, used to call people to prayer. In the old days, the *muezzin* (prayer leader) would climb the tower five times a day and chant, "There is only one God, and Muhammad is his prophet." In modern times, loudspeakers are used instead. Climbing the minaret's 89 claustrophobic, spiral stairs is a memorable experience, rewarding you at the top with the best views over Mostar—and the Old Bridge—that you can get without wings.

Because this mosque is accustomed to tourists, you don't need to take off your shoes to enter (but stay on the green carpet), women don't need to cover their heads, and it's fine to take photos inside. Near the front of the mosque, you may see some of the small, overlapping rugs that are below this covering (reserved for shoes-off worshippers).

Once **inside,** notice the traditional elements of the mosque. The niche *(mihrab)* across from the entry is oriented toward Mecca

MOSTAR & NEARBY

The Muslims of Bosnia

Muslims have been an integral part of Bosnia's cultural tapestry for centuries. During the more than 400 years under
Ottoman rule, the Muslim Turks did not forcibly convert their
subjects (unlike some Catholic despots at the time). But many
local Slavs were persuaded to become Muslims, for lower
taxes and better business opportunities. Within 150 years of
the start of Ottoman rule, half of the population of Bosnia-
Herzegovina was Muslim. These people constitute an ethnic
group called "Bosniaks," and many of them are still practicing Sunni Muslims today. Most Bosniaks are Slavs—of the same
ethnic stock as Croats and Serbs—but some have ancestors
who married into Turkish families.

The actions of a small but attention-grabbing faction of
Muslim extremists have burdened Islam with a bad reputation
in the Western world. But judging Islam based on ISIS and al-
Qaeda is a bit like judging Christianity based on the Oslo gun-
man and the Ku Klux Klan. Visiting Mostar is a unique opportunity to get a taste of a fully Muslim society, made a bit less
intimidating because it wears a more-familiar European face.

Here's an admittedly simplistic outline designed to help
travelers from the Christian West understand a very rich but
often misunderstood religion that's worthy
of respect:

Muslims, like Christians and Jews, are
monotheistic. They call God "Allah." The
most important person in the Islamic faith is
Muhammad, Allah's most important prophet,
who lived in the sixth and seventh centuries
A.D. Jesus is also one of the most revered
prophets in Islamic tradition.

The "five pillars" of Islam are the same
among Muslims in Bosnia-Herzegovina, Turkey, Iraq, the US, and everywhere else. Fol-
lowers of Islam should:

1. Say and believe, "There is only one
God, and Muhammad is his prophet."

2. Pray five times a day, while facing Mecca. Modern Muslims explain that it's important for this ritual to include several
elements: washing, exercising, stretching, and thinking of God.

3. Give to the poor (one-fortieth of your wealth, if you are
not in debt).

4. Fast during daylight hours through the month of Rama-
dan. Fasting is a great social equalizer and helps everyone to
feel the hunger of the poor.

5. Visit Mecca. This is interpreted by some Muslims as a
command to travel. Muhammad said, "Don't tell me how edu-
cated you are, tell me how much you've traveled."

Good advice for anyone, no matter what—or if—you call a
higher power.

(the holy city in today's Saudi Arabia)—the direction all Muslims face to pray. The small stairway *(mimber)* that seems to go nowhere is symbolic of the growth of Islam—Muhammad had to stand higher and higher to talk to his growing following. This serves as a kind of pulpit, where the cleric gives a speech, similar to a sermon or homily in Christian church services. No priest ever stands on the top stair, which is symbolically reserved for Muhammad.

The balcony just inside the door is traditionally where women worship. Historically, Muslim men decided prayer would go better without the distraction of bent-over women between them and Mecca. These days, women can also pray on the main floor with the men, but they must avoid physical contact.

Muslims believe that capturing a living creature in a painting or a sculpture is inappropriate. (In fact, depictions of Allah and the prophet Muhammad are strictly forbidden.) Instead, mosques are filled with ornate patterns and Arabic calligraphy (of the name "Muhammad" and important prayers and sayings from the Quran). You'll also see some floral and plant designs, which you'd never see in a more conservative, Middle Eastern mosque.

Before leaving, ponder how progressive the majority of Mostar's Muslims are. Most of them drink alcohol, wear modern European clothing (you'll see very few women wearing head scarves or men with beards—and those you do see are likely tourists from the Middle East), and almost never visit a mosque to pray. In so many ways, these people don't fit our preconceived notions of Islam...and yet, they consider themselves Muslims all the same.

The mosque's **courtyard** is shared by several merchants. When you're done haggling, head to the **terrace** behind the mosque for the best view in town of the Old Bridge (entrance included in mosque ticket).

• *Just beyond this mosque, the river-stone cobbles of the Old Town end. Take a right and leave the cutesy tourists' world. Walk up one block to the big...*

▲▲New Muslim Cemetery

In this cemetery, which was a park before the Yugoslav Wars, every tomb is dated 1993, 1994, or 1995. As the war raged, more exposed cemeteries were unusable. But this tree-covered piece of land was relatively safe from Croat snipers. As the casualties mounted, locals buried their loved ones here under cover of darkness. Many of these people were soldiers, but some were civilians. Strict Mus-

MOSTAR & NEARBY

lim graves don't display images of people, but here you'll see photos of war dead who were young, less-traditional members of the Muslim community. The fleur-de-lis shape of many of the tombstones is a patriotic symbol for the nation of Bosnia. The Arabic squiggles are the equivalent of an American having Latin on his or her tombstone—old-fashioned and formal.

• *For an optional sightseeing stop, you can head up the wide stairs to the right of the cemetery (near the mosque). At #4 (on the right, just before and across from the bombed-out tower), you'll find the...*

Museum of Herzegovina (Muzej Hercegovine)

This humble little museum is made worthwhile by a deeply moving **film** that traces the history of the town through its Old Bridge: fun circa-1957 footage of the diving contests; harrowing scenes of the bridge being pummeled, and finally toppled, by artillery; and a stirring sequence showing the bridge's reconstruction and grand reopening on that day in 2004—with high-fives, Beethoven's *Ode to Joy*, fireworks, and more divers. (This includes much of the same footage as the similar film at the Gallery on the Bridge, described earlier, but doesn't focus solely on the wartime damage.)

The museum itself displays fragments of this region's rich history, including historical photos and several items from its Ottoman period. There are sparse English descriptions, but without a tour guide the exhibits are a bit difficult to appreciate. Topics include the Turkish period, Herzegovina under the Austro-Hungarian Empire, village life, and (in the basement) local archaeology. One small room commemorates the house's former owner, Dzemal Bijedić, who was Tito's second-in-command during the Yugoslav period until he was killed in a mysterious plane crash in 1977. (If Bijedić had lived, many wonder whether he might have succeeded Tito...and succeeded in keeping Yugoslavia together.)

Cost and Hours: 5-KM museum entry includes 12-minute film, no narration—works in any language, ask about "film?" as you enter; Mon-Fri 8:00-16:00, closed Sat-Sun; Bajatova 4—walking up these stairs, it's the second door that's marked for the museum, under the overhanging balcony, tel. 036/551-602, www.muzejhercegovine.com.

• *Backtrack to where you left the Old Town. Notice the **Tepa Market**, with locals buying clothing and produce, in the area just beyond the pedestrian zone. Now continue into the modern town, with the market on your left (bear right at the fork). You'll head along the lively street called **Braće Fejića**. (There's no sign, but the street is level and busy with*

*cafés.) You're in the "new town," where locals sit out in front of boister-
ous cafés sipping coffee while listening to the thumping beat of distinctly
Eastern-sounding music. Stroll down this street for a few blocks. On the
left, just after the handy Konzum supermarket (a block or so before the
big minaret), side-trip a block to the left to reach...*

▲Bišćević Turkish House (Bišćevića Ćošak)

Mostar has three traditional Turkish-style homes that are open for
tourists to visit. The Bišćević House is the oldest, most interesting,

and most convenient for a quick visit, but two
others are described at the end of this listing.
Dating from 1635, the Bišćević House is typical of old houses in Mostar, which mix Orien-
tal style with Mediterranean features.

Cost and Hours: 4 KM, daily 9:00-19:00,
generally closed Dec-Feb—but you can arrange a visit by calling ahead to Fortuna Tours
at tel. 036/552-197; house is at Bišćevića 13.

Visiting the House: First you'll step
through the outer (or animals') garden, then
into the inner (or family's) garden. This inner
zone is surrounded by a high wall—protection from the sun's rays,
from thieves...and from prying eyes, allowing women to take off
the veil they were required to wear in public. Enjoy the geometrical
patters of the smooth river stones in the floor (for example, the
five-sided star), and keep an eye out for the house's pet turtles. It's
no coincidence that the traditional fountain *(šadrvan)* resembles
those at the entrance to a mosque—a reminder of the importance
of running water in Muslim culture. The little white building is a
kitchen—cleverly located apart from the house so that the heat and
smells of cooking didn't permeate the upstairs living area.

Buy your ticket and take off your shoes before you climb up the
wooden staircase. Imagine how a stairway like this one could be
pulled up for extra protection in case of danger (notice that this one
has a "trap door" to cover it). The cool, shady, and airy living room is
open to the east—from where the wind rarely blows. The overhanging roof also prevented the hot sun from reaching this area. The
loom in the corner was the women's workplace—the carpets you're
standing on would have been woven there. The big chests against
the wall were used to bring the dowry when the homeowner took
a new wife. Study the fine wood carving that decorates the space.

Continue back into the main gathering room *(divanhan)*. This
space—whose name comes from the word "talk"—is designed in
a circle so people could face each other, cross-legged, for a good
conversation while they enjoyed a dramatic view overlooking the
Neretva. The room comes with a box of traditional costumes—

MOSTAR & NEARBY

great for photo fun. Put on a pair of baggy pants and a fez and really lounge.

Other Turkish Houses: If you're intrigued by this house, consider dropping by Mostar's two other Turkish houses. The **Muslibegović House** (Muslibegovića Kuća) feels newer because it dates from 1871, just a few years before the Ottomans left town. This homey house—which also rents out rooms to visitors (see "Sleeping in Mostar," later)—has many of the same features as the Bišćević House. If they're not too busy, Zerina or Gabriela can give you an English tour (4 KM, mid-April-mid-Oct daily 10:00-18:00, closed to visitors off-season, just two blocks uphill from the Karađozbeg Mosque at Osman Đikića 41, tel. 036/551-379, www. muslibegovichouse.com). To find it, go up the street between the Karađozbeg Mosque and the cemetery, cross the busy street, and continue a long block uphill on the alley. The wall with the slate roof on the left marks the house.

The **Kajtaz House** (Kajtazova Kuća), hiding up a very residential-feeling alley a few blocks from the Old Bridge, feels lived-in because it still is (in the opposite direction from most of the other sights, at Gaše Ilića 21).

• *Go back to the main café street and continue to the...*

▲Karađozbeg Mosque (Karađozbegova Džamija)

The city's main mosque was completed in 1557, the same year work began on the Old Bridge. This mosque, which welcomes visitors, feels less touristy than the one back in the Old Town. Before entering the gate into the complex, look for the picture showing the recent war damage sustained here. You'll see that this mosque has most of the same elements as the Koski Mehmet-Pasha Mosque (described earlier), but some of these decorations are original. Across the street is another cemetery with tombstones from that terrible year, 1993.

Cost and Hours: 5 KM to enter mosque, 5 KM more to climb minaret, daily 9:00-18:00, Oct-April 10:00-16:00. You'll need to remove your shoes, but women don't have to cover their heads, and photos are allowed inside.

• *Now leave the tourists' Mostar and continue into modern, urban Mostar along the street in front of the Karađozbeg Mosque. This grimy, mostly traffic-free street is called...*

▲Braće Fejića

Walking along the modern town's main café strip, enjoy the opportunity to observe this workaday Bosniak town. Notice many cafés that serve drinks but no food. People generally eat at home before going out to nurse an affordable drink. (Café ABC has good cakes and ice cream; the upstairs is a popular pizza hangout for students and families.)

At the small mosque on the left, obituary announcements are tacked to the stone wall on the corner, listing the bios and funeral times for locals who have recently died. A fig tree grows out of the mosque's minaret, just an accident of nature illustrating how that plant can thrive with almost no soil (somehow, the Bosniaks can relate). Walking farther, look back and up to see a few ruins—still ugly more than two decades after the war. There's a messy confusion about who owns what in Mostar. Surviving companies have no money. Yugo Bank, which held the mortgages, is defunct. No one will invest until clear ownership is established. Until then, the people of Mostar sip their coffee in the shadow of these jagged reminders of the warfare that wracked this town a couple of decades ago.

Near the end of the pedestrian zone, through the parking lot on the right, look for the building with communist-era reliefs of 12th-century Bogomil tomb decor—remembering the indigenous culture that existed here even before the arrival of the Ottomans.

When you finally hit the big street (with car traffic), head left one block to the big **Trg Musala** (literally, "Place for Prayer"). Historically, this was where pilgrims gathered before setting off for Mecca on their hajj. This is a great scene on balmy evenings, when it's a rendezvous point for the community. The two busts near the fountain provide perfect goal posts for budding soccer stars.

• For a finale, you can continue one block more out onto the bridge to survey the town you just explored. From here, you can backtrack to linger in the places you found most inviting. Or you can venture into...

WESTERN (CROAT) MOSTAR

Most tourists stay on the Bosniak side of town. But for a complete look at this divided city, it's well worth strolling to the west side. While there's not much in the way of sightseeing here, and much of this urban zone isn't particularly pretty, it does provide an interesting contrast to the Muslim side of town. As this is the location of some of Mostar's new shopping malls, this area feels more vital each year, and a few of the tree-lined streets seem downright elegant.

Crossing the river and the Bulevar, the scarred husks of destroyed buildings begin to fade away, and within a block you're immersed in concrete apartment buildings. When the city became divided, the Muslims holed up in the original Ottoman Old Town, while the Croats claimed this modern Tito-era sprawl. The relative lack of war damage here makes it clear which side of town had it

MOSTAR & NEARBY

MOSTAR & NEARBY

The Dawn of War in Mostar

Mostar was always one of the most stubbornly independent parts of the former Yugoslavia. It had one of the highest rates of mixed-ethnicity marriages in all of Bosnia-Herzegovina. In the early 1990s, Mostar's demographics were proportioned more or less evenly—about 35 percent of its residents were Bosniaks, 34 percent Croats, and 19 percent Serbs. But this delicate balance was shattered in a few brutal months of warfare.

On April 1, 1992, Bosnia-Herzegovina—led by Muslim president Alija Izetbegović—declared independence from Yugoslavia. Very quickly, the Serb-dominated Yugoslav People's Army moved to stake their claim on territory throughout the country, including the important city of Mostar. On April 3, Serb forces occupied the east end of town (including the Ottoman Old Town), forcing many residents—predominantly Croats and Bosniaks—to hole up in the western part of the city. Meanwhile, Serbian and Croatian leaders were secretly meeting to divvy up Bosnian territory, and by early May, they'd agreed that Croatia would claim Mostar.

Several weeks later, when the joint Croat-Bosniak forces crossed back over the river, the Serb forces mysteriously withdrew from the city (having been directed to capitulate), and retreated to the mountaintops above town. The Croats and Bosniaks, believing they'd achieved peace, began putting their city back together. During this time, some factions also rounded up, tortured, and killed Serbs still living in Mostar. Many Bosniaks moved back to their homes on the east side of town, but, rather oddly, many of the Croats who had previously resided there instead stayed in the west—in many cases, moving into apartments vacated by Serbs who had fled.

On May 9, 1993—the Yugoslav holiday of "Victory over Fascism Day"—Mostarians were rocked awake by the terrifying sounds of artillery shells. Croat military forces swept through the city, forcibly moving remaining Bosniaks from the west part of town into the east. Throughout that summer, Bosniak men were captured and sent to concentration camps, while the Croats virtually sealed off the east side of town—creating a giant ghetto with no way in or out. The long and ugly siege of Mostar had begun.

worse. Also notice that there are more pizza and pasta restaurants than *ćevapčići* joints—even the food over here is more Croat than Bosniak.

Looking at a map, you'll notice that many streets on this side of town are named for Croatian cities (Dubrovačka, Splitska, Vukovarska) or historical figures (Kneza Branimira, Kralja Tomislava, and Kralja Petra Krešimira—for the dukes who first united the Croats in the ninth and tenth centuries). This side of town also has several remnants of Mostar's brief period of Habsburg rule (1878-1918). During this time, the empire quickly expanded what had been a sleepy Ottoman backwater, laying out grand boulevards and erecting genteel buildings that look like they'd be at home in Vienna.

All streets converge at the big roundabout (about a 15-minute walk from the Old Town) called the **Rondo,** which is a good place to get oriented to this neighborhood. Overlooking this lively intersection is the stately Hrvatski Dom ("Croatia House") cultural center. Notice how even the street signs are politically charged: *Centar* signs pointedly direct traffic *away* from the (Bosniak) Old Town, and many road signs point toward Široki Brijeg—a Croat stronghold in western Herzegovina.

The adjacent **Park Zrinjevac** is a pleasant place to stroll, and was the site of an infamously ill-fated attempt at reconciliation. In the early 2000s, idealistic young Mostarians formed the Urban Movement of Mostar, which searched for a way to connect the still-feuding Catholic and Muslim communities. As a symbol of their goals, they chose Bruce Lee, the deceased kung-fu movie star, beloved by both Croats and Bosniaks for his characters' honorable struggle against injustice. A life-size bronze statue of Lee was unveiled with fanfare in this park in November of 2005—but was almost immediately vandalized. The statue was repaired, and may or may not have been returned to its pedestal (which you'll still find in the park).

Several interesting sights lie close to this roundabout. A block toward the Old Town from the Rondo (on Kralja Višeslava Humskog), look for the big **Muslim cemetery** with tombstones from the early 1990s. These are the graves of those killed during the first round of fighting, when the Croats and Bosniaks teamed up to fight the Serbs.

If you head from the Rondo down Kneza Branimira (across from the park), you'll enjoy an inviting boulevard shaded by plane trees. When first built, this street was called **Štefanijino Šetalište**—"Stéphanie's Promenade," after the Belgian princess who married Austria's Archduke Rudolf (the heir apparent of the Habsburg Empire until he died in a mysterious murder-suicide pact with his mistress).

If you head up Kralja Petra Krešimira IV from the Rondo, after two long blocks on the left you'll see an abandoned, derelict park leading to a gigantic **Partisan Cemetery and Monument.** This socialist-style monument spreads all the way up the hill.

MOSTAR & NEARBY

It oozes with symbolism trumpeting the pivotal WWII Battle of the Neretva, when Tito and his Partisan Army turned the tables on Nazi forces (just 30 miles north of here). It was designed by Bogdan Bogdanović, who created many such monuments and memorials throughout Yugoslavia, and dedicated by Tito himself in 1965. From the terrace at the top, which is scattered with symbolic gravestones for those who gave their lives to free Yugoslavia from the Nazis, small streams once trickled down to the large enclosure at the bottom, ultimately flowing beneath a stylized broken bridge representing the Bridge at the Neretva. Today the monument is overgrown and ignored—a tragic symbol of post-Tito ethnic discord. Local Croats—who have little nostalgia for the Yugoslav period, which they now view as a time of oppression—seem to intentionally neglect the place. This formerly hallowed ground is a mess of broken concrete and a popular place for drunken benders, garbage dumping, and drug deals (be careful if you decide to explore, and avoid it after dark). A pensive stroll here comes with a poignant reflection on how one generation's honored war dead can become the next generation's unwanted burden.

Nightlife in Mostar

Though Mostar is touristy, it's also a real urban center with a young population riding a wave of raging hormones. The meat market in the courtyard next to the old Turkish bathhouse (on "Hammam Square") is fun to observe. The Old Bridge is a popular meeting place for locals as well as tourists. A stroll from the Old Bridge down the café-lined Braće Fejića boulevard to the modern **Trg Musala** at the far end of town (described earlier) gives a great peek at Mostarians socializing away from the tourists. Wherever you wind up, order a cocktail or try a Turkish-style hubbly-bubbly (*šiša*, SHEE-shah). Ask to have one of these

big water pipes fired up for you and choose your flavored tobacco: apple, cappuccino, banana, or lemon.

Ali Baba is an actual cave featuring a fun, atmospheric, and mellow hangout scene (look for the low-profile entrance

along Coppersmiths' Street, just down from the Old Bridge—watch for signs tucked down a rocky alley).

Oscar Nightclub is a caravanserai for lounge lizards—an exotic world mixing babbling streams, terraces, lounge chairs, and big sofas where young and old enjoy cocktails and *šiša* (open "nonstop" as long as the weather is good—usually June-mid-Sept, closed off-season, up from the Old Bridge on Onešćukova street, near the Crooked Bridge at the end of the pedestrian zone).

Black Dog Pub, the brainchild of Seattleite Stefan (who moved to Mostar as part of a humanitarian NGO during the war), fosters a lively, youthful scene that feels more international than "traditional Bosnian." They serve more than 40 local microbrews (including several from the Oldbridz Brewery)—with some on tap—and have live music most nights from around 20:00. While they don't serve food, they can call in an order for you at a neighboring restaurant. Stefan makes a point of hiring locals from every different ethnic background, and his bar has become a hangout for Mostarians from both sides of town as well as tourists. Sit in the convivial interior, or head out to the riverside terrace (daily in summer 9:00-24:00, from 15:00 off-season, just across the Crooked Bridge from Onešćukova street).

Sleeping in Mostar

Most of my listings are small, friendly, accessible, affordable guesthouses in or very near the Old Town. Prices are deceptively low here—don't overlook my lowest-priced listings, which are essentially as comfortable as the pricier ones. Many hotels and pensions in town promise "parking," but it's often street parking out front—private lots are rare. Mostar's Old Town can be very noisy on weekends, with nightclubs and outdoor restaurants rollicking into the wee hours. If you're a light sleeper, consider Villa Fortuna, the Muslibegović House, or Shangri La, which are quieter than the norm. If you're looking for something more luxurious, check online for the new Marriott near the Old Bridge, which opened in the spring of 2018.

$$ The **Muslibegović House,** a Bosnian national monument that also invites tourists in to visit during the day, is in an actual

Turkish home dating from 1871. The complex houses 10 homey rooms and two suites, all of which combine classic Turkish style (elegant and comfortable old beds, creaky wooden floors with colorful carpets, lounging sofas; guests

remove shoes at the outer door) with modern comforts (air-con, flat-screen TVs). Situated on a quiet residential lane just above the bustle of Mostar's main pedestrian drag and Old Town zone, this is a memorable experience (includes a tour of the house, closed Nov–Feb, 2 blocks uphill from the Karađozbeg Mosque at Osman Đikića 41, tel. 036/551-379, www.muslibegovichouse.com, muslibegovichouse@gmail.com; Zerina, Gabriela, and stoic boss Tađudin).

$ **Shangri La Mansion** fills a gorgeously restored Austro-Hungarian building on a hill above the Old Town, accessed by a steep driveway next to a war ruin. The eight rooms come in all different sizes, but they're all modern and nicely appointed. Thoughtfully run with modern flair by Nermin, it also has a beautiful rooftop garden that's ideal for relaxing (breakfast extra, air-con, free parking, Kalhanska 10, mobile 061-169-362, www.shangrila.com.ba, info@shangrila.com.ba).

$ **Villa Anri,** between the Old Town and the Bulevar, feels bigger and a bit more hotelesque than other Mostar pensions. The stony facade hides eight rooms (six with balconies) combining old Herzegovinian style and bright colors. The big draw is the rooftop terrace, shared by two rooms, which enjoys grand views over the Old Bridge area (cash only, air-con, free parking, Braće Đukića 4, tel. 036/578-477, http://villa-anri-mostar-ba.book.direct, villa.anri@gmail.com).

$ **Pansion Čardak,** run by kind and gregarious Suzana and Nedžad Kasumović, has seven pleasant rooms sharing a kitchen in a stone house set just back from the bustling Crooked Bridge area. Their top-floor rooms, while a bit more expensive, are beautifully decorated and feel luxurious (cash only, breakfast extra at nearby restaurant, air-con, free parking, Jusovina 3, tel. 036/578-249, mobile 061-385-988, www.pansion-cardak.com, info@pansion-cardak.com).

$ **Pansion Nur,** run by Feđa, a relative of Suzana and Nedžad (above), has four simpler but cheaper rooms and a shared kitchen (cash only, no breakfast, air-con, free parking, Jusovina 8b, mobile 062-160-872, www.pansion-nur.com, info@pansion-nur.com).

$ **Hotel Kriva Ćuprija** ("Crooked Bridge"), by the bridge of the same name, is tucked between waterfalls in the picturesque gorge a few steps from the Old Bridge. It's more hotelesque, impersonal, and expensive than my other listings in this price range. The 26 rooms are stylish (though many suffer from nearby night-life noise), and their restaurant has atmospheric outdoor seating (RS%, air-con, call to reconfirm if arriving after 19:00, enter at Onešćukova 23 or Kriva Ćuprija 2, tel. 036/360-360, mobile 061-915-915, www.hotel-mostar.ba, krivacuprijamostar@gmail.com,

Sami). They also have three big apartments in a building across the river.

¢ **Villa Fortuna** is an exceptional value, located in a nonde-script urban neighborhood a few minutes' walk farther away from the Old Bridge. Owners Nela and Mili Bijavica rent eight taste-ful, modern rooms above the main office of Fortuna Tours. The courtyard in front offers free, secure parking, and in back there's a pleasant garden with a traditional Herzegovinian garden cot-tage (RS%, breakfast extra, nonsmoking, air-con, Rade Bitange 34, tel. 036/580-625, mobile 063-299-189, www.villafortuna.ba, villa_fortuna@bih.net.ba).

¢ **Villa Botticelli,** overlooking a charming waterfall garden just up the valley from the Crooked Bridge, has five colorful rooms at affordable prices (breakfast extra, air-con, Muje Bjelavca 6, enter along the street facing the Crooked Bridge, mobile 063-319-057, www.villabotticelli.com, info@villabotticelli.com, sweet Snježana and Zoran).

Eating in Mostar

Most of Mostar's tourist-friendly restaurants are conveniently con-centrated in the Old Town. If you walk anywhere that's cobbled, you'll stumble onto dozens of tempting restaurants charging the same reasonable prices and serving rustic, traditional Bosnian food. In my experience, the menus at most places are virtually identical—though quality and ambience can vary greatly. As eater-ies tend to come and go quickly here, and little distinguishes these places anyway, don't be too focused on a particular spot. Grilled meats are especially popular—read the "Balkan Flavors" sidebar, on page 151, before you dine. Most local wines are made with one of two indigenous grapes: *blatina* (literally "muddy"; a thick, heavy, earthy red) and *žilavka* (literally "root"; a bright, fairly acidic white).

ON THE EMBANKMENT, WITH OLD BRIDGE VIEWS

For the best atmosphere, find your way into the several levels of restaurants that clamber up the riverbank and offer perfect views of the Old Bridge. In terms of the setting, this is the most memorable place to dine in Mostar—but be warned that the quality of the food along here is uniformly low, and prices are relatively high (figure

8-18 KM for a meal). If you want a good perch, it's fun and smart to drop by earlier in the day and personally reserve the table of your choice.

To reach two of the most scenic eateries, go over the Old Bridge to the west side of the river, and bear right on the cobbles until you get to the Hammam Museum. To the right of the old Turkish bathhouse is the entrance to a lively courtyard surrounded by cafés. Crossing straight through the courtyard, you'll find stairs leading down to several riverfront terraces belonging to two different restaurants: **$ Babilon** (my choice for better food) and **$ Teatar.** Poke around to find your favorite bridge panorama before settling in for a drink or a meal. Two other places (including a pizzeria) are a bit closer to the bridge—to reach these, look for the alley on the left just before the bridge tower.

IN AND NEAR THE OLD TOWN

While they lack the Old Bridge views, these places are just as central as those listed earlier, and serve food that's generally a step up.

$ Restoran Hindin Han is pleasantly situated on a woody terrace over a rushing stream. It's respected locally for its good cooking—with a wide variety, from grilled meats to seafood—and fair prices (Sarajevsko beer on tap, daily 11:00-24:00, Jusovina 10, tel. 036/581-054). To find it, walk west from the Old Bridge, bear left at the Šadrvan restaurant, cross the bridge, and you'll see it on the left.

$ Tima-Irma, run by the frenetic one-woman show Irma, grills up the best *ćevapčići* and other meats that I've had in Mostar. Its touristy, very scenic location—along the main shopping drag, a couple of blocks from the Old Bridge—belies the quality of the food (long hours daily, Onešćukova b.b., mobile 066-905-070).

$ Nacionalni Restoran Aščinica Balkan ("Balkan National Restaurant/Cafeteria") is a convenient cafeteria-style eatery with two handy locations. They serve up tasty, home-cooked Bosnian specialties; you can order from the menu, but it's more fun to order a "mix" *(mješanac)* plate from the display case—the small 10-KM plate is plenty for a light meal (Bosnian coffee, tempting dessert display case, daily 10:00-23:00, one location right at the end of the Old Town cobbles before the market, the other a couple of blocks away on the new town's main drag at Braće Fejića 57, tel. 036/551-868).

$ Saray is an untouristy, nondescript little eatery just uphill from the Karađozbeg Mosque in the modern part of town. They have a basic menu of very cheap and very tasty grilled meats—specializing in the classic *ćevapčići*—and outdoor seating overlooking a playground that offers good people- and kid-watching while you eat (daily 7:00-23:00, Karađozbegova 3, mobile 062-062-301).

MOSTAR & NEARBY

$ Urban Grill's food is nothing special—it has basically the same menu as other places in town—but its terrace enjoys one of Mostar's best unobstructed views of the Old Bridge (Bosnian coffee, daily 8:00-22:00, enter along the main cobbled Old Town drag at Mala Tepa 26, tel. 036/552-235).

In the West (Croat) Side of Town: While less charming and romantic, a stroll to the west side of town (still inhabited primarily by Croats) offers an interesting contrast to the cutesy Old Town—and a completely different array of restaurants. Here you'll find more pizza and pasta than grilled meats, as well as shiny new shopping centers with modern food courts. For more on this neighborhood, see "Sights in Mostar," earlier.

Mostar Connections

BY BUS

Not surprisingly for a divided city, Mostar has two different, autonomous bus terminals, each served by different companies. Mostar's **main bus station** (called "Autobusna Stanica") is on the east/Bosniak side of the river, about a 15-minute walk north of the Old Town (for details, see "Arrival in Mostar," earlier). Most buses you're likely to take use this station; for information on the other station (on the west/Croat side of town), see the end of this section.

Schedules and Tickets: Tracking down reliable schedule information in Mostar is tricky, but you can research timetables (and purchase tickets) at www.getbybus.com, which usually succeeds in listing most of your options. At the main station, two primary companies (one Bosniak, one Croat) operate independent offices, providing schedule information and tickets only for their own buses. Because the companies are reluctant to cooperate, there's no single ticket office for all Mostar buses—if you're unclear on your options, visit both companies to get details before buying tickets. As you face the bus station, near the left end is the Bosniak company **Autoprevoz** (tel. 036/551-900, www.autoprevoz-bus.ba); they also sell tickets for a few other companies (including Eurolines and Bogdan Bus). Near the right end is the Croat-owned **Globtour** (look for *Mediteran Tours* sign, tel. 036/550-065, www.globtour.com), which sells tickets only for its own buses. Local and regional connections (not listed below) are operated by Mostar Bus, whose buses depart from across the street from the main bus station (www.mostarbus.ba). Note that buses to seasonal destinations (such as along the Dalmatian Coast) run more frequently in peak season, roughly June through mid-September.

From Mostar's Main Bus Station: Both Autoprevoz and Globtour operate buses to **Sarajevo** (7/day on Autoprevoz, 4/day on Globtour, 3 hours), **Zagreb** (3/day on Autoprevoz, 4/day

MOSTAR & NEARBY

on Globtour, 9 hours, includes a night bus), and **Split** (2/day on Autoprevoz, 8/day on Globtour, 4 hours; additional departures by Eurolines in summer). Globtour exclusively handles buses to **Međugorje** (5/day, 40 minutes), and **Dubrovnik** (5/day in summer, less off-season, 3-4 hours).

That important **Dubrovnik** connection is tricky: Most days, all Dubrovnik buses depart early in the day, making an afternoon return from Mostar to Dubrovnik impossible. However, in summer (June-Aug), Eurolines typically adds two more departures each day—including a handy 17:30 departure, which makes day-tripping from Dubrovnik workable (tickets sold at Autoprevoz office).

Globtour also runs a handy bus to Montenegro's **Bay of Kotor.** Two buses leave around the same time, at 7:00; one originates in Mostar and takes the inland route, via Herzegovina and Trebinje, passing only one border (but with much less coastal scenery). This takes longer but is more likely to be on time, arriving in Kotor around 16:00. The other option takes the coastal route via Dubrovnik, with four borders and more scenery, and is scheduled to arrive at 13:00—but often arrives late. Another connection to Kotor (using the inland route) leaves at 16:00, arriving around 1:00 in the morning.

From Mostar's West/Croat Bus Station: A few additional buses, mostly to Croatian destinations and to Croat areas of Bosnia-Herzegovina, depart from the west side of town. These use a makeshift "station" (actually a gravel lot behind a gas station) on Vukovarska street, called "Kolodvor." It's about a 15-minute walk due west of the main bus station. Most buses using the Kolodvor station are operated by the Euroherc company. In addition to one daily bus apiece to **Zagreb, Split,** and **Sarajevo,** this station has several departures to **Metković** (at the Croatian border, with additional connections to Croatian destinations) and to **Međugorje.** Additionally, some Croat buses leave from a bus stop near the Franciscan Church. But since the connections are sparse, the location is inconvenient, and the "station" is dreary, I'd stick with the main bus station and ignore this option unless you're desperate.

BY TRAIN

While the bus is preferable for almost every destination, a new train line between Mostar and **Sarajevo** is up and running that takes about as long as the bus and costs less. While you'll enjoy a higher vantage point for this scenic journey, the train spends more time in tunnels—so you'll wind up seeing less. As the schedule is in flux (likely 2/day, 2.5 hours), ask at the station or try checking www.zfbh.ba.

ROUTE TIPS FOR DRIVERS
FROM DUBROVNIK TO MOSTAR

You have two options for the drive between Dubrovnik and Mostar: easy and straightforward along the coast, or adventurous and off-the-beaten-path through the Herzegovinian mountains. I've narrated each route coming from Dubrovnik to Mostar, but you can do either one in reverse.

Option 1: Main Coastal Road

The vast majority of traffic from Dubrovnik to Mostar follows the coastal road north, then cuts east into Bosnia. Because this is one of the most direct routes, it can be crowded (allow about 2.5 hours, not counting photo and sightseeing stops, or border delays). It's also a bit inconvenient, as you have to cross the border three times (into and out of Bosnia at Neum, and into Bosnia again at Metković).

Crowd-Beating Tip: At busy times—particularly in the peak of summer (July-Aug), and especially on weekends—northbound traffic can back up at Neum (worst around 9:00-11:00, when day-trippers from Dubrovnik are clogging the roads). If busy borders have been the norm (you can try asking savvy locals—but it's hard to predict), try leaving Dubrovnik early (before 8:00) or later (around 10:00, or leave earlier but make some stops—such as Trsteno or Ston—en route; your goal is to reach the border after 11:00). Another way to beat the crowds is to take the lesser-known border crossing between the Croatian town of Slano ("Salty") and the Bosnian town of Ravno ("Flat")—you'll meet up with my "Rugged-but-Scenic" route, described later, near the Vjetrenica cave (see "Near Dubrovnik" map in the previous chapter). This misses the scenery of the Neretva Delta and the option of seeing the Roman museum near Metković, but if you expect the Neum borders to be backed up, it will save some time.

The Drive Begins: Head north out of Dubrovnik, passing some of the places mentioned in the Near Dubrovnik chapter: **Trsteno** (with its arboretum), and **Ston** and **Mali Ston** (with a mighty wall and waterfront restaurants, respectively). After passing the Ston turnoff, you'll see the long, mountainous, vineyard-draped **Pelješac Peninsula** across the bay on your left. (Note: Between Trsteno and Ston—about 30 minutes after crossing the bridge out of Dubrovnik—you'll curve around the bay town of Slano, where you can take the alternate border crossing to Ravno, Bosnia.)

Soon you'll come to a surprise border crossing, at **Neum.** Here you'll cross into Bosnia-Herzegovina—then, six miles later, cross back out again (for details on this odd little stretch of Bosnian coast, see page 84).

You won't be back in Croatia for long. Just north of Neum, the

main coastal road jogs away from
the coast and around the striking **Neretva River Delta**—the
extremely fertile "garden patch
of Croatia," which produces
a significant portion of Croatia's fruits and vegetables. The
Neretva is the same river that
flows under Mostar's Old Bridge
upstream—but in Metković,

it spreads out into 12 branches as it enters the Adriatic, flooding
a vast plain and creating a bursting cornucopia in the middle of
an otherwise rocky and arid region. Enjoying some of the most
plentiful sunshine on the Croatian coast, as well as a steady supply
of water for irrigation, the Neretva Delta is as productive as it is
beautiful.

At the Neretva Delta, turn off for the town of **Metković.** If
you're interested in Roman ruins, it's worth a brief detour to see
the Narona Archaeological Museum in Vid (see listing later in this
chapter). Otherwise, just carry on straight through Metković to
reach the border into **Bosnia-Herzegovina,** then continue straight
on the main road (M-17) directly into Mostar. As you drive, you'll
see destroyed buildings and occasional roadside memorials bearing the likenesses of fresh-faced soldiers who died in the Yugoslav
Wars of the mid-1990s.

Along the way are a few interesting detours, all described later
in this chapter: In Čapljina, you can turn off to the left to reach
Međugorje. If you stay on the main road, keep your eyes peeled
soon after the Čapljina turnoff for a mountaintop castle tower
(on the right side of the road), which marks the medieval town of
Počitelj. With extra time, just before Mostar (in Buna), you can
detour a few miles along the Buna River into Blagaj.

Approaching **Mostar** on M-17, you'll pass the airport, then
carry on straight toward *Sarajevo*. Be warned that GPS doesn't
have a good handle on Mostar, so follow these directions instead:
Skip the first turnoff for *Centar*, when you're still far from town.
Rather, stay on the main Sarajevo-bound road, and then, as you
begin to enter Mostar's urban sprawl, take the left turn for *Centar*
and *Posušje*. When you come to the traffic light, you can turn right
to reach the east side of the river (for the Muslibegović House or
Shangri La); or continue straight and then bear right onto the Bulevar to reach the west side of the river (for my other accommodations, or parking near the Old Bridge—see "Arrival in Mostar,"
earlier).

Once in town, signage can be confusing; if you get lost, try asking for directions to "Stari Most" (STAH-ree most)—the Old Bridge.

Option 2: Rugged-but-Scenic Backcountry Journey Through Serb Herzegovina

While the coastal route outlined above is the most common way to connect Dubrovnik to Mostar, I enjoy getting out of the tourist rut by twisting up the mountains behind Dubrovnik and cutting across the scenic middle of Herzegovina. This route feels much more remote, but the roads are good and the occasional gas station and restaurant break up the journey—and, because you're going through just one border crossing (instead of three), it takes about the same amount of time as the main route, described above.

I find this route particularly interesting because it offers an easily digestible taste of the **Republika Srpska** part of Herzegovina—controlled by the country's Serb minority, rather than its Bosniak and Croat majorities. You'll see Orthodox churches and monasteries, the Cyrillic alphabet, and various symbols of the defiantly proud Serb culture (such as the red, white, and blue flag with the four golden C's). You can't get a complete picture of the former Yugoslavia without sampling at least a sliver of Serb culture. (Because this road goes through the Serbian part of Herzegovina, it's not popular among Bosniaks or Croats.) If you want a little taste of Republika Srpska, consider just day-tripping into Trebinje—especially on Saturday, when the produce market is at its liveliest.

The Drive Begins: From Dubrovnik, head south toward Cavtat, the airport, and Montenegro. Shortly after leaving Dubrovnik, watch for—and follow—signs on the left directing you to *Brgat Gornji*. (Signage completely ignores the large Serb town of Trebinje, just past this obscure border village.) As you climb up over the mountains and cross the border into Bosnia-Herzegovina, notice the faint remains of a long-abandoned old rail line cutting sharp switchbacks up the slope. This once connected Dubrovnik to Mostar and Sarajevo. The charred trees you may see are not from the war, but from more recent forest fires.

Carry on across the plateau, where you may begin to notice Cyrillic lettering on signs: You've crossed into the Republika Srpska. About 20 minutes after the border, you'll come upon **Trebinje** (Требиње)—a pleasant and relatively affluent town that's a good place to stretch your legs, get some Convertible Marks (ATMs are scattered around the town center), and maybe nurse a coffee while

(MOSTAR & NEARBY)

people-watching on the big, leafy, inviting main square. Out on the square, a smattering of humble open-air market stalls sell local produce (Saturday is the biggest market day, but there's always some action). There's a welcoming TI on the square, but in this small-time town, they don't have much to do (closed Sun, Jovana Dučića b.b., tel. 059/273-410, www.trebinjeturizam.com). From the bottom of the square, you can stroll through the fortified gate into the sleepy, almost completely untouristy Old Town (called Kaštel), with more cafés and the town mosque (vengefully demolished during the war, but later rebuilt). The Trebišnjica River is spanned by the graceful, Ottoman-built Arslanagica Bridge.

Overlooking the town from its hilltop perch is the striking Orthodox Church of **Nova Gračanica,** built to resemble the historically important Gračanica Monastery in Kosovo. If you have time, drive up to the church's viewpoint terrace for great views over Trebinje and the valley, and step inside the church to immerse yourself in a gorgeously vibrant world of Orthodox icons.

Whether you stop in Trebinje or not, from here you'll follow signs for *Mostar* and *Ljubinje.* You'll trace the course of the Trebišnjica River into a high-altitude karstic basin, where evocative old waterwheels power a primitive irrigation system. From here, the river flows down to the coast—providing hydroelectric power for Dubrovnik—before detouring south and emptying into the sea near Herceg Novi, Montenegro...one river, three countries, in just a few miles. This area is blanketed with vineyards and dotted with old monasteries. Passing the village of Mesari ("Butchers"), you'll also see flocks of sheep. In this part of the Balkans, Croats were traditionally the city-dwellers, while Serbs were the farmers. There used to be sheep like these in the pastures near Dubrovnik, but when the Serbs left during the war, so did the sheep.

Pull over at one of the humble, slate-roofed Orthodox chapels by the road. (There's one in Staro Slano.) In the cemeteries, many of the gravestones are from 1991—when soldiers from this area joined the war effort against Dubrovnik.

The large, flat, sunken field you're driving along is called **Popovo Polje** ("Priests' Field"). Because it floods easily, the canal was built to remove floodwater. Watch for the turnoff to **Vjetrenica** (near Zavala), a karstic cave that was a big draw in Yugoslav times. Closed down during the war, it recently reopened. It's less spectacular than the famous caves in Slovenia, but has interesting water features that may be worth touring for spelunkers with time to kill (www.vjetrenica.ba).

At the fork, carry on straight to Ljubinje. Climbing up into the mountains, you may see garbage along the side of the road—an improvised dump in this very poor land, where a fractured government struggles to provide even basic services. Twisting up through even higher mountains, you'll wind up in the town of **Ljubinje** (Љубиње). In this humble burg, roadside stands with *med* signs advertise homegrown honey. Also keep an eye out for drying tobacco. The partially built houses are not signs of war damage (the war didn't reach here); they're a form of "savings" in the Balkans, where people don't trust banks: Rather than deposit money in an account, they spend many years using any extra funds to gradually add on to a new house.

Continuing toward Mostar, you'll pass through more desolate countryside, then your ears will pop (and you'll pass a red, white, and blue sign marking the "border" of Republika Srpska) as you drop down into the town of **Stolac** (Столац); the town's defiant mosque minaret tells you that you've crossed from Serb territory into Bosnia's Muslim-Croat Federation. Stolac is home to some fascinating history, and worth a stroll if you have the time (see later in this chapter). Leaving Stolac toward Mostar, keep an eye out (on the left, just before the *Poprati* sign) for its interesting **necropolis**— a cluster of centuries-old traditional Bosnian tombstones (worth a quick photo-op stop, and described later).

Past Stolac, you'll climb up the hill, going through the village of Poprati. Soon you'll have the option of either turning off to the right to head directly to **Mostar,** or continuing along the main road to reach Čapljina, where you'll turn right to go past **Počitelj** on your way into Mostar. Either way, **Blagaj** (see below) is worth considering as a detour before ending in Mostar. (If you want to go to **Međugorje**—described later—go through Čapljina and follow signs.)

Near Mostar

While Mostar has its share of attractions, there's also plenty to see within a short drive. Ideally try to splice one or two of these stops into your trip between Mostar and the coast (see my "Route Tips for Drivers," earlier, for tips on linking them up).

Blagaj

Blagaj (BLAH-gai, rhymes with "pie") was the historical capital of this region until the arrival of the Ottomans. This is the site of a mountain called Hum, which is topped by the ruins of a hilltop castle that once belonged to Herzog ("Duke") Stjepan, who gave Herzegovina its name.

Deep in Blagaj is an impressive cliff face with a scenic house marking the source of the Buna River. The building, called the

Near Mostar

Tekija, is a former monastery for Turkish dervishes (an order that emphasizes poverty and humility, famous for the way they whirl in a worshipful trance). Built in the 15th century and recently restored, the house is surrounded by a modern visitors-center complex with a café, gift shop, and pay WCs. It's free to enter and look around the Tekija, which feels similar to the tourable Turkish houses in Mostar (for a description, see the Biščević Turkish House listing under "Sights in Mostar"). You'll take your shoes off and tiptoe across a patchwork of small rugs from room to room. Gazing out the windows at the towering cliff stretching to heaven, and hearing the constant, steady flow of water, it's easy to imagine how this could be considered a very spiritual place.

After seeing the house, stroll a bit along the river, which is crossed by several footbridges offering a grand view back on the Tekija and cliff. A handful of sprawling, touristy restaurants—with open-air terraces right along the refreshing river—serve up traditional Bosnian food, including trout pulled from their own river-fed ponds.

Getting There: Blagaj is easiest to see on the way to or from Mostar—just turn off from the main road and follow the Buna River, following *tekija* signs to the big parking lot.

Počitelj

Počitelj (POTCH-ee-tell) is an artists' colony filled with a compelling mix of Christian and Muslim architecture. Ideally situated right along the main Mostar-to-Croatia road, it's one of the most popular rest stops for passing tour buses, so it's hardly undiscovered. But it's still worth a stop for its dramatically vertical townscape and beautifully restored Ottoman architecture.

Park your car and hike across the riverstone cobbles to the open square at the base of town, with a handy restaurant, lots of gift shops, and aggressive vendors. The multidomed building is an old hammam (bathhouse). Then hike up the steep stairs (dodging costumed vendors, and enjoying fine aerial views on those hammam domes) to reach the **mosque.** You can pay 3 KM to enter (women must cover their heads). The interior is bigger, though not necessarily better decorated, than the mosques in downtown Mostar (for a description of a typical Bosnian mosque interior, see the Koski Mehmet-Pasha Mosque listing under "Sights in Mostar"). A photo on the porch shows the building circa 1993, destroyed to its foundation.

Continue up the stairs behind the mosque, which lead steeply all the way up to the fortress, which was originally built in the 15th century by Hungarian King Mátyás Corvinus (who pushed the Ottomans back, briefly reclaiming some territory—including this region—for the forces of Christian Europe). There's virtually nothing to see inside (the stairs inside the tower are extremely steep and narrow—tread carefully), but the views are sensational. The best views are from the flat terrace out front. It's clear just how strategic this location is, between steep cliffs and with perfect views up and down the Neretva Valley.

Metković

This dusty and depressed Croatian border town—which sits where the lush Neretva River Delta meets a wall of limestone hills—is best-known as the place where most people cross the border into Bosnia. There's nothing to see in Metković itself, but if you're interested in ancient ruins, the nearby Narona Archaeological Museum is worth a short detour.

▲Narona Archaeological Museum (Arheološki Muzej Narona)

In Roman times, the province of Dalmatia (roughly today's Croatia and Bosnia) was sparsely populated. There were only two real towns of note. The main city was Salona, the birthplace of Diocletian, near today's Split. The second city was Narona, which stood on a plain at the foot of the mountains, powered by tributaries of the Neretva River. Today Narona is mostly unexcavated, sitting under a tiny village called Vid near Metković. In the 1990s, archaeologists discovered a treasure trove of Roman statues in a dilapidated barn here. They carefully excavated this cache—the largest collection of marble Roman statues from this period—and built a state-of-the-art museum to show them off in situ (with English explanations). The centerpiece is the foundation of a temple of Augustus, dating from around 10 B.C., with 15 Roman statues. You'll also see plenty of Roman carvings, pottery frag-ments, and good descriptions. Out front, under glass, is a mosaic floor. If you're intrigued by Roman ruins, it's worth a quick detour off the main road through Metković to take a look. The museum is in a blocky, can't-miss-it building that stands at the entrance to the otherwise ramshackle hill town of Vid. (The square in front of the museum was the site of Narona's forum.)

Cost and Hours: 40 KM; June-Sept Tue-Sun 9:00-19:00; Oct-May Tue-Fri until 16:00, Sat until 17:00, Sun until 13:00, closed Mon year-round; Naronski Trg 5 in Vid, tel. 020/691-596, www.a-m-narona.hr.

Getting There: Driving through Metković toward the Bosnian border, turn left over the last bridge before you reach the checkpoint. At the next roundabout, turn right, following signs for *Vid*. After crossing the river in Vid, the museum is straight ahead. It's a less-than-10-minute detour from the main road.

Eating: Across the street from the museum, **$$ Đuđa i Mate** is a rustic restaurant specializing in local Neretva River cuisine—that means frogs and eels (though they also have an extensive menu of typical Croatian dishes). There's a covered terrace near the restaurant, but I prefer the covered seating down by the river (daily 8:00-22:00, tel. 020/687-500).

Stolac

One of the most historic spots in Herzegovina, Stolac (STOH-lats) was a cradle of early Balkan civilization. Unless you're fascinated by archaeology, Stolac isn't worth a long detour—but since it's on the way between Mostar and Dubrovnik (on the back-roads route), consider stopping off if you have time to spare.

About 15,000 to 16,000 years ago—long before the Greeks or Romans arrived in this region—the Illyrians lived in this area's

caves, where they left behind some drawings. On a hill above the modern town are the overgrown remains of the once-fearsome dry-stone Illyrian fortress that watched over this strategic road in the third and fourth centuries B.C. The Romans were later supplanted by the local Bogomil civilization, an indigenous Christian society. Stolac's most impressive attraction dates from this era: On the outskirts of town (on the road toward Mostar), you'll find a **necropolis** with a bonanza of giant tombstones called *stećak*s (from the 13th-15th centuries), engraved with evocative reliefs. Soon after these were erected, the Ottomans arrived, and conversions to Islam followed.

Archaeological treasures aside, today's Stolac is a workaday village with little tourism—it trudges along, largely oblivious to the ancient treasures embedded all around. The town was particularly hard-hit during the Yugoslav Wars, when it was taken over by Croat forces and its majority Muslim residents forced to flee to Mostar. The war crimes tribunal in The Hague had an entire division devoted to "Stolac Crimes"—at least 80 civilians were killed here. The mosque and surrounding area were completely leveled; it's now

MOSTAR & NEARBY

rebuilt, and the town's population is divided evenly between Croats and Bosniaks. Tension still hangs heavy in the air. Local Croats have erected crosses in front of several buildings in town, and the main square features a giant monument engraved with the names of Croats killed in the fighting here. The new, super-modern Catholic church spire rockets up over town, evoking the one-upsmanship of the similar steeple in Mostar. In a recent soccer match between the Croatian and Turkish national teams, local Bosniaks backed the Turks...and things got very tense.

Local Guides: If you're interested in learning more, it's well worth hiring local guide **Sanel Marić,** who works for a local organization that strives to help the people of Stolac transcend the scars of the recent war. He can both show you some of the ancient sights around town, and fill you in on recent events (€40 for a tour around town, mobile 061-071-830, sanel.marich@gmail.com). If Sanel is busy, his colleague **Edin Buzaljko** also does great tours of Stolac (same price, mobile 061-308-476, edobuzz@gmail.com).

Eating in Stolac: To grab a bite here, consider two traditional eateries. **$ Restoran Han** is right in the heart of town, while **$ Old Mill** occupies a beautiful setting overlooking waterfalls on the road up the Bregava River.

Međugorje

Međugorje is an unassuming little village "between the hills" (as its name implies) that ranks with Lourdes, Fátima, and Santiago de Compostela as one of the most important pilgrimage sites in all of Christendom. To the cynical non-Catholic, it's just a strip of crassly commercial hotels, restaurants, and rosary shops leading up to a dull church, all tied together by a silly legend about a hilltop apparition. But if you look into the tear-filled eyes of the pilgrims who've journeyed here, it's clear that to some, the power of this place is real. Strolling through the grounds, you can hear the hushed sounds of prayer whispering through the bushes.

For true believers, Međugorje represents a once-in-a-lifetime opportunity to tread on sacred soil: a place where, for decades, the Virgin Mary has appeared to six local people. Even though the Vatican has declined to officially recognize the apparitions, that doesn't stop hundreds of thousands of Catholics from coming here each year. More than 30 million pilgrims have visited Međugorje since the sightings began—summer and winter, war (which didn't touch Međugorje) and peace, rain and

Međugorje Mary

What compels millions to flock to this little village in the middle of nowhere? The official story goes like this: On the evening of June 24, 1981, two young women were gathering their sheep on the hillside above Mostar. They came across a woman

carrying a baby who told them to come near. Terrified, they fled, only to realize later that this might have been a vision of the Virgin Mary. They returned the next night with some friends and saw the apparition again.

In the three-plus decades since, six different locals (including the two original seers) claim to have seen the vision, and some of them even say they see it regularly to this day. They also say that Mary has given them 10 secrets—predictions of future events that will portend Judgment Day. Written on a piece of parchment, these are kept safely at the home of one of the seers. They have said they will reveal each of these secrets, 10 days before the event occurs, to the local parish priest, who will then alert the world.

Doubting Thomases aren't convinced. One cause for suspicion is that the six seers, before witnessing the visions, were sometimes known to be troublemakers. (In fact, they later admitted that they went up the hill that fateful night not to chase wayward sheep, but to sneak a smoke.) One investigator suggested that they invented the story as a prank, only to watch it snowball out of control once they told it to the local priest.

For decades, the Vatican declined to confirm the sightings as miraculous in nature. (Priests were allowed to accompany pilgrimages to Međugorje, but not to *lead* them.) But in recent years, the Church has showed signs of movement. In 2017, Pope Francis suggested that he believes the earliest apparitions may have been authentic, and that they warrant further study. Stay tuned.

shine. People make the trek here from Ireland, Italy, Germany, Spain, the US, and just about anywhere else that has Catholics.

PLANNING YOUR TIME

Unless you're a pilgrim (or think you might be a pilgrim), skip Međugorje—it's an experience wasted on nonbelievers. The only "attractions" are an unexceptional modern church, a couple of hilltop hikes, and pilgrim-spotting.

If you do go, the easiest way is to take a day-trip excursion from the Dalmatian Coast (sold from Split, Dubrovnik, and Korčula).

By public bus, you can day-trip into Međugorje from Split, but not from Dubrovnik. Consider spending the night here, or sleep in Mostar two nights and day-trip into Međugorje.

Orientation to Međugorje

Međugorje (MEDGE-oo-gor-yeh, sometimes spelled "Medjugorje" in English) is basically a one-street town—most everything happens in the half-mile between the post office (where the bus stop is) and the main church, St. James (Crkva Sv. Jakova). On the hills behind the church are two trails leading to pilgrimage sites. Many travel agencies line the main strip; at any of these, you can find a room, rent a car, hire a local guide, buy ferry tickets for Croatia, and use the Internet.

Sights in Međugorje

The center of pilgrim activity is **St. James' Church** (Crkva Sv. Jakova), which was built before the apparitions. The interior, like the outside, is modern and monochromatic—with a soothing yellow color and stained-glass windows lining the nave. Out front are posted maps that are useful for getting oriented, and a white statue of the Virgin Mary that attracts a lot of attention from pilgrims. Notice the long row of multilingual confessional booths.

As you face the church, you'll see two trails leading up into the hills. Behind and to the left of the church is **Apparition Hill** (at Podbrdo), where the sightings occurred (a one-mile hike, topped by a statue of Mary). Directly behind the church is the **Great Hill** (Križevac, or "Cross Mountain"), where a giant hilltop cross, which predates the visions, has become a secondary site of pilgrimage (1.5-mile hike). If you wonder why they don't make these rocky paths easier to climb, remember that an act of pilgrimage is supposed to be challenging. In fact, pilgrims often do one or both of these hikes barefoot, as an act of penitence.

Around back of the church is a makeshift amphitheater with benches, used for outdoor services. Beyond that is a path, lined with scenes from the life of Jesus. Farther along, on the right, is an elongated, expressionistic statue of the **Resurrected Savior** (Uskrsli Spasitelj), also known as the "Weeping Knee." Miraculously (or not), the statue's right knee is always wet—go ahead and touch the spot that's been highly polished by worshippers and skeptics alike.

Believers and nonbelievers both appreciate the parade of kitsch that lines the **main**

street leading up to the church. While rosaries are clearly the big item, you can get basically anything you want stamped with Catholic imagery (Mary is particularly popular, for obvious reasons).

Sleeping and Eating in Međugorje

In Town: The main street is lined with straightforward, crank-'em-out eateries catering to tour groups. For something a little more atmospheric and fun, head for **$$ Gardens Restaurant** (near the post-office end of the main drag), with a drinks-only bar, a classy upstairs dining room, and a garden terrace (Antunovića 66, tel. 036/650-499, www.clubgardens.com).

Just Outside of Town: Herceg Etno Selo is an appealing "ethno-village" of new-but-old-looking Bosnian dry-stone buildings wedged between industrial areas and office parks. With slate roofs, inviting ponds, playgrounds, a vineyard, a small farm, and a big amphitheater, this sprawling complex includes an industrial-size **$$** restaurant (well-executed Bosnian and Croatian food) and a 71-room **$** hotel (Tromeđa b.b., tel. 036/653-400, www.etno-herceg.com, info@etno-herceg.com). Leaving town, follow signs for *Split/Ljubuški*, and look for it on the left between warehouses.

UNDERSTANDING YUGOSLAVIA

Americans struggle to understand the complicated breakup of Yugoslavia—especially when visiting countries that rose from its ashes. Here's an admittedly oversimplified, as-impartial-as-possible history to get you started. (For a longer version, see www.ricksteves.com/yugo.)

For starters, it helps to have a handle on the different groups who've lived in the Balkans—the southeastern European peninsula between the Adriatic and the Black Sea, stretching from Hungary to Greece. The Balkan Peninsula has always been a crossroads of cultures. The Illyrians, Greeks, and Romans had settlements here before the Slavs moved into the region from the north around the seventh century. During the next millennium and a half, the western part of the peninsula—which would become Yugoslavia—was divided by a series of cultural, ethnic, and religious fault lines.

The most important influences were three religions: Western Christianity (i.e., Roman Catholicism, first brought to the western part of the region by Charlemagne and later reinforced by the Austrian Habsburgs), Eastern Orthodox Christianity (brought to the east from the Byzantine Empire), and Islam (in the south, from the Ottomans).

Two major historical factors made the Balkans what they are today: The first was the split of the Roman Empire in the fourth century AD, dividing the Balkans down the middle between Roman Catholic (west) and Byzantine Orthodox (east)—roughly along today's Bosnian-Serbian border. Then the Ottoman victory at the Battle of Kosovo Polje (1389) began five centuries of Islamic influence in Bosnia-Herzegovina and Serbia, further dividing the Balkans into Christian (north) and Muslim (south).

Because of these and other events, several distinct ethnic identities emerged. Confusingly, the major "ethnicities" of Yugoslavia

Yugoslav Succession

AUSTRIA   HUNGARY

ITALY Ljubljana ⊛   SLOVENE ⊛ Zagreb   VOJVODINA   HUNGARIAN   ROMANIA
       SLOVENIA   CROATIA   Novi Sad •

                    BOSNIA-   ⊛ Belgrade
                 • Banja Luka
                 HERZEGOVINA   SERBIA
Adriatic Sea   S E R B O - C R O A T I A N
           Knin •   Sarajevo ⊛   BULGARIA

                          MONTE- Priština
                          NEGRO   ⊛
ITALY   ⊛ Podgorica KOSOVO

                              A L B A N I A N   ⊛ Skopje
                                        MACEDONIA

                           ALBANIA
                                        GREECE
                                    100 Kilometers
                                    100 Miles

───── Former Yugoslavia Border
───── Current Borders
·········· Province within Serbia
SLOVENE Language
         "Serbian Krajina" (Serb-Controlled Croatia 1991-1995)
         Republika Srpska (Serb territory in Bosnia-Herz.)

are all South Slavs—they're descended from the same ancestors and speak closely related languages, but they practice different religions. Roman Catholic South Slavs are called **Croats** or **Slovenes;** Orthodox South Slavs are called **Serbs** or **Montenegrins;** and Muslim South Slavs are called Bosniaks (whose ancestors converted to Islam under the Ottomans). The region is also home to several non-Slavic minority groups, including **Hungarians, Albanians,** and others. The groups overlapped a lot—which is exactly why the eventual breakup of Yugoslavia was so contentious.

The Kingdom of Yugoslavia ("Land of the South Slavs"—yugo means "south") was first formed after the Austro-Hungarian Empire fell at the end of World War I. It was an arbitrary union of the various, mostly Slavic groups of southeast Europe. But from the very beginning, the different ethnicities struggled for power within the new Yugoslavia. This continued through the interwar period, until the region was occupied by the Nazis during World War II.

At the end of World War II, the rest of Eastern Europe was "liberated" by the Soviets, but the Yugoslavs regained their independence on their own, as their communist Partisan Army forced out the Nazis. After the short but rocky Yugoslav union between the World Wars, it seemed that no one would be able to hold the southern Slavs together in a single nation. But one man could, and did: Communist Party president and war hero Josip Broz, better known as Tito. With a Slovene for a mother, a Croat for a father, a Serb for a wife, and a home in Belgrade, Tito was a true Yugoslav. Tito had a compelling vision that this fractured union of the South Slavs could function.

Tito's new incarnation of Yugoslavia aimed for a more equitable division of powers. It was made up of six republics, each with its own parliament and president: **Croatia** (mostly Catholic), **Slovenia** (mostly Catholic), **Serbia** (mostly Orthodox; also included the "autonomous provinces" of **Kosovo** and **Vojvodina**), **Bosnia-Herzegovina** (the most diverse—mostly Muslim Bosniaks, but with very large Croat and Serb populations), **Montenegro** (mostly Orthodox—a sort of a Serb/Croat hybrid), and **Macedonia** (with about 25 percent Muslim Albanians and 75 percent Orthodox Macedonians). Each republic managed its own affairs...but always under the watchful eye of president-for-life Tito, who said that the borders between the republics should be "like white lines in a marble column."

Tito's Yugoslavia was communist, but it wasn't Soviet communism. Despite strong pressure from Moscow, Tito refused to ally himself with the Soviets—and therefore received good will (and $2 billion) from the United States. Tito's vision was for a "third way," in which Yugoslavia could work with both East and West, without being dominated by either. While large industry was nationalized, Tito's system allowed for small businesses. This experience with a market economy benefited Yugoslavs when Eastern Europe's communist regimes eventually fell.

After Tito died in 1980, it didn't take long for his union to unravel. In the late 1980s, squabbles broke out in the autonomous province of Kosovo between the Serb minority and the ethnic-Albanian majority. Serbia, led by Slobodan Milošević, annexed Kosovo—causing other republics (especially Slovenia and Croatia) to fear that he would gut their nation to create a "Greater Serbia," instead of a friendly coalition of diverse Yugoslav republics. Over the next decade, Yugoslavia broke apart, with much bloodshed.

Slovenia declared independence from Yugoslavia on June 25, 1991. After 10 days of fighting and fewer than a hundred deaths, they were granted their freedom. But the situation in other republics—which were far more ethnically diverse—was not so simple.

In April 1990, a historian named Franjo Tuđman won Croatia's first free elections. Tuđman invoked the spirit of the last group to lead an "independent" Croatia—the Ustaše, who had ruthlessly run Croatia's puppet government under the Nazis (and had killed many Serbs in their concentration camps). The 600,000 Serbs living in Croatia began to rise up.

By the time Croatia formally declared its independence (also on June 25, 1991), war was imminent. Croatia's Serb residents immediately declared their own independence from Croatia. The Serb-dominated Yugoslav National Army swept in, supposedly to keep the peace between Serbs and Croats—but it soon became obvious that they were there to support the Serbs.

Fighting raged through the region. In a surprise move, the Yugoslav National Army even attacked the tourist resort of Dubrovnik. By early 1992, the Serbs had gained control over the parts of inland Croatia where they were in the majority, and a tense ceasefire began. Then, in 1995, the Croats swept back through Serb territory to reclaim it for Croatia. During this period, both the Serbs and the Croats carried out "ethnic cleansing"—systematically removing an ethnic group from a territory, by displacing or killing them. Finally, the 1995 Erdut Agreement brought peace.

Bosnia-Herzegovina declared its independence from Yugoslavia four months after Croatia and Slovenia did. But Bosnia-Herzegovina was even more diverse than Croatia, as it was populated predominantly by Muslim Bosniaks (mostly in the cities) but also by large numbers of Serbs and Croats (many of them farmers).

At first, the Bosniaks and Croats teamed up to fight against the Serbs. But even before the first wave of fighting had subsided, Croats and Bosniaks turned their guns on each other. A bloody war raged for years between the three groups: the Serbs led by Radovan Karadžić (with support from Serbia proper), the Croats (with support from Croatia proper), and—squeezed between them—the internationally recognized Bosniak government, led by President Alija Izetbegović, who desperately worked for peace.

Bosnia-Herzegovina was torn apart. Even the many mixed families were forced to choose sides. If you had a Serb mother and a Croat father, you were expected to pick one ethnicity or the other—and your brother might choose the opposite. As families and former neighbors trained their guns on each other, proud and beautiful cities such as Sarajevo and Mostar were turned to rubble, and people throughout Bosnia-Herzegovina lived in a state of constant terror.

Finally, in 1995, the Dayton Peace Accords carefully divided Bosnia-Herzegovina among the different ethnicities. Today—following the peaceful declarations of independence in Montenegro (2006) and Kosovo (2008)—there are seven countries where once was a single, united Yugoslavia. While tension still exists, the region is peaceful, stable, and welcoming to visitors.

Travelers to this region quickly realize that the vast majority of people they meet here never wanted these wars. And so finally comes the inevitable question: Why did any of it happen in the first place?

Explanations tend to gravitate to two extremes. Some observers consider this part of the world to be inherently warlike—a place where deep-seated hatreds and age-old ethnic passions unavoidably flare up. Others believe this theory is an insulting oversimplification. Sure, animosity has long simmered in the Balkans, but the conflict broke out because of the single-minded, self-serving actions of a few selfish leaders who exploited existing resentments to advance their own interests. It wasn't until Milošević, Karadžić, Tudman, and others expertly manipulated the people's grudges that the country fell into war.

Many people you'll meet here are eager to tell you their own story. But keep in mind that everyone in the former Yugoslavia seems to have a slightly different version of events. A very wise Bosniak told me, "Listen to all three sides—Muslim, Serb, and Croat. Then decide for yourself what you think."

PRACTICALITIES

This section covers just the basics on traveling in Croatia (for much more information, see *Rick Steves Croatia & Slovenia*). You'll find free advice on specific topics at www.ricksteves.com/tips.

This book also includes destinations that are in different countries: Bosnia-Herzegovina and Montenegro. You'll find most of the practicalities about traveling in each of those places (such as the local currency and telephone tips) in their chapters.

MONEY

In Croatia, credit cards are widely accepted, but day-to-day spending is generally more cash-based than in the US. If you need cash, Croatia uses a currency called the kuna: 6 Croatian kunas (kn) = about $1. To roughly convert Croatian kunas into dollars, divide by six. A kuna is broken into 100 smaller units, called lipas.

The standard way for travelers to get kunas is to withdraw money from an ATM (called a *bankomat* in Croatia) using a debit card, ideally with a Visa or MasterCard logo. Before departing, call your bank or credit-card company: Confirm that your card(s) will work overseas, ask about international transaction fees, and alert them that you'll be making withdrawals in Europe. Also ask for the PIN number for your credit card—you may need it for Europe's "chip-and-PIN" payment machines (see below; allow time for your bank to mail your PIN to you). To keep your valuables safe, wear a money belt.

Dealing with "Chip and PIN": Most credit and debit cards now have chips that authenticate and secure transactions. European cardholders insert their chip card into the payment slot, then enter a PIN. (Until recently, most US cards required a signature.) Any American card with a chip will work at Europe's hotels, restaurants, and shops—although sometimes the clerk may ask for a signature. But some self-service payment machines—such as those at train stations, toll roads, or unattended gas pumps—may not accept your card, even if you know the PIN. If your card won't work, look for a cashier who can process the transaction manually—or pay in cash.

Dynamic Currency Conversion: If merchants or hoteliers offer to convert your purchase price into dollars (called dynamic currency conversion, or DCC), refuse this "service." You'll pay more in fees for the expensive convenience of seeing your charge in dollars. If an ATM offers to "lock in" or "guarantee" your conversion rate, choose "proceed without conversion." Other prompts might state, "You can be charged in dollars: Press YES for dollars, NO for kunas" (or "euros" or "Bosnian convertible marks"). Always choose the local currency.

STAYING CONNECTED

The simplest solution is to bring your own device—mobile phone, tablet, or laptop—and use it just as you would at home (following the tips below, such as connecting to free Wi-Fi whenever possible).

To call Croatia from a US or Canadian number: Whether you're phoning from a landline, your own mobile phone, or a Skype account, you're making an international call. Dial 011-385 and then the phone number, minus its initial zero. (The 011 is our international access code, and 385 is Croatia's country code). If dialing from a mobile phone, you can enter a + in place of the international access code—press and hold the 0 key.

To call Croatia from a European country: Dial 00-385 followed by the phone number, minus its initial zero. (The 00 is Europe's international access code.)

To call within Croatia: If you're dialing from a Croatian landline within an area code, just dial the local number; but if you're calling outside your area code, dial both the area code (which starts with a 0) and the local number.

To call from Croatia to another country: Dial 00 followed by the country code (for example, 1 for the US or Canada), then the area code and number. If you're calling European countries with phone numbers that begin with 0, you'll usually have to omit that 0 when you dial.

Tips: If you bring your own mobile phone, consider signing up for an international plan; most providers offer a global calling plan that cuts the per-minute cost of phone calls and texts, and a flat-fee data plan.

Use Wi-Fi whenever possible. Most hotels and many cafés offer free Wi-Fi, and you'll likely also find it at tourist information offices (TIs), major museums, and public-transit hubs. With Wi-Fi you make free or inexpensive domestic and international calls via a calling app such as Skype, FaceTime, or Google+ Hangouts. When you can't find Wi-Fi, you can use your cellular network

---

Sleep Code

Hotels are classified based on the average price of a standard double room with breakfast in spring and fall. Prices may go up in summer, and down in winter.

$$$$	**Splurge:**	Most rooms over €150 (1,100 kn)
$$$	**Pricier:**	€110-150 (800-1,100 kn)
$$	**Moderate:**	€80-110 (600-800 kn)
$	**Budget:**	€50-80 (375-600 kn)
¢	**Backpacker:**	Under €50 (375 kn)
RS%	**Rick Steves discount**	

Unless otherwise noted, credit cards are accepted, hotel staff speak basic English, and free Wi-Fi is available. Comparison-shop by checking prices at several hotels (on each hotel's own website, on a booking site, or by email). For the best deal, book directly with the hotel. Ask for a discount if paying in cash; if the listing includes **RS%**, request a Rick Steves discount.

---

to connect to the Internet, send texts, or make voice calls. When you're done, avoid further charges by manually switching off "data roaming" or "cellular data."

Without a mobile device, you can make calls from your hotel and get online using public computers (there's usually one in your hotel lobby or at local libraries). Most hotels charge a high fee for international calls—ask for rates before you dial. For more on phoning, see www.ricksteves.com/phoning. For a one-hour talk on "Traveling with a Mobile Device," see www.ricksteves.com/travel-talks.

SLEEPING

I've categorized my recommended accommodations based on price, indicated with a dollar-sign rating (see sidebar). For most travelers, Croatian hotels are a bad value; instead, I focus my recommendations on what locals call "private accommodations": a rented apartment *(apartman)* or a room in a private home (*soba*, pronounced SOH-bah; plural *sobe*, SOH-bay). Private accommodations offer travelers a characteristic and money-saving alternative for a fraction of the price of a hotel. While most Croatian accommodations quote their rates in euros, when you check out, payment is expected in kunas (or by credit card).

Generally the more you pay for your *soba*, the more privacy and amenities you get: private bathroom, TV, air-conditioning, kitchenette, and so on (though telephones are rare). Apartments are typically bigger and cost slightly more than *sobe*, but they're still far cheaper than hotels. The prices for private accommodations generally fluctuate with the seasons, and stays of fewer than three nights usually come with a 20–50 percent surcharge (though

PRACTICALITIES

this is often waived outside of peak season).

The hotel situation is more straightforward in Bosnia, which has a wider range of small, reasonably priced hotels. Bosnian accommodations also quote their rates in euros.

Since the best-value *sobe* deservedly book up early, reservations are highly recommended. It's important to **book directly** with your host. The importance of this can't be overstated. Several *sobe* hosts I list in this book told me that some of my readers have emailed them to check availability and then proceeded to book through a third party. This frustrates them because it costs everybody more money—except the middleman. Making your reservation directly with the host by phone or email can result in a better price and also gives you the opportunity to ask any questions. Any special prices or discounts I've negotiated for this book are invalidated if you use a middleman.

Email the *sobe* host with the following key pieces of information: number and type of rooms; number of nights; arrival date; departure date; and any special requests. Use the European style for writing dates: day/month/year.

After you've reserved, keep in mind that your host loses money if you don't show up. For this reason, some hosts may request your credit-card number to secure the reservation. (They'll generally ask for payment in cash when you're there; your credit card won't be charged.) A few hosts might ask you to wire or mail money as a deposit. Because wiring money can come with substantial fees—which you (rather than the *sobe* host) will incur—it usually works better to mail them a check or travelers check, or pay them through PayPal. Ask your *sobe* host which options they accept.

Some *sobe* hosts and hoteliers are willing to deal to attract guests: Try emailing several to ask for their best price. In general, prices can soften if you stay at least three nights or travel off-season.

If you like to travel without reservations, during most of the year you'll have no problem finding *sobe* as you go (though late July and August are the exceptions). Locals hawking rooms meet each arriving boat and bus. The quality can be hit or miss, but many of these are good options. Be sure you understand exactly where the room is located (i.e., within easy walking distance of the attractions) before you accept. Because Europeans tend to dramatically lowball walking estimates, ask to see the location on a map.

Third-party aggregator sites such as Airbnb, FlipKey, Booking.com, and the HomeAway family of sites (HomeAway, VRBO, and VacationRentals) are another way to find a bed. As a last resort, enlist the help of a travel agency on the ground to find you a room—but you'll pay 10–30 percent extra (to search from home, try www.dubrovnikapartmentsource.com).

Restaurant Price Code

I've assigned each eatery a price category, based on the average cost of a typical main course. Drinks, desserts, and splurge
items (steak and seafood) can raise the price considerably.

$$$$ **Splurge:** Most main courses over €17 (125 kn)
$$$ **Pricier:** €13-17 (100-125 kn)
$$ **Moderate:** €10-13 (75-100 kn)
$ **Budget:** Under €10 (75 kn)

In Croatia, a takeout spot is **$**; a basic sit-down *konoba* or piz-
zeria is **$$**; a casual but more upscale restaurant is **$$$**; and
a swanky splurge is **$$$$**.

EATING

I've categorized my recommended eateries based on price, indicated with a dollar-sign rating (see sidebar). Croatian food has a
distinct Mediterranean flavor; you'll enjoy locally produced wine,
olive oil, and *pršut* (air-dried ham, similar to prosciutto). The
budget standby is pizza and pasta. For a splurge, try seafood: fish,
scampi, mussels, squid, octopus, and more. Prices for fish dishes
are listed either by the kilogram (1,000 grams) or by the 100-gram
unit; figure about a half-kilo, or 500 grams—that's about one
pound—for a large portion. Try the octopus salad, a flavorful mix
of octopus, tomatoes, onions, and spices.

You'll find similar fare in Bosnia-Herzegovina and
Montenegro, but there you're also likely to come across some
pan-Balkan elements. One staple is phyllo dough pastries—both
honey-drenched baklava and its savory cousin, *burek* (stuffed with
cheese, meat, or spinach). But the big item is grilled meat: *ćevapčići*
(cheh-VAHP-chee-chee), grilled minced meat shaped like a sau-
sage link; *pljeskavica* (plehs-kah-VEET-suh), grilled minced meat
shaped like a patty; and *ražnjići* (RAZH-nyee-chee), skewered
grilled steak similar to a shish kebab. Any kind of meat goes perfectly with the eggplant/red-pepper condiment called *ajvar* (EYE-
var).

Service: Good service is relaxed (slow to an American). You
won't get the bill until you ask for it: *"Račun?"* (RAH-choon). At
restaurants that have a waitstaff, it's common to tip after a good
meal by rounding up 5 to 10 percent. At some tourist-oriented restaurants, a 10 or 15 percent "service charge" may be added to your
bill, so an additional tip is unnecessary.

TRANSPORTATION

Since Dubrovnik has no train access, you'll generally get around
by car, bus, or boat.

By Car: A car is a headache to drive and park in Dubrovnik,

PRACTICALITIES

but is the most convenient way to side-trip to this book's other destinations. You can arrange a short-term rental on the fly in Dubrovnik (ask any travel agency), or—often cheaper—reserve it in advance from the US (several big rental-car companies have offices in Dubrovnik). Pick up and drop off your car in the same country: International drop-off fees are astronomical (usually several hundred dollars). For tips on your insurance options, see www.ricksteves.com/cdw. Bring your driver's license; in Croatia and Bosnia, you're also required to carry an International Driving Permit (IDP), available at your local AAA office ($20 plus two passport-type photos, www.aaa.com). As you approach any town, follow the signs to *Centar* (usually also signed with a bull's-eye symbol). Follow this book's parking advice, and get additional tips from your hotelier. If you want someone else to do the driving, hire a local driver.

It's mandatory to wear seat belts. For other rules of the Croatian road, ask your car-rental company, or check the US State Department website (www.travel.state.gov, select "International Travel," then "Country Information," then search for your destination and click on "Travel and Transportation").

By Bus: Without a car, buses are the best way to connect most of the destinations in this book. Confusingly, a single bus route can be operated by a variety of different companies, making it difficult to find comprehensive schedules. Your first stop should be www.getbybus.com, which includes many (but not necessarily all) bus connections in Croatia, and many in neighboring countries, and lets you book tickets online (for a small fee). You can also confirm schedules with a local TI or bus station (or try www.autobusni-kolodvor.com). For popular routes during peak season, either book ahead online or drop by the station to buy your ticket a few hours—or even days—in advance to ensure getting a seat (ask the bus station ticket office or the local TI how far ahead you should buy). You'll pay about $2 per bag to stow your luggage under the bus. Bus routes that cross borders can be subject to significant delays during peak times.

By Boat: Slow car ferries and speedy catamarans inexpensively shuttle tourists between major coastal cities and quiet island villages. The big ferries are operated by the national boat company, Jadrolinija (www.jadrolinija.hr). Walk-on passengers riding these boats don't need reservations, but drivers will want to line up their cars in advance (get advice locally about how early you need to arrive). A faster, private catamaran called *Nona Ana*—which takes only passengers (no cars)—also connects Dubrovnik to nearby islands (www.gv-line.hr). You'll be competing with lots of travelers for a few precious seats on the most convenient catamarans. Book your ticket as far ahead as possible; on the popular routes, tickets sell out—sometimes very quickly.

HELPFUL HINTS

Emergency Help: To summon the **police** or an **ambulance**, call 112. For passport problems, call the **US Embassy** (for Croatia it's in Zagreb—tel. 01/661-2200, https://hr.usembassy.gov; for Montenegro it's in Podgorica—tel. 020/410-500, https://me.usembassy.gov; for Bosnia it's in Sarajevo, tel. 033/704-000, https://ba.usembassy.gov).

If you have a minor **illness,** do as the locals do and go to a pharmacist for advice. Or ask at your hotel for help—they'll know of the nearest medical and emergency services. For other concerns, get advice from your hotelier.

Theft or Loss: To replace a passport, you'll need to go in person to an embassy (see above). Cancel and replace your credit and debit cards by calling these 24-hour US numbers collect: Visa—tel. 303/967-1096, MasterCard—tel. 636/722-7111, American Express—tel. 336/393-1111. In Croatia, to make a collect call to the US, dial 0800-220-111; press zero or stay on the line for an operator. In Bosnia, call 00-800-0010. In Montenegro, it's not possible to make collect calls—dial your credit card's number direct. File a police report either on the spot or within a day or two; you'll need it to submit an insurance claim for lost or stolen rail passes or travel gear, and it can help with replacing your passport or credit and debit cards. For more information, see www.ricksteves.com/help.

Borders: You'll have to stop and show your passport when you cross the border between Croatia, Bosnia-Herzegovina, and Montenegro. Drivers may be asked to show proof of car insurance ("green card"), so be sure you have it when you pick up your rental car. When you change countries, you change phone cards, postage stamps, and, in most cases, money.

Time: All three countries use the 24-hour clock. It's the same through 12:00 noon, then keep going: 13:00, 14:00, and so on. Croatia, Bosnia-Herzegovina, and Montenegro, like most of continental Europe, are six/nine hours ahead of the East/West Coasts of the US.

Business Hours: Business hours can fluctuate wildly, based on demand—shops are open long hours daily in summer, but might be closed entirely in winter. Most businesses close on Sundays except in Croatia, where some may be open in touristy areas or in large cities (especially near bus or train stations).

Holidays and Festivals: All three nations celebrate many holidays, which can close sights and attract crowds (book hotel rooms ahead). For information on holidays and festivals, check these websites: Croatia—http://us.croatia.hr, Bosnia-Herzegovina—www.bhtourism.ba, Montenegro—www.montenegro.travel. For a simple list showing major—though not all—events, see www.ricksteves.com/festivals.

Numbers and Stumblers: What Americans call the second floor of a building is the first floor in Europe. Europeans write dates as day/month/year, so Christmas 2020 is 25/12/20. Commas are decimal points and vice versa—a dollar and a half is 1,50, and there are 5.280 feet in a mile. All destinations covered in this book use the metric system: A kilogram is 2.2 pounds; a liter is about a quart; and a kilometer is six-tenths of a mile.

Smoking: Croatia has enacted smoking bans in most public places, though patrons at outdoor tables can still smoke. Bosnia-Herzegovina and Montenegro have no such bans.

RESOURCES FROM RICK STEVES

This Snapshot guide is excerpted from my latest edition of *Rick Steves Croatia & Slovenia*, which is one of many titles in my ever-expanding series of guidebooks on European travel. I also produce a public television series, *Rick Steves' Europe,* and a public radio show, *Travel with Rick Steves.* My website, www.ricksteves.com, offers free travel information, a forum for travelers' comments, guidebook updates, my travel blog, an online travel store, and information on European rail passes and our tours of Europe. If you're bringing a mobile device, you can download my free Rick Steves Audio Europe app, featuring dozens of self-guided audio tours of the top sights in Europe and travel interviews about Europe. You can get Rick Steves Audio Europe via Apple's App Store, Google Play, or the Amazon Appstore. For more information, see www.ricksteves.com/audioeurope. You can also follow me on Facebook, Twitter, and Instagram.

ADDITIONAL RESOURCES

Tourist Information: Croatia—http://us.croatia.hr; Bosnia-Herzegovina—www.bhtourism.ba; Montenegro—www.montenegro.travel

Passports and Red Tape: www.travel.state.gov

Packing List: www.ricksteves.com/packing

Travel Insurance: www.ricksteves.com/insurance

Cheap Flights: www.kayak.com or www.google.com/flights

Airplane Carry-on Restrictions: www.tsa.gov

Updates for This Book: www.ricksteves.com/update

HOW WAS YOUR TRIP?

To share your tips, concerns, and discoveries after using this book, please fill out the survey at www.ricksteves.com/feedback. Thanks in advance—it helps a lot.

PRACTICALITIES

Croatian Survival Phrases

In the phonetics, ī sounds like the long i in "light," and bolded syllables are stressed.

English	Croatian	Pronunciation
Hello. (formal)	Dobar dan.	doh-bahr dahn
Hi. / Bye. (informal)	Bok.	bohk
Do you speak English?	Govorite li engleski?	goh-voh-ree-teh lee ehn-glehs-kee
Yes. / No.	Da. / Ne.	dah / neh
I (don't) understand.	(Ne) razumijem.	(neh) rah-zoo-mee-yehm
Please. / You're welcome.	Molim.	moh-leem
Thank you (very much).	Hvala (ljepa).	hvah-lah (lyeh-pah)
Excuse me. / I'm sorry.	Oprostite.	oh-proh-stee-teh
problem	problem	proh-blehm
No problem.	Nema problema.	neh-mah proh-bleh-mah
Good.	Dobro.	doh-broh
Goodbye.	Do viđenija.	doh veed-jay-neeah
one / two	jedan / dva	yeh-dahn / dvah
three / four	tri / četiri	tree / cheh-teh-ree
five / six	pet / šest	peht / shehst
seven / eight	sedam / osam	seh-dahm / oh-sahm
nine / ten	devet / deset	deh-veht / deh-seht
hundred / thousand	sto / tisuća	stoh / tee-soo-chah
How much?	Koliko?	koh-lee-koh
local currency	kuna	koo-nah
Write it?	Napišite?	nah-peesh-ee-teh
Is it free?	Da li je besplatno?	dah lee yeh beh-splaht-noh
Is it included?	Da li je uključeno?	dah lee yeh ook-lyoo-cheh-noh
Where can I find / buy...?	Gdje mogu pronaći / kupiti...?	guh-dyeh moh-goo proh-nah-chee / koo-pee-tee
I'd like / We'd like...	Želio bih / Željeli bismo...	zheh-lee-oh bee / zheh-lyeh-lee bees-moh
...a room.	...sobu.	soh-boo
...a ticket to ___.	...kartu do ___.	kar-too doh ___
Is it possible?	Da li je moguće?	dah lee yeh moh-goo-cheh
Where is...?	Gdje je...?	guh-dyeh yeh
...the train station	...kolodvor	koh-loh-dvor
...the bus station	...autobusni kolodvor	ow-toh-boos-nee koh-loh-dvor
...the tourist information office	...turističko informativni centar	too-ree-steech-koh een-for-mah-teev-nee tsehn-tahr
...the toilet	...vece (WC)	veht-seh
men / women	muški / ženski	moosh-kee / zhehn-skee
left / right / straight	lijevo / desno / ravno	lee-yeh-voh / dehs-noh / rahv-noh
At what time...?	U koliko sati...?	oo koh-lee-koh sah-tee
...does this open / close	...otvara / zatvara	oht-vah-rah / zaht-vah-rah
(Just) a moment.	(Samo) trenutak.	(sah-moh) treh-noo-tahk
now / soon / later	sada / uskoro / kasnije	sah-dah / oos-koh-roh / kahs-nee-yeh
today / tomorrow	danas / sutra	dah-nahs / soo-trah

In a Croatian Restaurant

English	Croatian	Pronunciation
I'd like to reserve...	Rezervirao bih...	reh-zehr-**veer**-ow bee
We'd like to reserve...	Rezervirali bismo...	reh-zehr-**vee**-rah-lee **bees**-moh
...a table for one / two.	...stol za jednog / dva.	stohl zah **yehd**-nog / dvah
Is this table free?	Da li je ovaj stol slobodan?	dah lee yeh **oh**-vī stohl **sloh**-boh-dahn
Can I help you?	Izvolite?	**eez**-voh-lee-teh
The menu (in English), please.	Jelovnik (na engleskom), molim.	yeh-**lohv**-neek (nah **ehn**-glehs-kohm) **moh**-leem
service (not) included	posluga (nije) uključena	**poh**-sloo-gah (**nee**-yeh) **ook**-lyoo-cheh-nah
cover charge	couvert	**koo**-vehr
"to go"	za ponjeti	zah **pohn**-yeh-tee
with / without	sa / bez	sah / behz
and / or	i / ili	ee / **ee**-lee
fixed-price meal (of the day)	(dnevni) meni	(duh-**nehv**-nee) **meh**-nee
specialty of the house	specijalitet kuće	speht-see-yah-**lee**-teht **koo**-cheh
half portion	pola porcije	**poh**-lah **port**-see-yeh
daily special	jelo dana	**yeh**-loh **dah**-nah
fixed-price meal for tourists	turistički meni	**too**-ree-steech-kee **meh**-nee
appetizers	predjela	**prehd**-yeh-lah
bread	kruh	kroo
cheese	sir	seer
sandwich	sendvič	**send**-veech
soup	juha	**yoo**-hah
salad	salata	sah-**lah**-tah
meat / poultry	meso / perad	**may**-soh / **peh**-rahd
fish / seafood	riba / morska hrana	**ree**-bah **mor**-skah **hrah**-nah
fruit	voće	**voh**-cheh
vegetables	povrće	**poh**-vur-cheh
dessert	desert	deh-**sayrt**
(tap) water	voda (od slavine)	**voh**-dah (ohd **slah**-vee-neh)
mineral water	mineralna voda	**mee**-neh-rahl-nah **voh**-dah
milk	mlijeko	mlee-**yeh**-koh
(orange) juice	sok (od naranče)	sohk (ohd **nah**-rahn-cheh)
coffee	kava	**kah**-vah
tea	čaj	chī
wine	vino	**vee**-noh
red / white	crno / bijelo	**tsehr**-noh / bee-**yeh**-loh
sweet / dry / semi-dry	slatko / suho / polusuho	**slaht**-koh / **soo**-hoh / **poh**-loo-soo-hoh
glass / bottle	čaša / boca	**chah**-shah / **boht**-sah
beer	pivo	**pee**-voh
Cheers!	Živjeli!	**zhee**-vyeh-lee
More. / Another.	Još. / Još jedno.	yohsh / yohsh **yehd**-noh
The same.	Isto.	**ees**-toh
Bill, please.	Račun, molim.	**rah**-choon **moh**-leem
tip	napojnica	**nah**-poy-neet-sah
Delicious!	Izvrsno!	**eez**-vur-snoh

INDEX

Start your trip at

Explore Europe

At ricksteves.com you can browse through thousands of articles, videos, photos and radio interviews, plus find a wealth of money-saving travel tips for planning your dream trip. And with our mobile-friendly website, you can easily access all this great travel information anywhere you go.

TV Shows

Preview the places you'll visit by watching entire half-hour episodes of Rick Steves' Europe (choose from all 100 shows) on-demand, for free.

your travel dreams into affordable reality

Radio Interviews

Enjoy ready access to Rick's vast library of radio interviews covering travel

tips and cultural insights that relate specifically to your Europe travel plans.

Travel Forums

Learn, ask, share! Our online community of savvy travelers is a great resource

for first-time travelers to Europe, as well as seasoned pros. You'll find forums on each country, plus travel tips and restaurant/hotel reviews. You can even ask one of our well-traveled staff to chime in with an opinion.

Travel News

Subscribe to our free Travel News e-newsletter, and get monthly updates from Rick on what's happening in Europe.

Rick's Free Travel App

Experience maximum Europe

Save time and energy

This guidebook is your independent-travel toolkit. But for all it delivers, it's still up to you to devote the time and energy it takes to manage the preparation and logistics that are essential for a happy trip. If that's a hassle, there's a solution.

Rick Steves Tours

A Rick Steves tour takes you to Europe's most interesting places with great

with minimum stress

guides and small groups of 28 or less. We follow Rick's favorite itineraries, ride in comfy buses, stay in family-run hotels, and bring you intimately

close to the Europe you've traveled so far to see. Most importantly, we take away the logistical headaches so you can focus on the fun.

travelers—nearly half of them repeat customers—along with us on four dozen different itineraries, from Ireland to Italy to Athens. Is a Rick Steves tour the right fit for your travel dreams? Find out at ricksteves.com, where you can also request Rick's latest tour catalog. Europe is best experienced with happy travel partners. We hope you can join us.

Join the fun
This year we'll take thousands of free-spirited

A Guide for Every Trip

BEST OF GUIDES

Full color easy-to-scan format, focusing on Europe's most popular destinations and sights.

Best of England
Best of Europe
Best of France
Best of Germany
Best of Ireland
Best of Italy
Best of Spain

COMPREHENSIVE GUIDES

City, country, and regional guides with detailed coverage for a multi-week trip exploring the most iconic sights and venturing off the beaten track.

Amsterdam & the Netherlands
Barcelona
Belgium: Bruges, Brussels,
   Antwerp & Ghent
Berlin
Budapest
Croatia & Slovenia
Eastern Europe
England
Florence & Tuscany
France
Germany
Great Britain
Greece: Athens & the Peloponnese
Iceland
Ireland
Istanbul
Italy
London
Paris
Portugal
Prague & the Czech Republic
Provence & the French Riviera
Rome
Scandinavia
Scotland
Spain
Switzerland
Venice
Vienna, Salzburg & Tirol

THE BEST OF ROME

ome, Italy's capital, is studded with
oman remnants and floodlit-fountain
ares. From the Vatican to the Colos-
um, with crazy traffic in between, Rome
onderful, huge, and exhausting. The
ds, the heat, and the weighty history

of the Eternal City where Caesars walked
can make tourists wilt. Recharge by taking siestas, gelato breaks, and after-dark
walks, strolling from one atmospheric
square to another in the refreshing evening air.

ired **Pantheon**—which
gest dome until the
rly 2,000 years old
day over 1,500).

l of Athens in the Vat-
odies the humanistic
ce.

, gladiators fought
another, entertaining

his Rome **ristorante.**
ds at **St. Peter's**
rk seriously.

Rick Steves guidebooks are published by Avalon Travel,
an imprint of Perseus Books, a Hachette Book Group compa

POCKET GUIDES

Compact, full color city guides with the essentials for shorter trips.

Amsterdam	Paris
Athens	Prague
Barcelona	Rome
Florence	Venice
Italy's Cinque Terre	Vienna
London	
Munich & Salzburg	

SNAPSHOT GUIDES

Focused single-destination coverage.

Basque Country: Spain & France
Copenhagen & the Best of Denmark
Dublin
Dubrovnik
Edinburgh
Hill Towns of Central Italy
Krakow, Warsaw & Gdansk
Lisbon
Loire Valley
Madrid & Toledo
Milan & the Italian Lakes District
Naples & the Amalfi Coast
Normandy
Northern Ireland
Norway
Reykjavík
Sevilla, Granada & Southern Spain
St. Petersburg, Helsinki & Tallinn
Stockholm

CRUISE PORTS GUIDES

Reference for cruise ports of call.

Mediterranean Cruise Ports
Scandinavian & Northern European Cruise Ports

Complete your library with...

TRAVEL SKILLS & CULTURE

Study up on travel skills and gain insight on history and culture.

Europe 101
Europe Through the Back Door
European Christmas
European Easter
European Festivals
Postcards from Europe
Travel as a Political Act

PHRASE BOOKS & DICTIONARIES

French
French, Italian & German
German
Italian
Portuguese
Spanish

PLANNING MAPS

Britain, Ireland & London
Europe
France & Paris
Germany, Austria & Switzerland
Ireland
Italy
Spain & Portugal

Rick Steves books are available from your favorite bookseller.
Many guides are available as ebooks.

Avalon Travel
Hachette Book Group
1700 Fourth Street
Berkeley, CA 94710

Printed in Canada by Friesens.
Fifth Edition. First printing August 2018.

ISBN 978-1-63121-819-4

For the latest on Rick's talks, guidebooks, tours, public television series, and public radio show, contact Rick Steves' Europe, 130 Fourth Avenue North, Edmonds, WA 98020, 425/771-8303, www.ricksteves.com, rick@ricksteves.com.

Rick Steves' Europe
Managing Editor: Jennifer Madison Davis
Special Publications Manager: Risa Laib
Assistant Managing Editor: Cathy Lu
Editors: Glenn Eriksen, Julie Fanselow, Tom Griffin, Katherine Gustafson, Suzanne Kotz, Rosie Leutzinger, Teresa Nemeth, Carrie Shepherd
Editorial & Production Assistant: Jessica Shaw
Editorial Intern: Emily Burks
Graphic Content Director: Sandra Hundacker
Maps & Graphics: David C. Hoerlein, Lauren Mills, Mary Rostad

Avalon Travel
Senior Editor & Series Manager: Madhu Prasher
Editor: Jamie Andrade
Editor: Sierra Machado
Copy Editor: Maggie Ryan
Proofreader: Kelly Lydick, Patrick Collins
Indexer: Stephen Callahan
Production & Typesetting: Christine DeLorenzo, Krista Anderson, Lisi Baldwin, Jane Musser, Rue Flaherty
Cover Design: Kimberly Glyder Design
Maps & Graphics: Kat Bennett

Photo Credits
Front Cover: © Emicristea | Dreamstime.com
Title Page: Dubrovnik © Rick Steves' Europe
Full-page photos: p. 3, Dubrovnik; p. 101, Perast; p. 139, Coppersmiths' Street, Mostar.
Additional Photography: Dominic Arizona Bonuccelli, Cameron Hewitt, Sandra Hundacker, Pat O'Connor, Rhonda Pelikan, Rick Steves, Gretchen Strauch, Wikimedia Commons (PD-Art/PD-US). Photos are used by permission and are the property of the original copyright owners.

Let's Keep on Travelin'

Your trip doesn't need to end.

Follow Rick on social media!